The Forty Letters of Preparation for the End of An Age.

Horacio A. Villegas

I0011107

iUniverse, Inc.
New York Lincoln Shanghai

The Forty Letters of Preparation for the End of An Age.

iUniverse books may be ordered through booksellers or by contacting:

iUniverse
2021 Pine Lake Road, Suite 100
Lincoln, NE 68512
www.iuniverse.com
1-800-Authors (1-800-288-4677)

Because of the dynamic nature of the Internet, any Web addresses or links contained in this book may have changed since publication and may no longer be valid.

The views expressed in this work are solely those of the author and do not necessarily reflect the views of the publisher, and the publisher hereby disclaims any responsibility for them.

ISBN: 978-0-595-48542-0 (pbk)
ISBN: 978-0-595-60636-8 (ebk)

Printed in the United States of America

"Enter through the narrow gate; for wide is the gate and broad is the road that leads to destruction, and many will go that way. How narrow is the gate that leads to life and how rough the road; few there are the ones who find it." Matthew 7:13

Contents

Foreword

In the Name of the Father, the Son and the Holy Spirit. It is with great love and sense of urgency that I put forth the following message. I cannot, and do not attempt to take credit for the message, because it was not and never has been mine to begin with. It is a timeless message that has been given, heeded by few and ignored by the majority many times before throughout human history beginning with Noah and his great Ark. I merely put it forth and pray that whoever reads it, or hears it, heeds it. Sadly though, most will not.

It is also appropriate that at this time I acknowledge and give thanks to Mrs. Sheryl Rodgers for all she has done for me in getting this message out. I would also like to pray and give thanks to my very dear and loving parents, Pedro and Maria, for all their prayers and support during this time, as well as to my loving brothers and sisters in Christ, Lula Corley, Jeremiah Meroka and Chris Cortez. Thank you all for your support from the very beginning. Many thanks also to my loving family as well, Albert, Monica and Christina. May God almighty bless, protect and guide you and your families always. Amen, your loving brother Horacio.

Introduction

On a cool, dark March night in 2005, I experienced something that would forever change my life from that moment onward.

I couldn't sleep that night. Tossing and turning, I tried to sleep but found myself restless and frustrated. With each toss, I would glance over at the alarm clock on my nightstand and see the minutes ticking by. With my eyes shut and my senses perceiving the nighttime and its melodic creatures outside, I made futile attempts over and over to fall back to sleep.

Around 1:30 in the morning—with my eyes shut but still fully aware of my surroundings—I had the most profound experience. Still trying to find that elusive sleep, I suddenly felt a sudden burst of very strong—and at first—terrifying wind. It came from nowhere, and then—within what must have been seven to ten seconds—was gone. But what lasted for less than ten seconds still now affects my life for the better.

The wind was very strong and was blowing at me from behind my body. I felt it pushing and blowing around my feet, legs, arms, back and head. I, of course, was immediately frightened by what was happening but almost immediately my fear turned to peace. It felt similar to riding in the back of a pickup truck, driving about 50 miles per hour and standing up with your back to the wind. Your ears are deafened by the wind's rushing sound, and the force of the air pushes your body.

During this moment of great disturbance to me, I tried my hardest to open my eyes but couldn't. So instead I lay there and prayed, and immediately something or someone reassured me that everything would be fine.

It lasted only seconds, and as soon as it ended I immediately opened my eyes and turned to see if the candle I had next to my alarm clock had blown out. It hadn't. I also surveyed the room to see if anything else had been moved or blown over, but everything in the room remained completely intact.

Something inside me guided me to the Bible, and I opened it to Jeremiah 39-40. I read the Scriptures and knew immediately that what I was reading was only a little of what was to come.

The following morning, I began writing what would become this series of letters. From the very beginning, I knew they would have to be titled "Letters of

Preparation for the Coming Years," not just for my family and me but for all of us as a global family.

I do not profess to be a theologian, a minister, a priest, or, for that matter, anyone of great importance. All I am—and all that I will ever want to be—is a humble servant of Christ and my fellow man.

I do not have great learning, nor do I profess to have any titles, certificates or diplomas to my name. All I pursue—and forever want to pursue—is just a sliver of God's infinite wisdom so I may better serve Him by helping to lead others to Him.

Nearly a year almost to the day that I experienced that profound event, I finished all forty letters. Initially, when I began writing, I had no idea of how many there would be, nor what I would write about, or anything else for that matter. Everything that I questioned or sought was given to me or confirmed in one way or another.

I do not claim to be the origin of the message nor the creator. I was merely the instrument that was used to bring it forth for the current generation and the ones to come.

The message is the same one that has been given to us throughout history from He that is the Almighty. The only thing that has changed is the year, but the divine message of warning is the same. The reason why this message is necessary remains as relevant as in the days of Sodom and Gomorrah.

I do not know if this message will be accepted, much less heeded. I pray that it is, but realistically know that is not up to me but to those receiving it. Do not think that it is I who is making this call to you. Rather, it is a greater and more powerful being that calls you to repent and believe. I am nothing. He that is the creator is All.

Come to Him out of love and not from fear due to circumstances that will become more and more fearful throughout the world. As St. Augustine said, "Believe first, so that you might understand," and not vice versa.

I give all thanks and praise to God for allowing me to be one of many sounding the trumpets before the great battles that are just around the corner become fully realized.

I thank all those that have supported me in one way or another, and for their contributions to my knowledge that went forth into making this project into a book.

It has been a year since I finished writing. Since then, I was not sure about making it into a book. All the letters that were initially written were sent that very same day via e-mail to friends, family and coworkers. After much contemplation and continued support from friends and family, I decided to make the message that had been known to them accessible to you all as well.

May God bless, keep, guide and protect each and every one of us. Take care, my brothers and sisters in Christ, and have faith and trust in our Lord, especially during the coming years.

Your brother,
horacio

Letter I-A Call to All: First letter of Preparation

Greetings to all, and well wishes upon yourselves and your friends and families. I trust in Jesus Christ our Lord that you are all well.

The reason I am writing to you all this morning is to prepare you for what has been written in Scripture and to allow you all, my brothers and sisters in Christ, to continue more than ever to live a Christian lifestyle in the face of modern materialism and self-indulgence.

If your relationship with the Almighty is well and healthy, then help spread the wealth that you have amassed through Him. Talk to friends, family and neighbors who perhaps may not be as wealthy as you in Christ's love and teachings so they, too, can be prepared.

If on the other hand your relationship with God is not as healthy, begin to build it now before the flood comes for then it will be too late.

Read the Word of God as written in the Bible, and let its words and teachings grow within your hearts. Love your neighbors and pray for your enemies for they need prayers more than anyone else.

My dear friends, the time for preparation is now. The storm clouds are hanging low, the lightening is getting closer and louder, and the time to repent and be well with God through Christ is Now! Don't leave it for tomorrow.

Pray to God, and ask that the Holy Spirit guide and enlighten you. Do not continue being a Christian of Mouth, but be one of Heart. For many are the ones who say they believe in Christ, but how many of them live according to His moral teachings?

Simply look around you. Look at the society and the culture that are promoted within this country. Look at everything. Look at the movies Hollywood puts out for the entire world to see and be influenced by. Look at the music that is created and sold as a form of artistic expression but has no value whatsoever. Look at the television and the programs that are promoted and viewed through it. Can you honestly say that this culture is one with God?

Capitalism in its extreme forms (pursuit and pleasure of money) has replaced this country's relationship and moral code that once belonged to God.

Where people once feared and worshiped the Almighty, they now mock and criticize the religious and all that worship the Almighty. Where people once shared in community with their neighbors and looked out for one another, they now live in gated communities and fear their neighbors. Where once life and the protection of it was considered noble and sacred, today it has been reduced to the decisions of morally irresponsible individuals who believe their selfish choice is above that of an innocent life.

Money and the pursuit of it has enslaved this country and created a new Golden Calf for the current degenerative generation.

It seems that enough no longer seems enough. People simply want more. They want a bigger car or truck. They want a bigger house. They want the latest and most expensive fashions. They want and seek those things that are not of God's creation but rather of man's.

People everywhere have simply forgotten the meaning of the word Humble. There is no longer any humility but instead contempt for those that are.

But that is where the danger lies for those of us who are students of history and Scripture; we know how the Almighty has dealt with proud peoples and proud civilizations throughout history.

But it seems that most of these teachings are seen by the blind and heard by the deaf for they cannot understand what they can't see or hear until it is too late, which has been the case throughout human history.

Capitalism needs the poor to function. Whether it's the poor of this country or the poor nations of the world, this insidious form of policy takes full advantage of them.

This form of economic policy creates millions of marginalized people who are called the working class poor for without the poor this system of economic government could not function.

It seems that the wealthier and more powerful a country is, the less dependent it becomes on God and His teachings.

For who needs God and His Words when you have the world's best scientists working for you? Scientists who foolishly attempt to take the place of God and His creative powers. When you have the world's mightiest military arsenal at your disposal and believe that it is up to you as a nation to dispense of justice throughout the world when you see fit, instead of allowing God to dispense justice as it is written in Scripture? When you are considered the economic powerhouse of the Globe and give nations a preferred-nation status with added benefits when they play by your rules but take them off your list when they don't?

All human power is deceptive and illusionary. Don't be deceived by what man appropriates and gives you, but look for and seek with fervor the knowledge and wisdom that comes from God. For it is He and only He who can give you the secrets to everlasting life. The decision is yours. Ask and pray that the Almighty gives you eyes to see the truth and ears to hear it. For many can see and hear in the general sense of the word, but very few can see and hear the Truth as delivered by our Lord and Savior Jesus Christ. It is when people have lived in darkness for years that they begin to become numb and lose the ability to see. It is then that which lives and abides in this darkness begins to come out with little or no fear for lack of the light of truth.

The recent events that are currently occurring throughout the world have been foretold many years ahead of time, and they are now coming to be. Whether it is found in Scripture, Nostradamus, the Great Mayan Civilization, Edgar Cayce, Native American Prophecy, Hindu Prophecy, the Marian Apparition messages and, most recently, the codes found in the Bible, they all point to these years as the end of a cycle.

It appears God chose to give us these messages and warnings through many different people and civilizations, but even then, most will ignore the warnings.

In the Old Testament book of Daniel (which I highly suggest everyone read) chapter 12, verse 8, the prophet Daniel says, "I heard but did not understand. Then I said, 'My Lord, what will be the outcome of these things?' He said, 'Go, Daniel, for these words are secret and sealed until the appointed time of the end. Many will be purified, cleansed, and proved. The impious will go on doing evil, none of them will understand anything, only the learned will understand."

The Biblical codes have been kept sealed up and secret for 3,000 years until the age of computers came, and only now has the technology existed to decode this text and give us warning before it's too late.

Sir Isaac Newton attempted to decode the Bible, and he even wrote a book on this topic (something that really surprised me). But he couldn't break the code because God intended that it couldn't be broken until the advent of computers.

Finally, "Be strong in the Lord with his energy and strength. Put on the whole armor of God to be able to resist the cunning of the devil. Our battle is not against human forces but against the rulers and authorities and their dark powers that govern this world. We are struggling against the spirits and supernatural forces of evil. Therefore, put on the whole armor of God that on the evil day, you may resist and stand your ground, making use of all your weapons. Take truth as your belt, justice as your breastplate, and zeal as your shoes to propagate the Gospel of peace. Always hold in your hands the shield of faith to repel the flaming arrows of the devil. Finally, use the helmet of salvation and sword of the Spirit, that is, the Word of God. Pray at all times as the Spirit inspires you. Keep watch, together with sustained prayer and supplication for all the brothers and sisters." (Ephesians 6:10)

I thought this scripture reading was very appropriate for the message I was relaying to you all. Please forward this message to your friends and families so they, too, hear the words and may treasure them and allow them to give fruit within their hearts.

Please pray, my brothers and sisters in Christ, that God leads you closer to Him. Pray for those who don't believe and don't follow the teachings of Christ so that they have a change of heart and believe. Have faith, and be mindful always that God is with us (Emanuel) always. May peace and love with faith from God the Father and from Christ Jesus the Lord be with you, brothers and sisters. And may His blessing be with all who love Christ Jesus, our Lord, with undying love.

Your brother,
horacio

Letter II-Prophecy for America

Greetings to you all, my brothers and sisters in Jesus Christ our Lord. May His blessings be upon you and your loved ones, and peace be with you all today.

On the 28th day of the third month of this year 2005, the word of the Lord came to me, and He came through the Holy Spirit with such strength and tenacity that it rivaled the winds of a hurricane that blew around my body and awoke me from my slumber. The Lord had me open His book, and this is what I read and how He gave me to interpret it.

"My servant, look toward the leader of the free world, king of Freedom, and prophesy against all him. Say, This is the word of the Lord. I am against you, Leader, king of Freedom. Moan! Ah! The day is near; the day of the Lord is coming! It will be a day of clouds, a time of doom for the nations. The sword is brought to strike this land, and anguish will come to her. The slain will fall throughout her, and people will run off with its riches, and its foundations will be torn away. Throughout her, from coast to coast, the sword will strike people of the covenant. This is the word of the Lord.

"Those who support her will fall, too; her power will crumble! From New York to Los Angeles, people will perish, Word of the Lord. They will be numbered among desolate lands, and her cities among ruined cities. They will know I am the Lord when I set fire to her and when all her Allies are crushed.

"On that day, my messengers will leave in ships and planes to shake the people of America out of their complacency, and they will be in anguish on the day of her fall; for the day is coming. Thus, says the Lord, I will put an end to the hordes of America by means of a foreign invasion from the far East, the most feared among the nations, for I the Lord, will lead them here to destroy the land.

"They will draw their weapons and aim them against America and fill their land with victims. I will take away her strength and power she has found in her false wealth and hand her over to the wicked nation. I will use the hand of the foreigner to make the land and all it contains a waste. I, the Lord, have spoken.

"I will destroy the idols she made out of her abundance in wealth and wipe out the false masters she served throughout the land, from sea to shining sea. No longer will there be pride and contempt in the land of Freedom, but fear will reign throughout. I will make a wasteland of Los Angeles, set fire to New York and inflict punishment on its capitol. I will pour out my fury on Washington, the fortress of America.

"I will set fire to her. Washington will writhe in agony. They will enter her through a breach and take her by storm. The sons she bore will fall by the sword, and her daughters will be taken captive. What a dark day it will be when I break the leadership of America and destroy her arrogant might. As for this city, a cloud will cover it, and her daughters will be taken captive. I will inflict punishment on Her, and they will know I am the Lord."

The Lord continued to speak and said, "My servant, I have broken the arm of the leader of the Free World. No one has treated it for healing or bandaged it to enable him to hold a sword. That is why," thus says the Lord, "see, I am against this leader, king of Freedom. I will break his arms, both the one that is strong and the wounded one as well. I will scatter her children among the nations and disperse them in other lands. I will strengthen the arm of her enemies. Her enemies will come from the East. I will give the leader of the East a mighty sword, but as for the leader of Freedom, I will have broken his, making him moan like a mortally wounded man. Yes, I will strengthen the arm of the king of the East, but make Freedom's leader arm limp. Then they will know I am the Lord God Almighty, when I place my sword in the hands of the East. I will scatter freedom's children among the nations and disperse them in other lands, and they will then know I am the Lord.

"Say to America's leader, whom is comparable to you in your greatness? You are like a very tall majestic spruce with beautiful branches providing great forest shade with its top among the clouds. Throughout the years, the sapling that struggled to survive at first and depended on me for nourishment and protection early on grew. The waters of life that I provided made it grow, and the streams ascending from the deep springs that watered all the trees of the land flowed straight to its roots. It grew higher than all the other trees of the forest. Its boughs increased, and its branches grew larger because of the plentiful life giving water that I provided. The birds of the air nested in its boughs, and all the creatures, great and small, strong and weak, rich and poor, tired and wretched, brought forth their young under its mighty branches for shade and protection. Numerous nations lived under its shade, and all were one.

"It became majestic in height and in thickness of its branches for its roots were turned toward plentiful water. The other trees in the forest of God could not equal it. No other tree in the forest could equal it. I made it beautiful and unique.

I gave abundance to its branches, and it became the envy of all the other trees in the forest.

"That is why," thus says the Lord God, "Because it grew so tall and reached the clouds and became proud, I will now hand it over to the ruler of the nations who will treat it according to its wickedness. I have now rejected it and its entire proud splendor. Where it once allowed creatures, great and small, protection and shade if they needed it, it now turns its attention away from the meekest creatures and looks only for its self interest.

"Because I have now rejected it," says the Lord, "I will allow foreigners, the most terrible among nations, to cut it down. Its boughs and branches will lay strewn throughout the forest floor. All nations have fled from its shade and protection and have abandoned it. I do this to prevent well-watered trees from attaining such a height and reaching the clouds.

"The other nations were shaken at the noise of its fall. Those from among the nations who lived in its shade, they, too, went down together to those slain by the sword. O tree, splendid and glorious, which among the trees of the earth was comparable to you? But you were made to go down, just like so many other trees that have grown such as you did throughout the forest of history."

Brothers and sisters in Christ, I have provided the latter so as to continue your preparation. Do not be fearful when the earth shakes, the winds howl, and the branches of this mighty spruce begin to break, but rather turn to the Lord and praise him with all your heart and soul. Do not just provide Him lip service, but rather provide Him love. In this love, you should also provide love and respect for your bodies for they are His temples. Love your neighbor for is it not our duty to provide care and love for all of God's children and not just the ones pleasing to our eyes? Also love your enemies.

Pray for all those who have stone hearts that they may turn their hearts of stone to flesh. Pray for those that do not know God, and the Son, that they come back to communion with Him. And pray for those that mistreat the widow and the orphaned, for it is those that persecute the defenseless, the poor and meek that will have the most to account for in the Lord's eyes.

Many will be called, but few will be chosen.

Brothers and sisters, let us repent now and turn from our sinful ways. Call on the Lord Jesus Christ to give you strength and steadfastness that you may not sleep but rather stay awake.

The message that was just related to you was one that was not pleasing to the ear, but not all of the messages that are relayed from the Lord are pleasing. Rather they make us take notice and become aware of the truth. The truth is not always pleasing.

We live in a society promoted by a culture that blurs truth and fiction. So much so, that what many believe to be true is not. What many believe to be good is not. What many believe to be security and wealth is not.

Case in point: In this society everyone is under the misconception and false sense of security that is provided by insurers. Everyone has insurance for everything. Health, life, auto, home, et cetera. In a society such as this, who needs insurances from God, when you have State Farm? Who needs to pray for health, life, home and happiness when so many mistakenly believe in their own abilities to obtain strength and security through manmade policies? People have created the false notion that they are the source of their own glory.

Most of the message I just relayed to you was from a book in the Old Testament, but I felt moved by the spirit to relay to you all through modern places and people. The book is from Ezekiel, chapters 30-31. The original warning was to the mighty Egypt, but the prophet also warns the modern day might of America (modern-day Rome/Egypt).

Continue to pray, pray and pray some more. This message will fall on some deaf ears and blind eyes, but many will take it and water it so that it may grow and spread. I pray for you all, and ask that you pray for me. I also ask for intercessions on behalf of the Saints and the Virgin Mary to keep all of your friends and family well.

Letter III-Paths to Salvation

Greetings to you all, my brothers and sisters in our Lord Jesus Christ. May I find you and your loved ones doing well today, this fifth day of this fifth month in this 2005th year. I have been praying for you all and hope that your preparation has been going well and growing.

Brothers and sisters in the Lord, and those who are currently not in Him, I am speaking to all of you this day. Not just to those who follow His words and teachings but mainly to those that do not. For did not our Lord Jesus say that He came down to Earth to heal the sick? Who needs a doctor when one is healthy? He was sent down to earth and became man for the sake and salvation of all, not just the healthy. Not just the Jews who believed in His message and became followers of His. Not just for Christians who follow the Law of Christ but for everyone who believes, loves and trusts in Him.

We often feel neglected and sometimes rejected by those who comply with the Law and Sacraments of the Church, regardless of the denomination. We sometimes feel and think that we are unworthy of His love because of how others judge and condemn us. They make us feel less of a Christian and more as an unworthy sinner.

It is true that human nature can be very cruel and often times very hurtful and divisive. People foolishly walk proud as followers of Jesus. They have amassed a great knowledge of doctrinal and theological laws and quote Scripture passages left and right. They judge some and condemn others because others are not as enlightened as they are.

But of what use is all this great affluent and arrogant learning if it is not properly applied to rooting out those habitual vices that separate us from God? If it does not further strengthen us spiritually and instead further creates pride and the fruits of pride within us?

Perhaps it was because they were not baptized that they judge them. Maybe it was because they do not follow the Sacraments as they interpret them or feel they should be followed that they condemn them.

But to these men and women of the Christian law, I ask: What is more important? To love and trust in the Lord Jesus Christ and believe in Him with all your heart or to be baptized? Surely there are many who have been baptized or con-firmed and anointed in His name but are far from being faithful to Him. One must adhere to one of the two before the other can be adhered to. I am not less-ening the act of being baptized for Jesus himself felt it was important enough to be baptized by John, and He was the Son of God. Baptism after all cleanses us of our sins and inducts us into God's family as His children.

All I am saying is that **true baptism** brings true conversion to Christ and vice-versa. Because in this life we currently live, we need both a physical and a spiritual birth.

It is up to us, my brothers and sisters in the Lord, to help bring those who have not been birthed through the Spirit so that they, too, can be beacons of light to the world.

Jesus came to overturn certain restrictive and prejudicial thoughts and beliefs of His time. For Jewish law is such that it, too, focuses more on tradition and protocol than it does on faith, love and forgiveness. How would a Jewish man answer the following: What is more important—to have faith and love in God or to be circumcised? For it is written, "Abraham believed in God who, because of this held him to be a just man." (Romans 4:9)

It was his great faith and not only his acts and strict interpretation of rules that allowed him to be the man whom God chose to father many nations.

Many throughout the Christian church, regardless of denomination, have fallen into this trap. Not just followers and congregation members, but the Shep-herd's as well.

For many are the ones who abide by all the doctrines and sacraments but dis-regard the most important one—love, forgiveness and compassion for their neighbors and their enemies, and love and trust in God.

For if we had love of God first and foremost, then we could begin to fulfill the first two.

Do not be fooled, my brothers and sisters, into believing you are saved just because you have been marked by baptism or circumcision or any other sacra-ment. But rather know that you are saved through the faith and love you demon-strate not only to God but also to your neighbors, regardless of their treatment toward you. For this is the beginning of true conversion and imitation of Christ.

In today's world, we often find that our ears and eyes are far more receptive to a toned down, sweet presentation of God's message rather than to one that speaks the truth. We tune in to what we like to hear, and tune out what is hard to hear.

In a similar fashion, we do the same thing with television programming, fast food places, radio stations, et cetera. We simply change the station, or change the fast food restaurant choice, or change the church. We go in search of a message and messenger that is to our liking.

We must be careful when doing this. For often times, we fall into traps set by shepherds who are looking out only for their self interest. Even the apostle St. Paul wrote in Romans 16:17: *"Brothers and Sisters, I beg of you to be careful of those who are causing divisions and troubles in teaching you a different teaching from the one you were taught. Keep away from them, because those persons do not serve Christ our Lord, but their own interest, deceiving with their soft and entertaining language those of simple hearts. Everybody knows that you are very obedient, and because of that I am happy, but I wish to warn you to do what is good and avoid what is evil."*

We must truly be careful for Jesus himself warned to not be in fear of those who can harm the body but rather those who can harm the spirit. We must not allow ourselves to be fooled by a shepherd who gives his flock opium to keep them happy and coming back for more instead of a true message of salvation, which is not always pleasing to the ear.

St. Paul says in First Corinthians 1:17: *"For Christ did not send me to baptize, but to proclaim his Gospel. And not with beautiful words! That would be like getting rid of the cross of Christ. The language of the Cross-remains nonsense for those who are lost. Yet for us who are saved it is the power of God."* No cross, no crown. No Good Friday, no Easter Sunday.

It is for this reason that I bring this point to the surface. It is vitally important that we continue to grow and become closer to God through Jesus Christ, especially in this day and age. But be wise in the Shepherd you choose or for that matter chooses you. Jesus said, *"You will know them by their fruits,"* and in this manner you will know where this person is coming from and where they intend to go.

Be wary and pray that the Holy Spirit gives you eyes to see, ears to hear, and a heart to feel and know what is the truth and what is of this world.

Do not be fooled by messengers who wear fine suits, drive luxurious cars, and live in extravagant homes, yet deliver soft and entertaining words as Paul puts it. For it is written, "One cannot serve two masters." By the same token, we should be careful of falling into the trap of believing that our good deeds and acts merit something in return from God. That just because we have fulfilled certain sacramental acts throughout our lifetime, we are entitled to certain rewards.

Love and faith, faith and love, these are the two issues at the heart of salvation through the Lord. For it is when we have love and faith that we begin to grow in mercy, trust and humility, not from having met and fulfilled certain Sacramental acts alone. They are merely the tools and instruments that are to be used, a means to an end, not an end in and of themselves.

The institution that is the Church, too, must be careful that it not becomes the rigid structure (if it hasn't already) that Jesus came to preach and prophesy against.

How does it treat the marginalized? Whether they are the homeless, the immigrants, the homosexual community, et cetera. Are they inclusive and loving toward these groups or condemning? I have personally witnessed members and shepherds of a congregation turn their backs on members of these groups.

For was it not the teachers of the Law (Pharisees) that did the same thing to Jesus and His followers?

We must remember that we are all brothers and sisters in Christ, even if the other person does not acknowledge our Lord.

Continue praying, my brothers and sisters, and pray on a daily basis so as to please our Lord Jesus Christ. I, too, will continue to pray for all of you, and ask that same in return. Pray especially for those who have hearts of stone that they may be turned to flesh for it is they who need these prayers the most.

Thank you and have a great and Spirit-filled day.

Letter IV-The Poor and Meek

Greetings to all of you, my brothers and sisters in our Lord Jesus Christ. May His peace, love and faith be with each and every one of you this fifth day of the fourth month of this year 2005.

It is with great pleasure that I offer you all my salutations today for I have just come back today from a short excursion I took here in our beautiful Texas Hill Country.

The trip was very tiresome, lonely and exhausting but well worth it. I took it to further my preparation and devotion to the Call, which our Lord sends to me. Having no food or companionship for a couple of days was a very spiritual experience.

The call is simply this: To continue preparing people through the Spirit so they, too, will be heavily armored and protected from the spiritual enemy's attacks coming from both within and outside themselves. They must also be heavily armed with the guidance of the Spirit, the love of the Father, and the faith of the Saints.

Brothers and sisters, being without food, shelter, companionship and guidance is very hard, especially in today's world. The lack of any of these personal needs can be very humbling and frustrating, especially when we are so accustomed to having them all met, plus more! Especially living in this more-than-privileged country, but that is where the problem arises. For it is when we have plentiful water, food, shelter, companionship and health that we most forget about God. Having and living in great affluence is the main factor in spiritual death.

Some of us thank Him for His bountiful gifts to us but do so sporadically and superficially. But take any one of these away, whether it's food, water, health or shelter, and we begin to knock incessantly on His door.

So why do many of us turn our backs on those who endure the lack of these basic needs on a daily basis?

The homeless not only have to survive days and nights with little or no food, shelter, clothing or water but also the constant gaze of contempt and indifference. Are they not our brothers and sisters in our Lord's eyes? Did not our Lord and

Savior set the standard by saying, "Whatever we did for the least of our brothers and sisters, we would have done for Him?"

St. James said, *"Brothers, what good is it to profess faith without showing works? Such faith has no power to save you. If a brother or sister is in need of clothes or food, and one of you says, 'May things go well for you, be warm and satisfied,' without attending to their material needs, what good is that? So it is for faith without deeds: it is totally dead."* (James 2:14-17)

Many of us make attempts—in our eyes—to help the poor and homeless by giving them our spare change. But most often times, we walk faster and look the other way when passing them so we don't have to acknowledge them.

It is not enough to hand out our extra pennies or ignore them completely. Instead, we must love them. Love them with a sincere and genuine heart. Love them and pray for them. That is what Jesus truly wants us to do. For when you do this, not only do you increase your wealth in heaven but your brothers and sisters in the Lord as well.

In today's society, it is becoming increasingly clear to me on a daily basis of the cruel and cold nature with which we treat our homeless brethren.

Cities are now passing laws and ordinances that prohibit them from sleeping, eating, and congregating in certain places or they'll be arrested and fined. To add insult to injury, their meager belongings, which many of them carry in bags, will be confiscated and destroyed. San Antonio is the most recent city to pass these ordinances, but I am sure many throughout the country have laws similar to that or are attempting the same.

These city council men and women do not know Jesus Christ, much less the Father. But I'm almost positive that most, if not all, call themselves Christians and attend some form of service or worship on Sunday or Saturday. They go to service, sing the praises, hear the sugar-coated teachings of their shepherds (that in some way or another further validates their own self interest as well as that of their flocks'), and the very next day go back to work by passing more of the same anti-Christian ordinances.

How blind can they be, Lord? How deaf can they be, Lord? How cold-hearted can they be, oh, Lord? They truly are great Christians who pay great "lip service" to the Lord. Unfortunately, that is all they do.

But I know and firmly believe that the poor and homeless do not need as many prayers as the people who rebuke and offend them. They are who we should truly pray for.

Pray for those that shun them. Pray for those that mock, abuse and humiliate them. Pray for those who attempt to steal their dignity. Pray for those who offer a slap on the face instead of a helping and loving hand. Pray for those who call themselves Christians and men of Godly faith during one day of the week but by their acts are contrary to the Gospels during the week. Pray for those who have foolishly replaced their values and morals in the Lord with those of the almighty dollar and political power.

Yes, my brothers and sisters, these are the men and women we should pray for the most! It is true, the poor and homeless do need intercessory prayers, but not as many as their foolish oppressors do. For does not Scripture tell us that the "meek and poor shall inherit the Earth?"

This is true. They will and they shall inherit it. That is why it is so important that we treat all of God's children the same but especially with love, genuine love and compassion. Perhaps you could fast for one day or maybe two (and offer it up to the Lord as penance) to fully understand what it means to be without food, just as our less fortunate brothers and sisters.

For it is when we suffer and face tribulations that the Lord makes a personal call to us. The poor and meek throughout the world are in close communion with God due to their lack of physical, emotional or spiritual needs. For when you have to do without certain needs on a daily basis, your faith in the Lord increases one hundred times.

On the other hand, when we have an excess or abundance of things to more than fill our needs, we become complacent and lazy in our faith and lives.

As material wealth increases, so does our pride, and in turn one's foolish belief of living without the need for God's always nourishing water of life. For it is this water that saves, nourishes, replenishes and purifies. It is this water that the poor throughout the earth have in abundance, but the people of privileged countries lack as though a drought. We begin to foolishly think and believe we are the source of our own glory.

Pray, my brothers and sisters, that the Lord our God increase your dependence on His water of life and not on the water that flows from empty wells. Pray that through our Lord Jesus Christ, you become all knowing in the things that are of God and reject those that are of this world. Pray that, through the Spirit, you receive the vision to see the truth in all, hear the truth in all, and feel and believe in the truth through Jesus Christ our Lord. Pray especially for those who oppress, rebuke the poor and meek, either personally or legislatively, that they may see the errors of their ways.

For it is far better to be poor and meek in material abundance than it is to be poor and meek in the Spirit. I will continue to pray for you, my brothers and sisters in our Lord Jesus Christ, and ask that you all continue to pray for me. Have a safe and peaceful day.

Your brother,
horacio

Letter V-Know Them By Their Fruits

Good morning to you, my brothers and sisters in the Lord. It is a beautiful morning here, and I hope that wherever you find yourselves reading this letter, it is just as beautiful.

"God, who made the world and all that is in it, does not dwell in sanctuaries made by human hands, being as He is Lord of heaven and earth. Nor does His worship depend on anything made by human hands, as if He were in need. Rather, it is He who gives life and breath and everything else to everyone." (Acts 17:25)

This is a Scripture quote from the New Testament that I came across the other day and thought it was appropriate for the time in which we are living and how certain Christians lead their lives.

The other day, I was watching one of these Christian television evangelists and was carefully listening to what he was saying. Everything that spouted from his mouth was "seed" this and "seed" that. "You cannot expect to receive from God if you do not give to Him!" he shouted. With sweat dripping off his brow, he continued to give his Spirit-induced (according to him) sermon. "We must plant our seed and water it, but we must make sure that it is a nice, big seed so that we may reap a big reward," he said. For two more hours, he continued to talk in this manner, always about giving. He would also cite Scripture to support and promote his message. The crowd loved it.

They couldn't get enough of both the messenger and his message. During his preaching, the program posted a number that viewers could call to give their "seed" of $205 a month. That amount was the price the minister and his company had decided was enough to start "gardening" in his church. Actually, $205 was the minimum; he really wanted closer to $2,000 a month.

My brothers and sisters in the Lord, often times we come across unscrupulous people who call themselves followers of God but are nothing more that wolves in sheep's clothing.

They even have the audacity to preach the Word of God and call themselves ministers and pastors of God. I know we should give to help our church and its leaders when we can and when we are financially stable. I also know about tithing that's advocated by many churches. But many of these churches are filled with people who are financially well off and can better contribute to their causes. But, my brothers and sisters, what about the poor? Will they be left out in the cold because they cannot give? Surely not, for it is they who have the ability to give the most pleasing to God … love and mercy through a compassionate heart.

In today's world of materialist consumerism, we often times confuse what the world wants and demands of us with what God wants and demands of us.

God is not about materialism. God is not about consumerism. Just like the Scripture passage I quoted from Acts 17:24-27: ***God does not dwell in sanctuaries made by human hands, being as He is Lord of heaven and earth. Nor does His worship depend on anything made by human hands, as if He were in need.***

Yet we are constantly bombarded with self-proclaimed messengers of God that tell us the exact opposite—that we need to give, give, and give some more just in case God doesn't think it's enough. Perhaps it may not be enough for them.

Yet what these false prophets talk about is manmade wealth that goes to help support their extravagant lifestyles. "You shall know them by their fruits," Jesus said.

Their words are soothing, and the message is enticing because giving some how creates the illusion that God is pleased, or at least that's what these unscrupulous ministers want you to think. These men and women have forgotten the true message of Christ and have fallen themselves into the trap that the world sets for men of worldly desires—the trap of illusionary fame, power and money. But that is not enough because in order to maintain this illusion, they must continue preaching the same message, week after week. Give money—not praise and thanks through daily prayer or fasting or some other sacrificial penance that brings true sanctifying and divine grace. Give what man has made of his own hands, as if God were in need.

How foolish for people to designate this kind of status to God, yet thousands do it on a weekly basis. It is foolish for the sheep, but deceitful for the so-called pastors and ministers of God to proclaim this message as they have packaged it.

My brothers and sisters, do not misinterpret this message. I am not saying it is wrong to support the church because financial support is a big part of our commitment to the church and its leaders, and should be done so. But it should be done within our limits and not what someone else has set as the appropriate limit.

Because was it not Jesus, when one day He sat down opposite the temple treasury to watch people dropping money into the treasury box and, watching many rich people put in large offerings, saw a poor widow woman put in two small coins. He turned to His disciples and said, *"Truly I say to you, this poor widow put in more than all those others who have given larger offerings. For all of them gave from their plenty, but she gave from her poverty and put everything she had, her very living."* (Mark 12:41-44)

There was also another time Jesus addressed a similar issue (Mark 10:17-22): *"Just as Jesus was setting out on his journey again, a man ran up, knelt before him and asked, 'Good master, what must I do to have eternal life* (something all good Christians seek)?' *Jesus answered him by repeating the Commandments to him, and he in turn replied that he had kept and obeyed all of them since childhood. Then Jesus looked steadily at him and loved him, and said, 'Go and sell what you have and give the money to the poor, and you will have riches in heaven. Then come and follow me.' On hearing these words from Jesus, he looked down and went away sorrowful, for he was a man of great wealth and did not wish to part with his worldly possessions."*

I wonder how many of these wealthy Christian pastors and ministers would react the same way as this wealthy man did? How many would actually sell everything to inherit eternal life as a follower of Christ?

My brothers and sisters, it is for these men and women, these pastors and leaders of flocks throughout, that we must pray for and hope that the true grace of God and spirit of Jesus come upon them so that they may begin to see the true meaning of being a follower of Jesus Christ and what is truly pleasing to Him and the Father, not what is pleasing to man.

The benefits and false security that wealth offers are very tempting and deceptive. It is here that many fall into the trap of believing that their wealth can save them from anything this world may throw their way. Therefore, they place more assurance on what they have than on what God can provide.

Just like leaves that are swept away by the wind across open fields, so are many people who continue to be swept away by the winds of society and culture. From whatever direction the wind blows, people who are not anchored and rooted in the Word of God and His teachings are swept away by the wind, regardless of what direction it blows.

But whatever has roots cannot blow away because it is anchored, just like reeds of grass. No matter how hard the wind blows, they are flexible and stand their ground because they are rooted firmly in the ground, yet are flexible enough to withstand the greatest winds.

On the other hand, we cannot be like the majestic but rigid oak. Because mighty winds can blow hard and break some of its branches or even cause the oak to break in half.

Continue praying, my brothers and sisters in our Lord Jesus Christ, that we may be strong and resilient when rejecting the lure of false hope and security that wealth offers. Pray, too, that people are not blinded and misled by unscrupulous pastors of God that provide their sheep only what they want to hear and not what they need to hear. For if many of these sheep actually heard what they needed to hear, those monthly $205 "seed contributions" might just cease and dry up their gardens of plenty. Then the pastors would be left with an empty pen.

I, in turn, will continue praying for you, my brothers and sisters, and hope that you continue to pray for me. Peace is with you all, and my deepest heart-felt wishes go to you all.

Your brother,
horacio

Letter VI-Suffering

Greetings and many blessings to you, my brothers and sisters in our Lord Jesus Christ on this beautiful 14th day of the fourth month of this 2005th year.

I come to you once again as has been the custom now to bring forth the Good News so we may share and further promote it to become better prepared before the coming lean years. In today's world, many of us are surrounded with constant scenes of sufferings, tribulations and scenes of pain throughout the world. Perhaps we have had our own sufferings that seem to have no real reason or purpose. Perhaps we are still going through them.

Often times, it is during these moments of personal pain and anguish that we are healed of our personal blindness and are then able to see who it is we have been ignoring for so long. But then again, there are a few who continue in their blindness and further curse and abandon God for what He has allowed to happen in their lives.

If anyone knows about pain, surely it is He. For if we are faithful to God and His teachings, then surely we are aware that He gave His only begotten Son to be ruthlessly mocked, tortured, and eventually killed for our sake.

Some of us—after going through these moments of pain and humiliation—realize what we have forsaken for so long. Perhaps it was a lack of love for our neighbors? Perhaps it was the absence of love and compassion for the least of our brothers? Maybe it was a lack of love for our parents or our family? But most often, it is the lack of love and faith in the Lord our God.

Many of us try everything and anything to heal our pain and soothe our spirit but find that something is still not right. Something is still missing. We turn to all kinds of doctors and therapists to help alleviate some of the pain but find the solution very short-lived. Or perhaps we bury the pain deep within ourselves, leave it there unresolved, and allow it to manifest bitter fruits that continue to affect our lives long after the fact.

How is it that people can be so blind for so long? Yet it happens on a daily basis, sometimes for a lifetime.

Brothers and sisters, must we be reminded of how our Lord treated His people, the ones He loved most. Read Deuteronomy 8:2-5: *"Remember how Yahweh, your God, brought you through the desert for forty years. He humbled you to test you and know what was truly in your heart, whether you would keep his commandments or not (turn against him). He made you experience hunger, but he gave you manna to eat, which neither you nor your fathers had known, but to show you that man does not live on bread alone, but on all that proceeds from the mouth of God, is life for man."*

It is during these times of pain, sorrow, and personal trials that our Lord puts us to the test and sees how we react to Him. It is a form of spiritual training, if you will, that allows us to work on and strengthen our spiritual muscle.

Many of us have so much pride within that it is almost impossible to acknowledge that we have been humbled or are in the process of being humbled. We continue to walk and live in blindness, even as everything around us has fallen apart, and yet we continue to wonder why?

We are reminded in Deuteronomy that He made His people experience hunger but gave them manna to eat.

In the same way, my brothers and sisters, He makes us experience hunger as well. Whether it is hunger for justice, hunger for love, hunger for faith, hunger for strength, or hunger for the soothing of pain that we each carry inside, it is this hunger that the Lord will always make us experience once we begin to stray from His shadow.

He will allow for this type of hunger to settle into us so we may be wise enough to understand that we do not live on bread alone (in other words, things that are made by human hands or come from humans) but instead on all that comes from the mouth of God.

For it is in Him and His words that we find true solace and comfort, not in what our own hands, money, security and insurances can provide. It is what He can provide for us. For it is He that gives us the true bread of life and does so through Jesus Christ our Lord.

In today's world, I often see and hear so-called messengers of God who preach about how the Lord doesn't want anyone to suffer and how He wants everyone to be happy, fruitful and wealthy. These sweet-to-the-ear talkers of God only want to emphasize the good but never the pain and suffering that it truly takes to be a follower of Jesus Christ.

Did not Jesus set the standard of pain and suffering when He carried His cross and thereby gave us the example that if we wish to follow in His footsteps, then we, too, should bear the weight of our cross?

In Luke 9:23 (also in Mark 8:34 and Matthew 16:24), Jesus says, *"If you wish to be a follower of mine, deny yourself and take up your cross each day, and follow me.*

For if you choose to save your life, you will lose it, and if you lose your life for my sake, you will save it. What does it profit you to gain the Whole World, while you destroy and lose yourself?"

Our daily cross is one that each and every one of us has to bear at some point in our lives, and Jesus reminded us of this. The cross that each one of us bears are the trials, tribulations and sufferings each one of us has at some point in our lives. These are the tribulations that either allow us to turn to Him or turn on Him, for many are the ones who blame God when these events begin to unfold in their lives. [God ways are not man's ways, and they never have, are or will be. His ways are like the mighty oceans of the world put together, and our capacity to understand is like a thimble that tries to take in all the oceans' water. It can't be done.] They constantly want to keep the focus on all that brings wealth and happiness through human hands and is of this world, yet abandon the heavy cross that has been set aside for us. Why do you think that is?

Maybe it has to do with the fact that people do not like to be reminded of the cross that has been set aside for them, so they search and search until they find a pastor who gives them the option of carrying their cross.

But my brothers and sisters, if this were really the case, then why throughout history and the Bible do we see the people that God loved most suffer and experience the most pain and persecution? Remember the Old Testament prophets and their personal trials and suffering? Moses and his people wandering through the desert? Jesus Christ and all of His apostles, and later the saints who led trying, financially impoverished, violently persecuted and painful lives?

It is because this was how they were able to find their path back to God, and His true message ... Stay by my side, and nothing or no one will harm you.

God speaks to us very quietly, and if we lead lives full of noise and distractions, His message will never reach us. That is why each one of us must have a time of preparation, where through suffering trials and tribulations we become stronger in faith and hope.

It is through suffering that we are able to fully comprehend God's message to us, whatever that may be.

We become self-centered and foolish when we attempt to deal with it through human means and methods. Worse yet is when we become blinder and harden our hearts and minds even more. We are similar to children who have been reprimanded or punished. We go off to sulk and allow anger and hatred to remain within our hearts.

It is pride, my brothers and sisters, that allows the ones who can see to be blind, and the lack of pride that allows those that are blind to see once again.

It is similar to the story in John 9:1-41 of the man who was blind since birth. The apostles asked whether it was him or his parents who had sinned to cause him to be born blind. Jesus simply said, *"Neither this man nor his parents sinned; he was born blind so that God's power might be shown through him."* He then made some paste in his hands with clay and spit, rubbed it on the blind man's eyes, and told him to go wash it off. After doing so, the man that had been blind since birth was able to see for the first time in his life. But the Jewish priest and the Pharisees, who had great contempt and disdain for Jesus, did not believe any of it. Even worse, they continued to condemn Jesus because He had performed the act on the Sabbath! They were more concerned that Jesus had broken the law than that He'd restored vision to someone who had never seen before. The man who had was healed of his blindness believed and found new faith in Jesus, but the ones who had always been able to see continued to be blind and have no faith.

My dear brothers and sisters, it is this blindness that continues to affect many of us today throughout the world.

It is usually our brothers and sisters who have more faith in what their wealth or what their own hands can do that are the most blind and continue living in darkness. Or perhaps we are like the Pharisees in the Scripture? Are we more concerned about the laws of the church and the sacramental rites that must or must not be performed than we are about true faith and loving acts of kindness and compassion?

Truly it is the blind, lame, poor and handicapped of this world that are always in the Lord's shadow for they are in constant need of help that only He can give them, and they understand this. He is with them, and they are with Him always. But as for the rest of us, my brothers and sisters, are we in His shadow?

You see, He is always with us, but can the truth be said about us? Let us also be reminded what is in James 1:2-4, *"Consider yourselves fortunate, my brothers and sisters, when you meet with every kind of trial, for you know that the testing of your faith makes you steadfast. Let your steadfastness become perfect with deeds, that you yourselves may be perfect and blameless without any defect."* For it was through these words that St. James (the first Catholic bishop of Jerusalem) reminds us that we must remain steadfast in our faith and not be tempted into being disloyal to our Lord.

Let us also be reminded, my brothers and sisters, that throughout history, although many people today are blind or ignorant of this, great evil and destruction has been allowed upon us or the world by God to bring about a greater good. He did, after all, bring about the greatest good upon all humanity only after allowing the greatest evil: the crucifixion of His only begotten Son to be fulfilled.

Continue to pray, my bothers and sisters in the Lord, that we have eyes to see, ears to hear, and hearts to feel the truth as given to us through the Holy Spirit. Pray for me, and I, as always, will continue to pray for you. The time for preparation is now, and we must continue to prepare ourselves for the coming lean years. Be good to one another, and love your neighbors and your enemies, for it is they that need the most love and forgiveness.

Your brother in Christ,
horacio

Letter VII-Love For One Family

Greetings to you this morning, my brothers and sisters in our Lord Jesus Christ! I am very glad to be alive this morning and filled with the Spirit as I write to you this loved-filled letter. I hope and pray that you are doing well this morning.

This letter of preparation is the seventh I am writing, and I give thanks to God for filling me with His breath, which is that of the Spirit, for allowing me the insight, love and faithfulness to fulfill what is contained in the following message.

My brothers and sisters in the Lord, there is truly no higher gift than love. In Corinthians13:1-8 we read, *"If I could speak all the human and angelic tongues, but had no love, I would only be sounding brass or a clanging cymbal. If I had prophecy, knowing secret things with all kinds of knowledge, and had faith great enough to remove mountains, but had no love, I would be nothing. If I gave everything I had to the poor, even gave up my own body, but only to receive praise and not through love, it would be of no value to me. Love is patient, kind, without envy. It is not boastful or arrogant. It is not ill mannered nor does it seek its own interest. Love overcomes anger and forgets offenses. It does not take delight in wrong, but rejoices in the truth. Love excuses everything, believes all things, hopes all things, and endures all things. Love will never end."*

It is truly these words that St. Paul wrote to us around two thousand years ago that still resonate in our minds and fill our hearts. They have not lost any of their meaning or been worn away by the years, but have remained strong throughout the centuries. Like fine wine, they have aged well to perfection.

It is truly this message, my brothers and sisters, that we should take to plant in our hearts and nourish with the living water that comes from Jesus so as to make the fruitful plant of love grow within us.

Why do we carry anger, hate, jealousy, envy and the like within us if we are all called to be children of the one true God? Why are there so many issues that affect and divide us? How would Jesus react if He were to come back today, this very day, and see for Himself the thousands of Christian sects and churches that abound throughout the world? Are we not all called to be His sheep? So why can we not accept our brother who prays while he stands while we pray sitting down? Why do we criticize our sister who is baptized in a river while we believe a sprinkling of water on the head? Who are we to judge someone who does the work of Jesus on Sunday instead of going to mass and resting? Did not Jesus Himself address this issue of doing God's work on the Sabbath by healing?

Brothers and sisters, it is truly this message that is calling to all of us today. We must break down these barriers that hold us back from truly acknowledging and worshiping God the Father through our Savior Jesus Christ.

For Jesus Himself taught that a house divided cannot stand. The same is true for a nation, a family and even religious structures. It is these divisions that cause so much unnecessary pain and suffering. The same is true of the Christian faith. Religion and evangelization many times go hand in hand, but they, too, can be at odds with one another. This can clearly be seen where one church is more concerned with religious practices and doctrine while another evangelizes the word of God to the masses. One depends on its hierarchical structures for support, and the other leans on its ever-changing demographical congregations for support.

But the winds are beginning to blow from a new direction, and the direction is coming from within individuals like ourselves, my brothers and sisters. We are the new direction from which this new wind blows. We will be the sewing string that is used to hem up the rifts between the old and the new and create one true to the gospel faith. We are currently living in the "Time of the nations," and/or the last days, the period referred to by both Paul and Luke. [We live in the period that started at the inception of the Church at Pentecost and will continue until Jesus Christ returns in glory.]

It is during this time, my brothers and sisters, that we as true disciples of Christ and the Gospels have begun to go and spread the Good News to all peoples and all nations.

We will do so without religious barriers and prejudices and with true love, faith and kinship for one another as brothers and sisters in Christ. Not as Baptist, Lutherans or Catholics but as one family under Christ our Shepherd. This is the time when we as followers of Christ find ourselves led back in time to the period of Jesus and His apostles. It is the time to think outside the structural limits, which have imprisoned many of us for so many years, and be followers, students and imitators of Jesus Christ, our one and true Master.

The rift between the Protestants and Catholics can almost be seen like the rift between a mother and child.

During the infancy stages of Christianity, the church took on the responsibility of taking care of everything. Feeding, supporting, protecting, and loving her children were the church's main responsibilities. The church also reprimanded children when they did wrong and did her best to teach them in the faith.

Somewhere along the way, the church (just as any parent) committed a few things it later regretted but continued to oversee and protect the child. The child eventually grew and changed into a rebellious adolescent who began to talk back to her mother. Although the mother knew she had made mistakes, she was still the parent and, therefore, continued to set the rules of the household. The adolescent rebelled more and more, and reached a point where she felt she was being hindered by her mother's strict rules. So she decided to move out. She grew and matured, and experienced many things while living on her own, things that her mother probably never experienced but perhaps talked about. She married and had many children but felt she was missing something.

The mother, too, became older and wiser, and regretted that she perhaps had been a bit too overly concerned on her rules and regulations as a young mother, that she had neglected to love her child with true unconditional love, mercy and compassion.

She reflected that she had set her love with conditions and perhaps a few too many rules, so much so that her child had felt the need to leave the house many years ago. But both mother and child began to realize that they were both family and shared a common link and bloodline. They both had made foolish mistakes many years ago, but that now was a time for forgiveness and reconciliation with one another.

This is where we find ourselves today, my brothers and sisters in the Lord our Christ.

We are beginning to realize that there is something missing. That we cannot truly fulfill the calling of Jesus without making amends with one another and becoming one family again.

St. Paul in his many letters always warned us of being divided amongst ourselves or of being weary of those that caused divisions.

Jesus, too, told us that a house divided cannot stand. This is true.

This is why, my brothers and sisters, it is so important to recognize and admit to our own faults. To ask for forgiveness and to give it, especially when it is called upon us to do so. But none of this can be obtained without love, just as St. Paul reminded us in his letter to the Corinthians.

We must have love within ourselves to accept and forgive those who have wronged us. Pride can be an obstacle, and many times stands as a barrier to true reconciliation, but that is where true love overcomes.

It is this love that comes from the Father through the Spirit that will enable us to begin to mend these rifts within our Christian family. Because even though we might not live in the same house, following the same house rules, we are still related to one another and share a common belief in our Lord Jesus Christ and His salvation.

The time is upon us now, even as I write this letter, to begin this reconciliation with our family. Whether we belong to the rebellious child's family or the proud mother's, the time is now.

Let us pray, my brothers and sisters in our Lord Jesus Christ, that we have the love and compassion to receive one another as we are. Not as we would like them to be but simply as children of God and believers in Christ. Time has passed, and both families need to realize that wholeness is necessary in order to be prepared to receive the Lord. We are all one family and shall go about evangelizing as one, not as many.

I will continue to pray for you all, my friends and family in the Lord, that we continue in our task of becoming prepared for the coming lean years. That He may guide, enlighten and protect you all always. But more importantly, that He give you the love that comes from Him so that you in return share it with all you come in contact with. I ask this through Christ our Lord. Amen.

Your loving friend and brother,
horacio

Letter VIII-Would You Recognize Him?

Greetings to you, my brothers and sisters in Christ, on this beautiful morning of the 26th day of this fourth month in 2005. May the Lord and His blessing descend upon you and your families.

I truly hope that these letters of preparation have been serving a useful purpose.

Brothers and sisters in the Lord, I come to you today to present a possibility to you. It stems from this question: would you recognize Christ if He presented Himself to us today or in the future?

Do not be too quick to answer this question, my brothers and sisters. First, let us sit and ponder this a while. The following is an excerpt from one of the many messages given to Melanie, a child who the Virgin appeared to in France in 1846, otherwise known as the Apparitions of La Salette[1] (if you read all of the messages included in the Virgin's apparition, you will note that they reflect the scripture writings in the Book of Revelation). "*Woe to the inhabitants of the earth! There will be bloody wars and famines; pestilences and contagious diseases; there will be rains of a dreadful hail of animals, thunders which will shake cities, earthquakes which will engulf countries; voices will be heard in the air, men will beat their head against the walls, they will call upon death, and on another side death will be their torture; blood will flow on all sides. Who will be able to overcome, if God does not shorten the time of the ordeal? By the blood, the tears and the prayers of the just, God will let Himself be swayed, Enoch and Elie (similar to the two witnesses in Revelation chapter 11) will be put to death; pagan Rome will disappear; fire from Heaven will fall and will consume three cities; all the universe will be struck with terror, and many will let themselves be misled because they have not adored the true Christ living among them. It is time; the sun darkens; faith alone will live.*"

---

1. http://www.geocities.com/ourlady_dal/lasallete2.htm

The Virgin here indicates something that concerns me: many will let themselves "be misled, because they have not adored the true Christ living among them. It is time; the sun darkens, and faith alone will live."

Many of us, my brothers and sisters, are so certain of how He will come again and what will appear at His entrance that many of us might not recognize Him if He came and lived in our midst without all the symbolism that accompanied the metaphorical writing styles of the Evangelist. Long ago, many who considered themselves true followers of God and His law did not recognize Him the first time He came because they, too, expected a Messiah who would come through the clouds with a sword in His hand to smite the nations and peoples who were enemies of God's chosen people. They expected a Messiah who would be as King David had been. They expected that Messiah to restore Israel just as David had restored the tribes into one powerful nation. They expected a fierce and combative warrior, just as David had been. They expected the Messiah to come and be brought forth from the belly of heaven for all to see. But was that how He came?

I merely present a point of view that not many Christians, regardless of their denomination, have. There are times when the Bible can be taken literal, but other times when it cannot.

The writers of those past times wrote in allegorical styles that varied from time to time, just as writing and artwork have always varied with each passing generation. Some used direct writing styles while others used symbolic and metaphorical styles.

The first time around, many of the prophets, [Jer. 30:9, Is. 4:2, 9:1-7, 11:1-9, Is. 25:6-10, 7:12, 63:19, Zep. 3:3-14, Jer. 23:4, Mic 5:4, Ezk. 34:11-25, Ps 132, 72, Ps 2, Ps 110, Is 49:1-6, 50:1-9, 52: 13-53:12, Zec.2:14, Zec 12:10-12, Dn 7:13, 7:27] announced the Messiah's coming the way it would actually happen, and how it would happen.

They went further and prophesized how He would actually die for our sins, without saying a word. They spoke of His humility and His humble origins. They spoke of how He would endure pain and suffering for our sake. They did their best to let the world know how He would come, live and die. But they (the prophets of God), too, were rejected, tortured and killed by the very people they were trying to prepare.

The people that condemned many of these prophets were a stubborn people that had their minds made up and closed to any outside message that went against their paradigms (world view/preconceived notion). This is precisely why whenever He was presented to this world, the Jewish people—His Father's chosen people—did not recognize Him. They were completely appalled at the thought of a carpenter's son being the Messiah. How could this man lead them back to prosperity? How could this man lead them against the might of Rome or any other foreign invader? How could this man attempt to teach them anything regarding that pertains to God? He was just a carpenter. How dare He teach them when He himself has never been formally taught. This man did not come in a blaze of Glory down from heaven. They saw and heard no angels and trumpets blowing at His arrival. He had no legions of armies behind Him. He spoke of loving one's enemy instead of fighting and driving them away. Surely this man was not the Messiah.

That was how Jesus Christ, the only Son of the Father, was treated when He came among us the first time. Many began to believe when they saw the things He did, and He spoke the way He did, but still many did not.

It is somewhat ironic, my brothers and sisters, how God's chosen did not recognize their true Messiah when they had Him in their midst. Their pride and learned arrogance made them blind, and continues to make them blind, to the fact that He came as a carpenter to redeem us of our sins.

So again I ask the question that I asked at the beginning of this letter: would you truly recognize Him if He were to present himself today or in the future? Would you know it was truly Him if He didn't come with trumpets blaring from the heavens riding with legions of angels at his back? Or would you allow your fixed precepts/paradigms of how He has to come to dictate whether or not you accept Him (similar to what happened the first time he came)?

The point is this, my brothers and sisters in the Lord. The first time He came, He came to preach, and teach Hs message to His own people (the Jews), and they did not recognize Him. They were His people and His Father's chosen; yet they did not recognize Him because He did not appear to have any majestic or royal qualities about Him. They were expecting someone or something else.

Let us not fall into that same trap as well, my brothers and sisters, but let us pray for discernment that we may know the truth when we see, hear or feel it.

It would be a sad day if during His second coming to His people of the New Covenant (us Christians), the same thing happened. Whenever that glorious day occurs, whether it is ten years or two hundred years away, let us not be blinded by our own precepts, similar to how the great priests of the Jewish law were.

They had great knowledge and understanding of Scripture and the law but had very little faith and love in one another, and most importantly for God.

That's similar to some Christians today or self-proclaimed followers of Christ. They have great understanding and knowledge of Scripture and what the Gospels teach but have very little need or use for actual application of Jesus' most important commandments: love for one another, forgiveness, and true love and faith in Him.

What I have just presented to you all is a theory for discernment.

I am simply allowing for the presentation of possibilities that may or may not occur, but that at least one has taken and seen the presentation from several view points and not just one.

Enclosed paradigms throughout history have kept people from acknowledging certain truths or possibilities because they were so certain in their own ideas or beliefs that they had no use for other potential possibilities. Ideologues have no need for facts, only for those that bend and mold to their viewpoints.

At one time, people swore on their lives that the earth was flat or that the sun orbited the earth. They called anyone who presented something different as mad or crazy.

The same is true today, with just different issues.

Something that I go back to that seems to present this point is what the Virgin's message was to Melanie at La Sallete, specifically when she states, **"Many will be misled because they have not adored the True Christ living among them."**

This seems to indicate that many people (Christians and Jews) will allow themselves to be misled by a false Messiah, and/or his cohorts, and at the same time not recognize the true Christ in their midst.

I have no doubt in my mind that we will all be witnesses of Jesus' second coming, whether we are part of the living or the dead when it happens. The real question is: will we truly recognize Him when He comes or will we be like stubborn, blind people who did not recognize the Son of God in the body of a carpenter? Will we, too, put Him aside if He doesn't come in a blaze of glory through the clouds with trumpets blaring?

Rev. 19:11-21 speaks very clearly about His second coming, but what if He comes to us in our midst? Again, we must keep in mind the symbolic and metaphoric language the evangelists of the time used in order to relay their messages to a simpler people. Jesus Himself spoke in parables to help His disciples understand certain concepts and messages because they, too, were simple people of the land.

My dear brothers and sisters in the Lord, I know that some of you are well versed in Scripture and in the laws of God, and that others are perhaps are not.

We must remain prayerful and vigilant during these days before the storm. We must not allow ourselves or our friends, family and descendants of ours to fall into the trap that the Jewish people fell into two thousand years ago when they, too, denounced, ignored, rejected, mocked, abused, and finally killed the Messiah in the name of God. He had been the one that all of the prophets had foreseen and prophesized about, and yet they completely rejected Him because He had failed to meet their standards as far as having come in a glorious way and had failed to live like a king on earth in majestic form.

He wasn't born like a king, He hadn't lived like a king, and, therefore, to them He had merely been an imposter. For in their eyes, they did not see His true wealth and majesty; they just saw a poor man who socialized with all the undesirables. They did not see that His true power and authority came not from wealth, influence and power as the world sees it, but rather through selfless sacrifice, humble servitude and spiritual wealth that is further strengthened through poverty.

Let us not commit the same mistake, my brothers and sisters. Although I am well aware that it is written, "He will come again in glory to judge the living and the dead, and his kingdom will have no end." Let us keep in mind this is how the prophets had described Him prior to His first visit. Only those who knew how to interpret the glorious revelations that occurred were able to witness and give accounts to his glorious resurrection and ascension into heaven.

What the words glory and wealth mean to someone can have a completely different meaning to another.

To a materialist, these words could mean man-made wealth and glory while to a spiritual person, they mean something completely different.

My brothers and sisters in our Lord Jesus Christ, I continue to pray for you all on a daily basis. I pray that the good Lord give you strength, wisdom, courage, protection, guidance, and the ability to discern the truth. I, too, ask that you continue praying for me. We must pray especially for those who have no relationship or connection with the Lord, that they, too, begin to see, hear and feel the hunger pains for His Word and thirst for His life-giving water. Pray, and do penance, and pray some more.

Thank you all for being my brothers and sisters through the Lord our God. Amen.

Your brother,
horacio

Letter IX-Seeds of Words

Greetings once more, brothers and sisters in our Lord Jesus Christ, on this beautiful second day of the fifth month of this 2005 year. I truly hope this letter finds you all well and healthy, both in the physical and spiritual sense. That you, your family, friends and neighbors all continue to dwell on and live within the shadow of God for it is there one finds true solace, comfort, security, love and warmth.

Today, my brothers and sisters, I come to bring to light what many of us are guilty of doing on a daily basis. Many of us in today's world are more concerned with good food, a sculpted physique, outside appearances, and things of that sort (at least in this country and in many others) than we are with what reigns in the heart.

We are more preoccupied with what goes into our body, highlights the body, and preserves the body, than what comes out of it.

What I am referring to is none other than our words that come out and pollute not only ourselves but others as well.

What are the words that we use on a daily basis and in everyday conversations? Are they constructive, affirming, positive and optimistic, or are they destructive, negative, pessimistic and condemning? That old saying of "you are what you eat" also applies here: you are what you say.

Let me refer you to something that Jesus encountered when He and His apostles sat down one day to eat a meal together (all of Mathew 15). Just then, some of the Pharisees came and gathered around Jesus and asked him, *"Why don't your disciples follow the traditions of the elders? In fact, they don't even wash their hands before they eat."* [The Pharisees (Jewish priests who maintained themselves separate from the masses), as always, had been more concerned with what makes a person clean or unclean from the outside in. Their constant emphasis on what goes in or what is worn on the outside had always been one of their primary focuses. This in essence had become a smokescreen of sorts and continues to this day with some religious groups—where an over emphasis on customs and traditions becomes the main focus of worship and the message of God's calling is lost in the protocol. The true message of God gets lost in the pomp and ceremony of the occasion. Rites and traditions can be the tools to fine tune and center, keep and maintain the focus of worship, but that is all. They are the means within the infrastructure to the end. They should not be ends in and of themselves.]

Jesus goes on to give His apostles a lesson, *"Listen and understand: what enters into the mouth does not make a person unclean, what defiles him is what comes out of his mouth."*

He went on to clarify to some who did not understand this (Matthew15:17): " *Do you not see that whatever enters the mouth goes into the stomach, and then out the body? But what comes out of the mouth comes from the heart, and that is what makes a person unclean. Indeed, it is from the heart that evil desires come from—murder, adultery, immorality, theft, lies, slander. These are the things that make a person unclean; but eating without washing one's hands does not make a person unclean."*

With this message, Jesus shows not only His apostles at that time, but even us today, that true purity and cleanliness come from the heart and not from outside appearances, rituals, customs, or traditions.

This is where the fuse is lit that later goes and lights up the external aspects of one's faith and not the other way around. The heart must correspond to the open call to grace that God makes to each and every one us. Once the heart does so, then we begin to correspond to the rites, customs and traditions of our faith. But we must be moved by the heart first.

This is why, my brothers and sisters, we should be very attentive to our vocabulary and the terminology that we use on a daily basis. The words we use not only within ourselves but also with our friends, family, co-workers or perfect strangers.

Often times we do not even realize the words that we use in common everyday conversation, but if we stopped and really focused on what they were, we would probably stun ourselves at how negative, divisive, hurtful, foul and cynical they really are.

Words are like the seeds of a dandelion flower. They come out from the mouth of the flower and are taken by the wind. Wherever they happen to land, if the conditions are right, they sprout roots and begin to grow.

Words are exactly the same. They are carried by the wind, and if the conditions are right in the person receiving them, they sprout roots and begin to grow. But this is where the danger lies, for if the plant is a good one, then wherever the seeds sprout roots, more of the same good flower/plant can be expected. But if the flower is a weed (like the dandelion), then more of the same can be expected. ("You shall know them by their fruits.")

This is why we have to be careful, my brothers and sisters. Without even realizing it sometimes, we can either positively or negatively influence the people around us with the words we use on a daily basis (if the conditions are right in the receptor for those seeds to grow).

That is why people who are constantly spewing hate-filled, harmful words from their mouths are allowing the seeds of hate to be taken and planted in many different minds, thereby allowing the cycle to continue.

Young minds especially are vulnerable because they are fertile grounds for seeds of love or hate to take root in.

But if words of patience, love, kindness, understanding, compassion and unity are allowed to flow from our mouths, then good fruit-bearing plants are to be expected. Both old and young minds are vulnerable, but the young are most often the captive audiences of parents, teachers, coaches and family members.

Words are very powerful, my brothers and sisters, and Jesus knew this. He came to set the perfect example for us. Granted we were not created exactly like He was, but we can strive to be like Him and live as close to possible as He did.

We can begin by making a conscience effort in altering our everyday vocabulary and terminology. We should ask ourselves, before we speak, are these words going to help or hurt? Is this message a compassionate one or a careless one? Are these words cynical/sarcastic, or are they sweet and soothing?

We should ask ourselves these questions from now on, especially if we realize that our mouths are in need of some fine-tuning.

Sometimes a firm and assertive message needs to be said, but let's be aware of how we deliver this message. Jesus often times rebuked and corrected those who tried to entrap Him, but He did so with wisdom and knowledge that came through the grace of the Spirit.

Our tongues sometimes are as sharp as a double-edged sword. With them we use words to cut and slice people down to size.

When we feel our pride has been injured or hurt, we retaliate by doing the same. Is this what Jesus did?

This is the message that our good Lord has given me today to relay to you, my brothers and sisters, so that together we continue down this path of preparation.

If anyone of you who is receiving these letters from me is in need of prayers, please let me know so that not only I, but also this large circle of friends and family can pray for you.

Continue praying, my brothers and sisters in the Lord, that we can continue building bridges toward those lost and stranded sheep that have left the flock, maybe recently or maybe a long time ago, that they may once again find their way back to the one true Shepard. Please continue to forward these letters, or make copies of them, and distribute them to friends or family members so that they, too, can partake.

I, too, continue praying for you all, my brothers and sisters, and ask that you do the same for me. May your house be filled with peace and love, and that the Spirit reigns throughout your temples. These are the sincere wishes of your brother in Jesus Christ.

horacio

Letter X-Prayers of Intercession Through our Mother

Greetings, my brothers and sisters, on this morning of the third day of the fifth month.

I hope and pray that you are all doing well and are in good spirits. May the Lord our God descend upon your homes and your hearts to give you peace and love today, tomorrow and forever.

This is the tenth letter of preparation I bring to you all and do so with joy and anticipation that I am reaching you all with the good news. So that all who read these letters be comforted, enlightened, and more importantly prepared internally and spiritually for the coming lean years.

Prayer, and all that is concerned with prayer, is a vital and very important part of being a true, faithful and loving Christian. We must not forget to pray to God and do so on a daily basis so as to please Him and give thanks for all that He has given us.

Living in today's fast-paced and modern world can be difficult, and sometimes it's hard to find the time for prayer. Nevertheless, it must be a part of our daily experience. Whether we pray in the morning, afternoon or evening, we must do so with heartfelt expression and sincere devotion.

We must not do so out of a routine reaction but a genuine heartfelt one. Whether it is one simple and concise prayer, or a long, well thought-out and contemplative series of prayers, it is all the same as long as it comes from the heart.

Prayer is often—especially in today's world of modern sciences and technology—seen as a last resort, underestimated, or sometimes not even attempted for lack of faith and trust in the all-powerful creator. People attempt to try everyone (doctors, therapists, scientists) and everything rather than the most powerful means. For did not Jesus Himself say, *"Truly I say to you, if you had faith, and did not doubt, not only could you have done with the fig tree what I have done, but you could even say to that mountain: Go and throw yourself into the sea! And it would be done. Whatever you ask for in prayer full of faith, you will receive."* (Mathew: 20-22, Mark 11: 20).

Throughout the Bible, both in New and Old Testaments, we see how important the power of prayer was for God's people. We see the faithfulness and trust in prayer that Jesus had before He had to make very important decisions (please refer to Mark 1:35, Mark 14:36, Matthew 11:25, Luke 3:21, 6:12, 9:18, 29, 23:46, 22:32, 23:33, John 8:29,11:42).

He also demonstrates how He performs miracles and helps people in a bind when those who ask Him do so with faith (Luke 7:1, Mark 10:46, John 2:1-10).

But more importantly, He shows us how constant and repetitious petitioning can bring what we ask for from the Father (Matthew 7:24).

But what about prayers of intercession? When we ask others to pray for us? Does God listen? Is He moved to help us through these prayers? Of course, He is. Throughout the Old and New Testaments, there are endless examples of this. As early as Genesis 18:16-33, Abraham interceded for the city of Sodom to help avoid its destruction.

We see the same thing happen when Moses intercedes for his people (Exodus 32:9-14) just as Yahweh is about to destroy them. *"And Yahweh said to Moses, 'I see that these people are a stiff-necked people. Now just leave me that my anger may blaze against them. I will destroy them, but of you I will make a great nation. But Moses calmed the anger of Yahweh, his God, and said, 'Why O Yahweh, should your anger burst against your people whom you brought out of the land of Egypt with such great power and with a mighty hand?"* [Other examples of prayers of intercession from Moses can be found in Exodus 33:12, Numbers 11:11, 14:13. Likewise, throughout the Old Testament there are countless other examples of prayers of intercession, such as Elijah in 1 Kings 18:36, Amos 7:1, Jeremiah 10:23, 14:7, 37:3.]

Often, during these periods of intercession, the prophets had mixed thoughts and feelings between interceding for people who chastised and mocked them, and allowing the will of God to be done, even if it meant total destruction of their towns or people.

Likewise, throughout the Epistles, in St. Paul's letters, we see, too, the call for prayers of intercession on both his behalf and that of his readers for him and his mission.

Prayers of intercession come in all forms and from many sources. They can be from friends, family, clergy, the saints in heaven and the Virgin Mary. So why do many of our Christian brethren act hostile to prayers of intercession by the saints and Mary when it has been clearly demonstrated that not only is it acceptable but mandatory to pray for those whom we love as well as those that hate us?

Many of these people have been instructed incorrectly, and thus this is where the trouble lies. For it is in these misunderstandings that people fail to see eye to eye with something that is so simple to understand.

Many of our Christian brethren have been taught to believe that we worship the saints and Mary as if they were gods. I'm sorry to disappoint, but all true and devout Christians, regardless of denomination, should know that there is only one true God the Father. He is the one true omnipotent, omniscient and omnipresent creator for us all. We understand and acknowledge that Mary as well as all the saints throughout history have merely been servants of the one true God. (Mary herself acknowledged and affirmed herself to be servant of the Lord in Luke 1:38). They, like many of us today, were called to perform and act as the vessels and tools for what the great Creator had in mind. We do not ask them for something that God does not want to give us, but instead we ask for their intercession and that through our prayers and their prayers the will of God be done.

Perhaps we ask for mercy on a person or group of persons, just like Abraham and Moses did for their people during God's vengeful moments.

Although Mary and the saints throughout history were all called to be servants of the Lord, Mary was called for a very special purpose, and it has been this purpose that the world has acknowledged her with devout faith. She herself knew to some degree the importance and honor she would be given by man throughout history. In Luke 1:46 the prayer of the Mary, *"My soul proclaims the greatness of the Lord, my spirit exults in God my savior! He has looked upon his servant in her lowliness and people forever will call me blessed."*

Similar to what had been the Ark of the Covenant that housed the Laws of God (Ten Commandments), so, too, was Mary the New Ark of the New Covenant that housed our Lord Jesus Christ. Just as Moses and his people wandered throughout the desert carrying and protecting the Ark wherever they went for forty years, so, too, did Mary the Mother of Jesus house and protect Him for the forty weeks of pregnancy. For it was through her that the child known as Emmanuel came to be with us (Isaiah 7:14). It was she that taught Him, comforted Him, protected Him and loved Him with all her heart and soul, and still so many belittle her importance in the grand scheme of God's mysterious plan for humanity.

Psalm 16:9-10 is also similar and relevant to Mary's exultation canticle, *"My heart therefore, exults, my soul rejoices; my body too will rest assured. For you will not abandon my soul to the grave, nor will you suffer your holy one to see decay in the land of the dead."*

This particular Psalm, brothers and sisters, describes exactly why neither Jesus nor his holy Mother Mary experienced corruption after death. How could the Mother of Jesus our Savior ever have been abandoned by her son to experience the death, decay and corruption that is brought by sin and the devil himself? Jesus, in union with the Father and the Holy Spirit, would never have allowed the enemy the pleasure of being victorious through death over His precious mother.

This is precisely why God almighty created her, selected and protected her for this most precious purpose from before time ever began. For before there was anything, He is and always will be.

This is why so many of us (myself included) believe that Mary always has and will continue to play a pivotal role in the work for our salvation. For just as God Almighty through the Holy Spirit was Father to our Savior, we must also not forget and dishonor whom His mother was. For in doing so, we become guilty of breaking one of the original commandments: Honor thy Father and thy Mother.

I am well aware of the awesome power and might that our God has and His ability to use it for creating and destroying. I am also aware that He could have sent His only begotten Son to us any way He wished. But let's be reminded how He did. He chose a young Jewish woman for this great and honorable task. A woman filled with the grace of God (Luke 1:28) and whom God protected. She was blessed among women, and blessed was the fruit of her womb. Holy mother of Jesus she was, and through her we ask for her prayers of intercession, just like the countless prayers she must have prayed for Jesus from childhood until His death. Through the Holy Spirit, He was conceived and was born a man of flesh and blood, her flesh and blood. For it was through her that the prophecies of old were fulfilled (Isaiah 7:14, Isaiah 9:6, Mic. 5: 1, 2 Samuel 5:2, Isaiah 60:1-6, Palms 72).

In the following excerpt, we see the first example of Mary's intercession on behalf of others, John 2: 1-5: *"Three days later, there was a wedding at Cana in Galilee and the mother of Jesus was there. Jesus was also invited to the wedding with his disciples. When all the wine provided for the celebration had been served and they had run out of wine, the mother of Jesus said to him, 'They have no wine.' Jesus replied, 'Woman, your thoughts are not mine! My hour has not yet come. However, his mother said to the servants, 'Do whatever he tells you.'"*

Here we clearly see Mary's intercession on behalf on the wedding hosts. Even though Jesus was initially not inclined to provide what seemed as a trivial request, He conceded to his mother's request and provided the first miracle out of seven in John's gospel.

This is exactly how Mary has always interceded for us and on our behalf to her Son. Let us also be aware of what she told the servants at the wedding, *"Do whatever He tells you."*

In similar fashion, she tells each and every one of us: after we request a favor from her, do whatever He tells you to do. [Many that claim Mary had other children do not take into consideration the following: Would God, considering the being that He is, and the purity, holiness, and omnipotent force that He is, have allowed His only begotten Son to have been conceived and been born of anyone or anything less than pure herself? Furthermore, wouldn't it be logical to conclude that after having given birth to God in the flesh, the temple, which housed our Lord, would have been preserved and kept from iniquity and any impurity for all eternity?]

This is why both her and her memory deserves honor and devoutness. Not worship, like so many of our brethren that have been misinformed about, but honor. Jesus himself reminds us of honoring our fathers and mothers, and he that does not will be put to death (Matthew 15:3-4).

We should not turn away from her but rather ask for her prayers of intercession to both the Father and the Son so that she might help to calm God's vengeful wrath for this world that overflows with sin and wickedness. For it was through her that God invited us to know him in the flesh of Jesus Christ his Son. For it was through Jesus, that God who is unseen, became seen to us all. [The analogy I can best introduce here is the following. Let's take the scenario of a mischievous young boy who gets into trouble with his father for whatever reason. Just as the father is on the verge of disciplining the child with a mighty belt or a sturdy rod, the child's mother intercedes on behalf of the child and calms him down and reasons with him. He then listens to the maternal advice, drops the rod and instead gives the child a warning. The child goes on but has been warned. The same thing happens with us. We have been warned several times through her apparitions throughout history. Whether it was La Salette, Fatima, Lourdes, and the warnings have been given. That is why it is vital we pray for intercession because sometimes the corporal punishment can be prevented and a warning is given, but only for so long; soon the father says enough is enough.]

We also see where and when it was that Jesus gave not only the apostles His mother to look after her but to all of us as well. Where now we can all have the privilege of calling her our mother.

In John 19:25, *"Near the cross of Jesus stood his mother, his mother's sister Mary, who was wife of Cleophas, and Mary of Magdala. When Jesus saw the mother and the disciple, he said, **'Woman, this is your son.'** Then he said to the disciple, **'There is*** *your **mother**.' And from that moment the disciple took her to his own home. With that Jesus knew all was now finished."*

It was here, brothers and sisters, that Jesus gives His mother not only to that one disciple on that one day, but to all who call themselves disciples and brothers and sisters of Christ.

From that day on, Mary would live with the rest of the apostles and was even present at Pentecost, the day the Church was born (Acts 1:14) through the coming of the Holy Spirit. She continues to look over and protect us.

She is concerned for us and our welfare, too, especially when it comes to eternal salvation. She can be found in the first book of the Bible (Genesis: 3:15) and the last book in the Bible (Revelations 12), *"A great sign appeared in heaven: a woman, clothed with the sun, with the moon under her feet (image of Our Lady of Guadalupe, for she too is clothed with the sun, and has the moon under her feet) and a crown of twelve stars on her head* (represents her position in heaven, as mother/head of all the saints. Twelve stars represents the twelve apostles, just as she had been in their midst on the day of Pentecost.)

Brothers and sisters, do not be concerned by trivial matters that concern those that have only a mind for this world. Be strong in faith, love and hope, and continue to pray, and pray daily. I, too, will continue to pray for you all. Continue in your missions, whatever they are, but do not place them above Him. Keep faithful in the Word, and pray for me as well.

Your brother,
horacio

Letter XI-The Light of Truth

·

Greetings to you this morning, my brothers and sisters, on this beautiful morning of the 17th day of this fifth month.

I come to you once again to bring the message of preparation so you may continue either preparing yourselves or help prepare others who perhaps may be in need of spiritual strengthening.

I have been praying constantly and vigilantly for you all and hope that you, too, keep me in your daily prayers as well.

Brothers and sisters, in today's world many of us are constantly bombarded with all types of messages from all types of sources. Some come from the media, others from our ministers or priests, some from our families, and still others from complete strangers.

Even though the quantity and availability of these messages is increasing dramatically, the clarity of the messages at times can be very misleading, vague and ambiguous. It is hard to discern if the message is a good or bad one. Is it black or white? Is it right or wrong? Often times we find ourselves falling for ambiguous messages that are neither black nor white but gray.

The enemy has been hard at work in the past few years doing his job of leading many astray. People become deceived by what looks right and feels right but is not. Just because we can do or say something doesn't mean we should. This is where silent and wise discernment comes in. [Just because we have a car that can go up to 150 miles per hour doesn't mean we should travel at this speed through towns and cities. With more knowledge, power and technology comes the need for the proper wisdom to use it.]

Others who say and do what **is right** continue to be persecuted for their beliefs. But therein lies the sign that this is truly the right path. For Jesus said, *"If you want to follow me, deny yourself, take up your cross and follow me. For if you choose to save your life, you will lose it, and if you lose your life for my sake and for the sake of the gospel, you will save it. What good is it to gain the whole world, but destroy yourself?"* (Mark 9:34-36)

It was with these words that Jesus our Lord and Savior taught us and lived by example so we, too, could become more like Him. Through these words, He attempts to show us that to follow Him is to follow the same path that led Him to the cross. The path that is very often the least chosen. That to reach spiritual maturity within ourselves, it is necessary to renounce our materialism and the life that this world tries to promote and perpetuate as ideal.

It is a risk we must take, a leap of faith. What good will it do us to gain the whole world but destroy ourselves in the process of obtaining it? This question Jesus posed to us more that two thousand years ago is still as relevant as ever, if not more so today.

Jesus came to define with clarity and complete absoluteness what was black and what was white. What was right and what was wrong. He did not speak in ambiguous terms. He did not live an ambiguous life. He did not smile at you, then speak badly about you the moment you left His presence. He did not preach one thing and later do another. He did not speak in terms that would grant Him favor or flattery with the majority of the people, or with the ones that yielded great power and influence. He did not speak to gain popularity by the masses, nor did He speak in blue terms when speaking to a blue crowd and then in red terms when speaking to a red crowd. He was not a chameleon like so many are today. He came to speak, live and abide in the truth.

Jesus tells us, *"You are the light of the world. A city built on mountain cannot be hidden. No one lights a lamp and covers it; instead it is put on a lamp stand, where it gives it's light to everyone in the house. In the same way your light must shine before others, so that they may see the good you do and praise your Father in Heaven"* (Matthew 14:16)

In a similar way, Jesus says in the gospel of Mark, *"When the light comes, is it to be put under a tub or a bed? Surely it is put on a lamp stand. Whatever is hidden will be disclosed, and whatever is kept secret will be brought to light. Listen then, if you have ears!"* (Mark 4:21-23)

Jesus here clearly shows us what the truth does and how it does it. The truth comes as a light into the world. Wherever or whatever the truth shines upon, it will make visible for all to see. The truth will not always be pretty or soothing to the ears, but then again it rarely is.

The truth is like a pregnancy: it can only be kept hidden for so long before it is shown to the world and disclosed for all to see, and when the time comes for the pregnancy to end and give birth, it is painful, just like the truth can also be painful at times.

That is why, my brothers and sisters who read this message, it is to all of us that our Lord Jesus Christ is imploring to be like beacons of light to any and everyone we meet. Jesus told us, *"In the same way your light must shine before others, so that they may see the good you do and praise your Father in Heaven."*

When you speak, do not speak in gray terms but in black and white. The truth will not settle kindly on all who hear it or see it, but then again, it's not supposed to. It will convert some to become strong faithful followers of Christ. Yet to many, the truth will become a like a stumbling block; they will trip because of it and in turn will curse you.

Many in today's society compromise their core values, ethics and principles for what they will gain from this material world, such as honor, prestige, fame, money and power. They in essence attempt to gain the whole world by destroying themselves.

Truth becomes a nuisance to them, and whoever reminds them or blinds them with the light of truth, they attempt to extinguish, like a light that causes them pain or discomfort.

This is why throughout history many that have carried the torches of truth have become martyrs for the sake of it.

St. Paul reminds us of how we can know and tell when someone speaks and lives through the flesh (selfish, of this world interest), and when someone speaks and lives through the Holy Spirit and proclaims the truth: *"Immorality, impurity, shamelessness, idol worship, magic, hatred, jealousy, violence, anger, ambition, division, factions, envy, drunkenness, and orgies and the like. I again say to you what I have already said; those who do these things shall not inherit the kingdom of God. But the fruit of the Spirit is charity, joy, peace, patience, understanding of others, kindness/ fidelity, gentleness and self-control. Those who belong to Christ have crucified the flesh with its vices and desires. If we live by the Spirit, let us live in a spiritual way. Let us not be conceited, let there be no rivalry or envy of one another."* (Galations 6:9-26)

This is truly one way for us to create reference points and live by a standard that promotes and supports the truth. Let us do away with the gray messages (political correctness) this man-made world tries to impose on us, brothers and sisters. When in doubt, we must ask ourselves, "Is this law in keeping with man's law or God's divine/natural laws?" Which of the two is more important? If you answer this correctly, there will be no doubt in your mind, body and soul.

We, too, must be careful not to fall into ambiguous gray areas ourselves. We must strive to live a life according to our principles, morals and values that go according to Christ's moral and divine teachings.

Man will always attempt to change or bend the rules. It's human nature to do that. But let no one deceive you when they attempt to change God's natural and divine laws for their own selfish interest. Whether it's for money, political power, sexual perversion or any other egocentric whim, men will always try to bend and shape God's laws to suit them and their lifestyle.

This is why Jesus came to be the light and give us the light to shine upon all that is hidden, dark and perverse in the world, and in man's heart. He came to set the standard for all. Let us, too, become beacons of light for others that need to be guided to the path of truth, especially in a world that has been over taken by a moral and spiritual darkness. For if you live in darkness long enough, you will lose the use of your senses, starting with your eyes.

Brothers and sisters, I pray that this letter reaches all of you in good mental and physical health. I pray for you on a daily basis and ask that you continue to pray for me as well. Remain strong in faith and in the word of God. Be black or white, but stay away from those who are gray and want to infect you with the message of ambiguity and vagueness. I pray that the good Lord blesses you all and keeps you safe from the enemy's snares. I ask this through Christ our Lord and Savior. Amen.

Your brother in Christ,
horacio

Letter XII-Shepherds of the Faith

Greetings and good morning to all of you today, my brothers and sisters in the Lord. I hope and pray that you, your family and your friends are doing well today, this twenty-third day of this fifth month. May the love, patience and blessing of the Lord be upon you today and tomorrow as well.

Today I come to you with the message of how to be a leader through Christ, and how He calls each and every one of us, whether we are leaders or not, to promote and spread the faith.

For not all can be leaders, and not all can be followers; for if all were leaders, there would be no one to lead, and if all were followers, there would be loss and confusion.

That is why all of us, through what we do best, make up the body of Christ. It is the sum of the parts that make up the whole and give value and importance to the whole.

The hand cannot say to the foot, "You are not important, be gone," and vice-versa. The foot cannot say, "I want to be just like the head, nor the ears say the same to the eyes." They all fulfill certain tasks and roles that lead to the greater good of the whole. Not all can be the head and not all can be the hands and feet. They all depend on one another for the proper function and survival of the whole. The left hand cannot say, "I want the same power, prestige and recognition that the right hand gets all the time." This would not be feasible or constructive if we had two right hands.

Yet today, we have so many in the church that no longer like their roles or tasks as being the hands and/or feet of the body. They demand the body to give them the same power and authority as the head (in reference to the clergy and laity).

Throughout Biblical history from Genesis to Revelations, we are shown how our Trinitarian God (Father, Son, Holy Spirit), delivers the message to those He has designated as heads and leaders of His people. In Genesis 17, we see how God came to Abram, *"When Abram was ninety-nine years old, Yahweh appeared to him and said, 'I am God Almighty. Walk in my presence and be without blame! I will make a Covenant between myself and you, and I will multiply your race.' Abram fell face down and God said to him, 'This is my covenant with you: you will be the father of a multitude of nations. No longer will you be called Abram (meaning venerated father), but Abraham, because I will make you the father of many nations."* With this, God the Father established His first covenant with Abraham and disclosed to him exactly what he and his descendants would become. We also see how God changed Abram's name to Abraham (meaning father of many nations) and made him the head of His people, a great honor and responsibility.

We see the same thing happen to Jacob in Genesis 32:24-31 when he struggles with another man. *"Then a man wrestled with him until daybreak. When the man saw that could not get the better of Jacob, he struck him in the socket of his hip and dislocated it as he wrestled with him. The man said, 'Let me go for day is breaking,' but Jacob said, 'I will not let you go until you have given me your blessing.' The man then said, 'What is your name?' 'Jacob' was the reply. He answered, 'You will no longer be called Jacob, but Israel, for you have been strong with God as you have been with men and prevailed.'"*

Here, too, we see how after having struggled with God, Jacob prevails, and therefore God accepts this result and grants His blessing on Jacob. But also notice how God changes his name to Israel (meaning strong with God/men and prevails). Jacob finally realizes and understands that his trials and tribulations up to this point have been more than a confrontation with society and men but a struggle with God. It is also here where we as individuals can relate to Jacob's struggles against men, society, or in our own case, our own personal trials. For it is these struggles that allow us to see sometimes that before we can be blessed by God in life, we have to acknowledge our errors, repent of them, and in the process be humbled by these life experiences.? It is also because of this wrestling match with God that Jacob now better understands the One he has been struggling against, and blocks his path, is the one who can change Esau's (Jacob's brother) disposition, for it was Esau that became angry and ran him off in the first place for stealing his father's (Isaac) blessing.

The leadership role of Jacob and what it would represent to the Jewish nation would further be solidified and strengthened once again in Genesis 35:9-13: *"God appeared again to Jacob when he arrived from Paddan-aram and blessed him and said, 'Your name is Jacob, but longer will you be called Jacob, for Israel will be your name.' So he was called Israel. Then God said to him, 'Be fruitful and grow in number! A nation, or rather a group of nations will come from you. The land I gave to Abraham and Isaac I will give to you and to your descendants after you.' Then God left him."* [Jacob had twelve sons, representing the twelve nations of Israel. But more than this, God created and appointed through him the First Covenant and his leadership role as the patriarch cal figurehead. We shall see this happen again in the New Covenant.]

Nations, families and even we need leaders and individuals who can meet and fulfill these leadership roles and tasks. Christ is that foundation for us all. He came down from heaven and was sent by the Father to establish His New Covenant for the forgiveness of sins. But just as God had done so in the past with Abraham and Jacob, He needed to establish a clear visible leader for the church; and He did.

In Matthew 8:24-27, we have the first indication of how Jesus was beginning to lay the foundation for His message and His church: *"So, then, anyone who hears these words of mine and acts accordingly, is like a wise man who built his house on rock. The rain poured, the rivers flooded, and wind blew and struck the house, but it did not collapse because it was built on rock. But anyone who hears these words of mine and does not act accordingly, is like a fool who built his house on sand. The rain poured, the rivers flooded, and the wind blew and struck the house; it collapsed and the ruin was complete."*

In Matthew 10:2, we have the first naming of the twelve apostles with the first one being Simon called Peter. Just as Jacob had twelve sons, each representing a tribe of Israel as well as the Old Covenant, here, too, we see that Jesus, in selecting twelve apostles, was essentially doing the same thing. He was selecting twelve men who would be foundation stones of the early church. But just as God the Father needed a visible Shepherd for His sheep in the past, as in Abraham and Jacob (Jesus alludes to this in Matthew 22:32-33), God the Son needed a visible lead shepherd for His new flock. Furthermore, just as God the Father had designated and changed the names of the early head patriarchs of the faith, God the Son would also designate and personally change the name of His new leader.

In Matthew 16:15-19, Jesus asked, *"'But you, who do you say I am?' Peter answered, 'You are the Christ, the son of the living God.' Jesus replied, 'It is well for you, Simon Barjona, for it is not flesh or blood that has revealed this to you, but my Father in Heaven. And now I say to you, you are Peter (Cephas in Aramaic, meaning rock and no longer Simon) and on this rock I will build my Church and never will the powers of death overcome it. I will give you the keys of the kingdom of Heaven and whatever you bind on earth shall be bound in Heaven and what you bind unbind on earth shall be unbound in Heaven.'"*

We also see Peter's profession of faith in Jesus as the Christ (anointed one) in Mark 8:27, Luke 9:18, and John 6:69.

It is also interesting to note the appointment and responsibility Jesus gives to Peter in giving him the keys of the kingdom. If we look in Isaiah 22:22, we see the importance of this precedence(pre-figurement/biblical type) early in Jewish custom. Whoever was given these keys was responsible for being the steward or caretaker of the palace. He would have possession of the keys and be in charge of binding or unbinding, forgiving or not forgiving, allowing or not allowing certain people, ideas, and/or other concepts that would be left to his judgment/discernment.

We find in Isaiah 22:22, *"Upon his shoulder I will place the key of the House of David: what he opens, no one will shut; what he shuts, no one will open. I will fasten him like a peg in a sure spot, and he will be a seat of honor in the house of His father."*

This responsibility of binding/unbinding, forgiving/holding forgiveness, can also be found in Matthew 16:18, 18:18 and John 20:21. Even St. Paul speaks of the power and authority of the sacrament of reconciliation (absolving/withholding forgiveness of sins) that has been entrusted upon them by the elders Peter, James and others of the early Christian church in Corinthians II 5:18-21. St. Paul says, *"All of this is the work of God, who in Christ reconciled us to himself, and who entrusted to us the ministry of reconciliation. Because in Christ, God reconciled the world with himself, no longer taking into account their trespasses/sins and entrusting to us the message of reconciliation. So, we present ourselves as ambassadors in the name of Christ (priest also are representatives of Christ), as if God himself makes an appeal to you through us. Let God reconcile/forgive you. This we ask in the name of Christ."*

We clearly see the faith in Christ, the Son of God, which Peter, among the apostles is the first to proclaim, really comes from God. This faith does not come from our own human condition but rather from the Father, who has chosen each and every one of us to be brought forth to a life in Christ. [We also see how Jesus transfers the power, not only to Peter, but also to the rest of the apostles in reference to binding/forgiving, and unbinding/not forgiving. This special grace allows the apostles and those that have succeeded them ever since (the clergy throughout history) the ability to forgive and pardon sins in the name and as representatives (as St. Paul referred to) of Jesus Christ. They have the ability to absolve sins and/or withhold absolution of them. This is precisely why priests can forgive sins through the sacrament of reconciliation. Jesus Himself relayed the authority and grace to do this in His name. For it is through the sacraments that the material act, through efficacious work, becomes spiritual. This is why we base our faith on the community of saints and the succession of authority, through apostolic succession, throughout two thousand years of history from Christ himself.]

The change of name for Peter is also very significant. In John 1:40-42, we read, *"Andrew, the brother of Simon Peter, was one of the two who heard what John (the Baptist) had said and followed Jesus. Early the next morning he found his brother Simon and said to him, "We have found the Messiah," (the Christ), and he brought Simon to Jesus. Jesus looked at him and said, "You are Simon, son of John, but you shall be called Cephas"* (which means Rock in Aramaic).

This change of name for Peter attests that a mission will be given to him, as had been the case with Abraham and Jacob after their change of name. Further reference texts attest to the special relationship and mission that Jesus had in store for Peter. [Matthew 10:2, 14:28, 17:4-5,17:25, 18:21-22, 20:27-30, Mark 3:16-19, Luke 5:8-10, 22:32, John 6:68, 21:15-19]

Throughout the four gospels, we see these and countless other examples of Peter's significance and role in the grand scheme of God's plan. We see how God chooses leaders for His people that are perhaps a bit lacking in one or two areas but have the faith, perseverance and fortitude to complete His desired mission. A bit lacking in faith at times, as was the case with Abraham who took it upon himself to have a child through his wife's servant seeing how God was taking too long to fulfill His promise to him. And a bit crafty and cunning as was the case with Jacob, who stole the blessing that was to be given to Esau, and who after struggling with man and God, received God's blessing. And a bit of all these things put together in one, as was the case in Peter. He, too, was rebellious, lacked faith at times, but he also possessed attributes and strong personality characteristics that enabled him to become the leader and fisher of men who God the Son had envisioned him to become (Matthew 15:27-29, 27:29-75, Acts 2:14-40).

Jesus Christ came to lay the foundation and was the architect and creator of the church. But this is precisely why after the foundation and the church had been initiated, He had to leave the pillars of support in place to maintain and further promote the livelihood of the church.

It was through the twelve apostles that He did this. From among the twelve, it was Peter/Cephas the rock who was selected as the visible head of the church, and through apostolic succession, the church that is today. For Peter is considered to have been the first Pope, and to this day, remains the seat of the Catholic Church's visible head under which the tombs of Peter and Paul can be found.

Jesus reminds us of this in John 21: 15-25, *"After they finished having breakfast, Jesus said to Simon Peter, 'Simon, son of John, do you love me more than these?' He answered, 'Yes Lord, you know that I love you.' And Jesus said, 'Feed my Lambs.' A second time Jesus said to him, 'Simon, son of John, do you love me?' And Peter answered, 'Yes, Lord, you know that I love you.' Jesus said to him, 'Look after my sheep.' And a third time he said to him, 'Simon, son of John, do you love me?' Peter was saddened because Jesus asked him a third time, 'Do you love me?' and he said,*

'Lord you know everything; you know that I love you.' Jesus then said, 'Feed my sheep.'"

Brothers and sisters in our Lord Jesus Christ, today I, too, invite you to become pillars of the body of Christ. As I mentioned earlier, the parts are not greater than the whole. Every one of us brings something unique and different when called upon by God. Not everyone can be the head, and not everyone can be a hand or a foot. But rather it is through the combined effort of all these parts that help create the desired work for our Lord.

Spread the message, and let others see your strong faith, love and devotion so they, too, become inspired and begin down the path of true conversion.

Our Lord God knows and accepts that we are not perfect. He does not expect us to be. The example of the leaders He has chosen throughout history clearly shows this to us. They have been individuals with faults and cracks in their personal character but strong in faith, even though sometimes that faith did waver.

For how can one find reconciliation with God if one is perfect? If that is the case, then the person has no need for God anymore. But it is rather through our fallen state that we should continue to seek forgiveness and guidance from the Almighty.

We, too, are called today by God to be leaders in His church in whatever category we choose to participate. Whether it is through evangelization, social work or charity, the invitation has been sent.

This is the twelfth in a series of letters that I have titled (from the very first one) "Letters of Preparation." I thought it significant to treat this twelfth letter with symbolism and reference to the number twelve because it is a number of completeness in both the Old and New Testaments. The completeness in the context of the pillars God has left behind as key figures to the foundation of the faith. Whether it was through the twelve sons of Jacob (the twelve tribes of Israel) or the twelve apostles of Jesus.

I continue to pray for you and have you in my thoughts and prayers every night. I, too, ask that you continue to pray for me so that the Lord continues through the Holy Spirit to give me eyes to see the truth, ears to hear the truth, and a heart to feel and know what is true. I also ask as a favor to you to forward these letters to others so they, too, become enriched in the message of preparation for the years to come. This message of preparation is for all, not just some or a few, but for all. God bless you all, and have a great work week.

Your brother,
horacio

Letter XIII-Love and Mercy above Sacrifice

Good morning to you all this beautiful morning on the thirtieth day of the fifth month. I hope and pray that you, your friends and families are doing well. Let us rejoice and be glad for today is the day that the Lord has made for our benefit as well as for His.

Brothers and sisters, I truly hope that your preparation has been going well and that you find yourself growing and strengthening your minds and souls on a daily basis.

In today's world, as was the case in Jesus' time, we find or come across brethren that attack us, our faith and beliefs, in order to challenge and cause us to doubt our faith. Be careful that you don't become defensive when addressing them, but at the same time be wise when answering their pointed questions. That is why, my brothers and sisters, we must be strong in the Word of God and our traditions as handed down by the apostles, for even Jesus said, *"Man does not live on bread alone, but on every word that comes from God."*

The focus and inspiration for this letter comes from a conversation I had with a sheep from another flock the other day. She did not attack me, but many within her flock are known for doing this. Instead, we had a pleasant exchange of ideas and shared our beliefs. We talked for a couple of minutes, and afterward went our separate ways. But something she mentioned stayed with me, and I thought it was important enough to bring to light and set it upon the table for all to see.

That day we spoke, she mentioned (among other things) how her brethren do not celebrate Christmas or any other days of celebration because they consider them pagan holidays and to do so would be wrong and go against what is pleasing to God. So a few days followed, and I began to search through the Good News as well as the epistles for answers so I could enlighten myself and other sheep such as herself.

In Matthew 12:1-13, Jesus becomes Lord of the Sabbath [also found in Mark 2:23, 3:1, Luke 6:1, 14:1]: *"It happened that Jesus walked through the wheat fields on a Sabbath. His disciples were hungry and began to pick some heads of wheat and crush them to eat the grain. When the Pharisees noticed this, they said to Jesus, 'Look at your disciples, they are doing what is prohibited on the Sabbath!' Jesus answered, 'Have you not read what David did when he and his men were hungry [1 Samuel 21:2/Leviticus 24:5]? He went into the house of God and they ate the bread offered to God, although neither he nor his men had the right to eat it, but only the priest. And have you not read in the Law that on the Sabbath, priests in the temple break the Sabbath rest, yet they are not guilty? I tell you, there is something greater than the temple here. If you really knew the meaning of the words: It is love and mercy, not sacrifice [Hosea 6:6], you would not condemn the innocent. Besides, the Son of Man is Lord of the Sabbath.' Jesus then left that place and went into one of their synagogues. A man was there with a paralyzed hand, and they asked Jesus, 'Is it permitted to heal on the Sabbath?' But these people (the Pharisees) just wanted to bring charges against him. But Jesus said to them, 'What if one of you has a sheep and it falls into a pit on the Sabbath? Will you not take hold of your sheep and lift it out? But a human person is much more valuable that a sheep! It is therefore permitted to do good on the Sabbath.' Jesus then said to the man, 'Stretch out your arm.' He stretched it out and it was completely restored, as sound as the other one."* In Mark 3:3, Mark expands his questions just a bit more, *"Jesus said to the man with the paralyzed hand, 'Stand here in the center.' Then he asked them (Pharisees), 'What does the Law allow us to do on the Sabbath? To do good, or to do harm? To save life, or to kill?' But they were silent."*

Through this exchange, we see Jesus expanding on what had been the acceptable norm up to that time. According to the pharisees and the Jewish law, it was considered unlawful to work on the Sabbath, even if it was a question of saving someone in danger of death. But for Jesus, not to do good is to do evil. Not to cure is to kill (this is highlighted in Mark's version). The reason the Pharisees remained silent after Jesus asked these questions was because they knew Jesus was right, but to confirm this would be very unsettling to their personal and religious pride.

We often come across people who are exactly like the Pharisees. They condemn actions that help someone or a group of people, yet they cannot accept that they are wrong because of their stubborn pride. People throughout the world may have the capacity and the means to better their personal conditions and well being, but they misappropriate them because they remain prisoners of principles or institutions (religious and political) that are considered sacred, and in order to preserve these sacred ideas, principles and institutions, they allow half of the world to suffer and/or die.

This is precisely what Jesus made reference to. "Is it better to do good, or to harm? To save life, or to kill?"

In the same light, today we have sheep from other flocks that would have us believe that to celebrate days such as birthdays and even Jesus' birthday is not right but wrong. That partaking and celebrating such days is not pleasing to God but that it is pagan worship, which should not be tolerated.

Circa 312 AD, Christianity became the official religion of the Roman Empire after a vision had assured Constantine II (and his 20,000 men) that he would triumph against Maxentius and his 100,000-troop army. He was to do this in the sign of Christ, and his men carried Christ's monogram on their shields as they marched toward the Tiber. Constantine's army won, and the rest is history. Shortly before he died in 337, he received baptism and authorized Christianity to be a legitimate form of worship throughout the Roman Empire

The point, my brothers and sisters, in the Lord is this. Would it have been better to not have converted pagan Rome? Would it have been better to allow the continuance of Christian persecution and killing by the Roman Empire? Would it have been better to continue to have allowed further bloodshed and killing of sheep from Christ's flock? You be the judge.

Throughout history we find many examples of Christian worship replacing pagan worship through cultural and ethnic customs and traditions that have been assimilated into Christian worship. We see this throughout the world. Whether it is in Mexico, where the indigenous people dance and celebrate the apparition of the Virgin Mary (through whom most of Mexico's indigenous populace converted to Christianity), or whether it's Africa, Asia, and/or elsewhere. The question to pose is this: if we are doing God's work, then who can stop us? Let God Himself confirm your mission.

Even St. Paul in Acts 17 was in Athens, a city full of idols. We see in verse 22, how Paul attempts to reach the pagan Greeks: *"Then Paul stood up in the Areopagus Hall and said, 'Athenian citizens, I note in every way you are very religious. As I walked around looking at your shrines, I even discovered an alter with this inscription: To an Unknown God. Now, what you worship as unknown, I intend to make known to you."* We see here how he does not attack or condemn them for what they worship and believe, but instead let us look at the grace with which he addresses them. Let us also look at how he uses their own worship of an unknown god to relay the message that he has for them. He attempts to supplant and replace their worship to an unknown god with that of his God, through our Lord Jesus Christ.

He attempts to make this connection so that they become followers of the one true God. He does not go and begin to criticize, condemn or insult their beliefs and their worship. Instead he wisely sees an opportunity to use their own structures and beliefs to further support and promote what he has to say. This is key. For even he knew that one gets nowhere with vinegar but far with honey. In verses 32 of Acts 17, we see the results of Paul's evangelizing, *"When they heard Paul speak of a resurrection from death, some made fun of him, while others said, 'We must hear you on this topic some other time.' At that point Paul left. But a few did join him, and believed."* We also may encounter the same, but that is to be expected.

We also see how throughout history pagan forms of worship have been replaced by Christian worship through the use of previous and former means, structures, and traditions. The Romans, Aztecs and countless other ancient civilizations once worshiped the sun and other celestial bodies but later worshiped and honored the one true God. This was accomplished by allowing and permitting certain customs and traditions to remain in place. What has changed is knowledge and worship of our Lord our God. [We also see examples of this in Judaism where pagan feasts in accordance with certain rhythms and cycles of nature became associated with and adopted by the Jewish faith as a new means of celebrating God's wonders and His intervention throughout history for His people, whether Christian or Jew. Even the Passover feast was at one time a pagan celebration, called the Pasch of the Lamb, which was the traditional feast of the shepherds. They would practice animal sacrifice on the first moon of the spring, an important period during which the ewes (female sheep) had just given birth. The lamb was then set aside for several days next to the shepherding families so that it could better be identified with the families and carry the sins of all its members. Later, the shepherd's camps were sprinkled with its blood to drive away the "deadly" spirits that threatened people and animals. But God almighty wanted to change this ancient feast and adopt it for His will and purpose. He wanted the Passover at the time of the exodus from Egypt. It would create a new feast of commemoration for the Jewish people and would always be there to remind them of their liberation and true worship of the one true God.[1]]

In Christmas, we see basically the same thing. It originated in pagan tradition. But God later had in mind another plan for this pagan feast, just as before. Except now, we would commemorate and be reminded of the birth of a different lamb, "The lamb of God," which takes away the sins of the world. We even see

---

1.   Christian Community Bible. Phillippines:Bernardo Hurault, 1994.

the shepherds and wise men from the east [not of Jewish descent or faith, but probably of Zoroastrian religion, which symbolize all non-Biblical/Jewish religions] come partake, celebrate and honor the birth of He that would be king. We see how, through this example, God came not only for the Jews, or even for Christians, but also for all. Notice how God did not communicate this information to the Jewish priests or authorities, but rather to some of His friends in pagan world, and they came when called. Jesus came for all, not just for some. God's ways are not our ways.

God almighty perfects the imperfect. He builds upon an incomplete structure, using His perfect tools and/or materials. He has done this throughout time and history.

It is for this reason, my dear brothers and sisters in the Lord, that I say the following. When confronted by someone who does not share your beliefs and attitudes in our Lord our God, do not become defensive, frustrated or abusive. Let us pray that the grace of God, through the Holy Spirit fill our hearts and minds, and address them with respect and honor, even if the same is not true of them.

Brothers and sisters, again I ask, "If we are doing God's will, who can stop us? If are spreading God's word, who can silence us? If we are celebrating God's existence and birth, who can say that it's wrong to do so?"

Even in celebrating our own days of birth, do we as Christians not give thanks and praise to the Lord for allowing us this wonderful gift of life? Surely it is always right to give Him thanks and praise. Just as Jesus asked the pharisees, "Is it better to do good, or to harm? To heal/save life, or to kill/let die?" This is the same question that I pose to our misinformed brethren. For they would rather allow the latter to happen, if it meant going against their sacred ideas and/or beliefs.

For even Jesus had love and compassion on the pagan captain who demonstrated his faith in Jesus by healing his sick servant. Jesus says, *"I say to you, not even in Israel have I found such great faith."*[Luke 7:1-10, Matthew 8:5, John 4:46]

Sometimes it is this type of faith that exists in those that are not baptized Christians, rather than in those that are.

My brothers and sisters, again I give thanks and praise to God for having such good friends and family such you all are. Every day I pray for you all, and ask that you, too, pray for me.

As always, pray to our Lord almighty that He may give you eyes to see the truth, ears to hear the truth, and hearts and minds to feel and know the truth. Continue preparing yourselves spiritually, and read the Word of God on a daily basis. Thirst and hunger for it, for it is truly that bread and life giving water that if we come to truly know it, we will never hunger or thirst again. May God bless and continue to enlighten you all in Jesus Christ's name.

Your brother,
horacio

Letter XIV-One Taken One Left

Greetings and a very good morning I wish upon you all on this great day that the Lord has made. Today, on the second day of the sixth month, I come to you once again, my brothers and sisters in the faith, to share with you the following message. I pray that both you and your families are doing well and continue doing well.

Brothers and sisters in the Lord, I come to you this morning to bring to the table the following bits of information for your senses to partake in and digest so you can make an informed decision on what I relay to you. What I present is not what I force upon you, but rather as has been the case with every one of my messages, I freely offer it to you all, and allow you to come to your own conclusions. The Holy Spirit moves me to deliver these messages; I continue to do what has been asked of me.

In Revelation 8:10-12, the following is written, *"When the third angel sounded his trumpet, a great star fell from heaven, like a ball of fire, on a third of the rivers and springs. The star is called Wormwood, and third of the waters were turned into wormwood, and many people died because of the water which had turned bitter. The fourth angel blew his trumpet, and third of the sun, the moon and the stars was affected. Daylight decreased one-third, and the light at the night as well."* We then continue to see the effects of the angels and the broken seals, and then chapter 9:18 describes the following: *"Then a third of humankind was killed by these three plagues: fire, smoke and sulfur which the horses released through their mouths (similar to tanks), for the power of the horses was both in their mouths and their tails. Their tails in fact, look like serpents, and their heads are able to inflict injury as well."*

We then read the following scripture passages of the Gospel, still within the same context, the day our Lord comes: Matthew 24:29-31, Mark 13:28, Luke17:20, *"For later, after that distress, the sun will grow dark, the moon will not give its light, the stars will fall from the skies and the whole universe will be shaken. Then, the sign of the Son of Man will appear in the Heaven; as all the nations of the earth beat their breasts, they will see the Son of Man coming in clouds of heaven with divine power and the fullness of Glory. He will send his angles to sound the trumpet and gather the chosen ones from the four winds, from one end of the earth to the*

61

other." [Notice here, Jesus alludes to the sign, which will appear in heaven, just as the third secret of Fatima[1] describes it.]

We see in Luke 17:26, where Jesus expands a little on how during the days of His return, people will be living: "*As it was in the days of Noah (Genesis 7:7), so will it be on the day the Son of Man comes. Then people ate and drank, they took husbands and wives, but on the day Noah entered the ark, the flood came and destroyed them all. Just as it was in the days of Lot; people ate and drank, they bought and sold, planted and built. But on the day Lot left Sodom, God made fire and sulfur rain down from heaven which destroyed them all. So will it be on the day the Son of Man is revealed. On that day, if you are on the rooftop, do not go down into the house to get your belongings, and if you happen to be in the fields, do not turn back.*"

Remember Lot's wife (Genesis 19:26)? [What Jesus states here is key to the rest of this letter. We must remember what happened to Lot's wife; that is why I reference the Book of Genesis.] "*Whoever tries to save his life will lose himself, but whoever gives his life will be born again. I tell you, though two men are sharing the same bed, it may be that one will be taken and the other left. Though two women are grinding corn together, one may be taken and the other left.*"

[What I have just written and referenced is key to understanding the following point I will make. Many people today have taken and misinterpreted what Jesus has said. They have taken these words out of context and perpetuated the notion of a rapture, where people will be raptured up into heaven during these days of tribulation. But let me, if I may, present the following for your discernment, then you can knowingly come to your own conclusions. Also, see how Jesus describes the way people will be living in a state of self-indulgence and self-amusement when He returns].

In Acts 2:17, Peter addresses the crowd and says, "*In the Last days (refers from the time after Pentecost and the initiating of the Church up to the Second Coming), God says, 'I will pour out my Spirit on every mortal. Your sons and daughters will speak through the Holy Spirit; your young men will see visions, and your old men will have dreams. In those days, I pour out my spirit even on my servants, both men and women, and they will be prophets. I will perform miracles in the sky above and wonders on the earth below. The sun will be darkened and the moon will turn red as blood, before the great and glorious Day of the Lord come. And then, whoever calls upon the Name of the Lord will be saved.*" We see here how Peter was referencing the Prophet Joel, for if we read Joel 3:1; we read basically the same text as said by Peter on Pentecost.

---

1.   http://www.fatima.org/thirdsecret/

If we then go from Joel to Amos 5:18, we see how he, too, points to the following: *"Woe to you who long for Yahweh's day! Why should you long for that day? It is a day of Darkness, not of dawn, as if a man fled from a lion only to run into a bear; or as if he entered his home, rested his hand against the wall, only to be bitten by a viper. Will not the day of Yahweh be darkness and not light, gloom without a glow of brightness?"*

Brothers and sisters in our Lord Jesus Christ, what I have just written demonstrates how throughout the Old and New Testament, it was clearly indicated for those that have wisdom and discernment, how the days to come will be of darkness and woe. They will be days of sorrow and repentance. Take note of this.

I illustrate how we have been warned through Scripture, but even more recently, how we have been warned through Our Lady's apparitions. This is why I sent to you the Third Secret of Fatima. If we read the message of Our Lady, not only from Fatima, but Lourdes and La Sallete, we find how the message she has been delivering to us directly correlates to that of Scripture. We see how she warns of us of the "Days of Darkness." Read what she has said and compare to what has been written through the prophets, the Gospel accounts, as well as the Book of Revelation. Read and see for yourself when she warns us of the destruction, the darkness, the cold, and the sign of hope. When she says the following, **"Hurricanes of fires will rain forth from Heaven and spread over all the earth, fear will seize mortals at the sight of these clouds of fire, and great will be their cries of lamentation, many godless WILL BURN IN THE OPEN FIELDS LIKE WITHERED GRASS. God's wrath will be poured out upon the whole world, the 'chastisement' will be terrible, SUCH AS NEVER BEFORE, and will afflict the ENTIRE EARTH,"** refer to Revelation 9:7. Both visions basically refer to the same thing, similar to that of a nuclear holocaust aftermath.

The following is an excerpt from Our Lady's apparition at La Sallete (this occurred in France in 1846, and has been recognized by the Vatican as being one of the authentic, supernatural occurrences, as was her apparition at Guadalupe Mexico, Lourdes, France, Fatima, Portugal and Akita Japan in 1968). *"The earth will be struck all kinds of plagues [in addition to pestilence and famine which will be general]; there will be wars until the last war, which will then be made by the ten kings of the antichrist, which kings will have all one same design and will be the only ones who will rule the world. Before these arrive, there will be a type of false peace in the world; one will think only about amusing oneself; (remember Jesus' words in the former paragraphs about living in self indulgence) the wicked will deliver themselves over to all kinds of*

sin, but the children of the holy Church, the children of the faith, my true imi-
tators, will grow in the love of God and in the virtues which are dear to me.
Happy the humble souls guided by the Holy Spirit! I will fight with them until
they arrive at the fullness of the age.' The seasons will be changed, the earth
will produce only bad fruits, the stars will lose their regular movements, the
moon will reflect only a feeble reddish light; water and fire will give to the
globe of the earth convulsive movements and horrible earthquakes which will
cause to be engulfed mountains, cities. 'Woe to the inhabitants of the earth!
There will be bloody wars and famines; pestilences and contagious diseases;
there will be rains of a dreadful hail of animals, thunders which will shake
cities, earthquakes which will engulf countries; voices will be heard in the air,
men will beat their head against the walls, they will call upon death, and on
another side death will be their torture; blood will flow on all sides. Who will
be able to overcome, if God does not shorten the time of the ordeal? By the
blood, the tears and the prayers of the just, God will let Himself be swayed,
Enoch and Elie will be put to death; pagan Rome will disappear; fire from
Heaven will fall and will consume three cities; all the universe will be struck
with terror, and many will let themselves be misled because they have not
adored the true Christ living among them. It is time; the sun darkens; faith
alone will live.'

Notice throughout the excerpt what I have highlighted, or italicized; where people will only think about amusing themselves, just as Jesus said in Luke 17:26-28.

We also see a reference to God shortening the time of the ordeal, just as Jesus said in Matthew 24:20-22 and Mark 13:17-20, where Jesus describes how God the Father will shorten this time for His chosen ones for if He does not do so, then no one will survive.

Mark 13:19-20 reads, *"For this will be a time of distress such as was never known from the beginning when God created the world, until now and is never to be known again. So that if the Lord had not shortened that time, no one would survive, but he decided to shorten it for the sake of his chosen ones."* We see Jesus' words reflected by what was said earlier in Biblical history to Noah (Genesis 6) and with Abraham (Genesis 18-19).

Earlier in the letter, I made a reference to the rapture and how this notion or belief has been perpetuated for basically the last century and a half. I also referred to Lot's wife and how this is key to understanding the following. Jesus references Lot's wife when describing how it will be during His second coming for a very important reason. If we look at Genesis 19:15-17, we see how God had mercy on

Lot and his family, and how they were allowed to flee the city before it was destroyed. But God relayed a very important warning to him through the angels and told him not to look back and not to stop anywhere but to flee to the mountain lest he perish. Lot did so, but asked for a small favor before he left—to be able to flee to the small town of Zoar and be safe. He was granted the request, and he fled, but just as they were leaving, his wife looked back, and she immediately became a pillar of salt. Where Lot was left to live another day and continue to give thanks and praise to God, his wife was taken. There were two, yet one was taken and one was left. This is key because here we truly see the context in which Jesus was talking. Furthermore, let's look at some of the following: Matthew 24:17-18, Mark 13:15-16, Luke 17:31-35, *"If you are on the housetop, do not come down to take anything with you. If you are in the field, do not turn back to fetch your cloak."* In Luke He also says, *"Whoever tries to save his life will lose himself, but whoever gives his life will be born again."*

This is the key to understanding the truth. For it is here where and how Jesus truly lets us know the truth about the coming times. For it is the selfish that try to go back and save their belongings. It is the selfish that think about and look only for ways of saving their lives. It is the selfish (Lot's wife) who look back and are taken or converted to pillars of salts. It is the selfish that think only about this life but not in the one that has been promised to us as good followers of Christ. But it is the selfless that do God's will and follow His ways and heed His warnings that will be born again in the Holy Spirit (Edgar Cayce, the sleeping prophet was, too, asked about the end times in reference where people could move to be saved from disaster, and he would tell them, "It's not so much where you live that will matter, but how you are living.")

For to be baptized through the Holy Spirit in true conversion is to be born again (as Jesus references this) and to be a true follower of His. This is precisely why Jesus said these words and gave them to us in the context in which He did. **If one is taken and one is left**, then it is up to us to make sure we are not consumed with things of this world when that day comes, as was the case with Lot's wife. She looked back and was concerned about what she was losing and the way in which she lost it. Therefore she was taken, and Lot was left. Where do we fall? Would we look back? Would we try to save our lives? Let us be more concerned about our spiritual livelihoods than our temporal and limited ones.

Many today believe in the rapture, and there is nothing wrong with believing in this theory, as long as you live your life according to Christ's teachings and precepts. But we must also keep in mind and take into account that nowhere in the Gospels does Jesus actually refer to this rapture of the physical taking of the human body. Remember what is written in Genesis 3:19, *"With sweat on you face you will eat your bread, until you return to clay, since it was from clay that you were taken, for you are dust and to dust you shall return."* God makes it known to us that this earthly temple we inhabit is of the earth and from the earth. For it is corruption, decay and death that are the consequences of sin, and it is only those that are immaculately conceived that will/have never experienced this.

[The whole rapture movement was basically started and promoted by a Scottish preacher named Edward Irving; I highly suggest you look into this man's biography and how C.I. Scofield (an American) took this theory and introduced it in a reference Bible early in the early 20th Century. He became very rich in selling this new Christian theory during his lifetime, and it still influences millions of people in this country today because so many have taken it as an infallible truth. (For further reference to this, I highly recommend you search the following site: truthkeepers.com). The truth shall set you free. I strongly urge that you look into this (if you are a Rapture believer), and see for yourselves what so many others have found out about the founders of this theory.]

Another point I want to leave for your discernment is the following. Throughout the Gospel accounts, as is the case with the Virgin's messages to us, we see how Jesus refers to the shortening of this chastisement. *"For if it was not shortened, then no one would survive."* But Jesus says that He will shorten this time for *"His chosen ones."* This reference continues in the same path as seen throughout Biblical history. We see how God warns His people ahead of time of what is to come. Whether it was through Noah, Moses, the prophets, Jesus, the apostles, and now the Virgin, people have always been warned ahead of time through God the Father's messengers but to little or no avail. Throughout, it has always been shown how God had mercy on His chosen ones and protected those He loved and in turn loved and obeyed Him.

Nowhere in the Bible do find examples of people being raptured prior to God's wrath. Were Abraham and Lot raptured? Were Moses and his people raptured? Was Noah and his family raptured? Was Jesus, the Son of God, raptured prior to His suffering?

Nor does Christ in the Gospel accounts, or the Virgin in all of her messages, ever refer to anything that would lead one to believe this notion. They were all warned, just as we have been. They were all shown a way to protect and save themselves, just as we have. But nowhere was the option of being lifted up (in the physical body) to be spared this tribulation ever offered. We have hope, the hope that comes from knowing that God has mercy, and can be swayed by strong prayers of intercession on our behalf, by the saints and the blessed Virgin.

Brothers and sisters in the Lord, just as Moses interceded and warned his people about the coming of God's wrath in Egypt, so, too, the Virgin is warning us and has been doing so for the past century and a half. See how/what God said to Moses in Exodus 11:6-7, *"There will be great wailing throughout all Egypt, such as has never been before and never will again. But among the Israelites not a dog will howl for the death of either man or beast. This is what you may understand that Yahweh makes a distinction between Egypt and Israel."* He also added in chapter 12: 6-7, *"On that evening all the people will slaughter their lambs and take some of the blood to put on the doorposts and on top of the door frames of the houses where you eat."* He (God) used this method of recognition to spare the Israelites from sharing the same fate the Egyptians did that tragic night the angel of death swept through the valley.

Similarly, we see how the Virgin in her message from Fatima states, **"As soon as you perceive the disturbed signs of the very cold night: Go inside, shut and lock all doors and windows, pull down the shades, keep the doors and windows well covered, go and stay away from doors and windows. Do not look out, do not go outside for any reason, and do not talk to anyone outside. ANYONE WHO LOOKS OUT OR GOES OUT WILL DIE IMMEDIATELY! The wrath of God is holy and He does not want us to see it. All will be black, and the only thing, which will give light, will be blessed wax candles; even these will not burn in the houses of the godless scoffers. Once lit, NOTHING WILL PUT THEM OUT IN THE HOUSES OF THE BELIEVERS. Be sure to keep a supply of blessed wax candles in your homes—also Holy Water to be sprinkled freely around the house, especially at doors and windows. Bless yourself and others with it. Drink it and anoint your 'senses' with it (eyes, ears, nose, mouth) and hands, feet, and forehead."**

Notice now that it is no longer blood from a lamb, but holy water that is to be sprinkled for we are no longer bound to the Old Covenant, but have been made whole through our knowledge and worship of Christ through his New Covenant. Also, notice how those God chooses to protect those that are His here on earth and not in some raptured like state.

In Exodus 12:22-23, Moses says, *"Take a twig of hyssop dipped in its blood and sprinkle it on the door post, and the top of the door frame: from then on no one will go out of the door of the house before morning. Because God will pass through to strike Egypt and when he sees the blood on the lintel and the door posts, he will pass over the door and not allow the destroyer to enter your houses and kill."*

Notice the warning Moses gives his people, as relayed by God, and notice the warning as given by the Virgin at Fatima. This was the message then, and is the message today once again.

We must remain strong in the faith, and pray, my brothers and sisters, that we may be strong and not fall into temptation.

This letter is merely to pass along the message that I have been given for you all. It is up to you and your discernment, whether or not you believe any of it. But I ask this favor of you: inquire and find out to the best of your ability to see if what I have said is true or not.

Read for yourselves and become curious in the Word of God, as well as the warnings that have been given to us by the Virgin. She is our intercessor. You decide whether or not what I say is true or false. My job has been to give you what I have been giving you over the last several weeks and months and to prepare you for what is to come. Pray for me, just as I have been praying for you, my brothers and sisters in the Lord. Be strong in your faith. I pray that God give you the strength, heart and wisdom to discern what is true from what is not. Be kind and good to one another, and pray, pray, pray that you have strength.

Your brother,
horacio

Letter XV-To Err is Human, To Forgive Divine

Greetings and good morning to you, my brothers and sisters. May the Lord be with you today on this eighth day of this sixth month of 2005. I hope and pray that you, your friends and loved ones are doing well on this day that the Lord has made.

Brothers and sisters, today I bring forth a message of mercy, acceptance, love and forgiveness. For after all, this is the message that Jesus came to give us by example. He taught us both physically and verbally how to treat one another and how to have mercy and forgiveness for one another. It is often times very difficult to forgive when we feel we have been wronged or hurt.

By the same token, it is always equally as difficult to ask for forgiveness when we were the ones who perpetrated the act of hurt or wrongdoing.

We often times allow the wall of pride to be erected between us and the other person, thereby creating a very difficult barrier to overcome. I have been personally culpable of this myself, as I am sure all of you have at some point or another in your lifetime. We feel ashamed, hurt and embarrassed, and if we allow these emotions to settle and take root, then we could have an unforgiving spirit for a very long time.

Sometimes the person who wronged us wasn't a person at all but rather an institution. I have often met people that feel they were wronged by the church, the schools, the state, you name it. They then begin to form and allow an unforgiving spirit to settle into their minds and spirits. They form a grudge.

Once this grudge settles into them and is allowed to take firm roots, they then begin to see and encounter its fruits—pride, egocentrism, hate, anger, selfishness and depression. Whether they were the ones wronged or the ones who committed the wrong, they begin to hide and stay away from their brothers or sisters against whom this was perpetrated to or from (just as Adam and Eve hid from God in the Garden of Eden after they pride fully went against God).

The same is true if the guilty party was a church community or even a priest. We begin to avoid the person or institution that wronged us. There is nothing wrong with getting angry with what actually transpired because anger is a God-given human emotion. Even Jesus became angry when He turned over the tables in the temple (John 2). It is only when we begin to allow this anger to settle into us wherein the danger lies; for it is here that the enemy begins to have fertile soil to plant his seeds within us.

Brothers and sisters, remember what Jesus taught about forgiveness in Matthew 18:21 and Luke 17:3: *"Then Peter asked him, 'Lord, how many times must I forgive the offenses of my brother? Seven times?' Jesus answered, 'No, not seven times, but seventy-seven times.'"*

We clearly see here how Jesus was trying to demonstrate to His apostles and to us as well that no matter how many times someone wrongs us—and each time comes back to ask forgiveness—we should forgive him/her every time.

How many times do we have the same conviction to forgive someone even after the first offense? Much less seventy-seven.

For many of us, the initial desire we have is for revenge. We want to see the other person in pain as well and to settle the score [this is precisely what society and pop culture through movies, television and music promote. They all further the notion of settling the score and obtaining vengeance through a vindictive spirit]. We begin to have scheming thoughts and desires that lead us astray and far from the grace of forgiveness.

Another good example Jesus left for us is also found in Matthew 18:23, the unmerciful servant parable. *"This story throws light on the kingdom of Heaven. A king decided to settle the accounts of his servants. Among the first was one who owed him ten thousand pieces of gold. As the man could not repay the debt, the king commanded that he be sold as a slave with his wife, children and all his goods in payment. The official threw himself at the feet of the king and said, 'Give me time, and I will pay you back everything.' The king took pity on him and not only set him free but cancelled his debt. This official then left the king's presence and he met one of his companions who owed him a hundred pieces of silver. He grabbed him by the neck and almost strangled him, shouting, 'Pay me what you owe!' His companion threw himself at his feet and asked him, 'Give me time and I will pay everything.' The other did not agree, but sent him to prison until he had paid all his debt. His companions saw what happened. They were indignant and so they went and reported everything to the king. The King then summoned his official and said, 'Wicked servant, I forgave you all that you owed when you begged me to do so. Weren't you bound to have pity on your companion as I had pity on you?' The king was now angry, so he handed his servant over to be punished, until he had paid his whole debt.' Jesus added, 'So will my heavenly Father do with you unless each of you sincerely forgives his brother.'"*

Here Jesus clearly illustrates how sometimes we may ask for forgiveness from God for all that we have done to offend Him. Yet when one of our brothers or sisters asks the same of us, we turn our back on them and throw them to the lions. Where God forgives us and cancels our whole debt, we do the opposite when it comes time to forgive and cancel the debt owed to us.

That is why when we pray the Lord's Prayer, we say, "Forgive us our trespasses/debts, just as we forgive those who trespass against us." We say these words every time we pray the Lord's Prayer, but how often do we actually do/mean this? For some this may be easy, but for many it is not.

But how about when we are the ones who are seeking forgiveness? Jesus also gives the parable of the prodigal son (Luke15:11): *"There was a man with two sons. The younger said to his father, 'Give me my share of the estate.' So the father divided his property between his two sons. Some days later, the younger son gathered all his belongings and started off for a distant land where he squandered his wealth in loose living. Having spent everything, he was hard pressed when a severe famine broke out in that land. So he hired himself out to a well-to-do citizen of that place and was sent to work on a pig farm. So famished was he that he longed to fill his stomach even with the food given to the pigs, but no one offered him anything. Finally coming to his senses, he said, 'How many of my father's hired men have food to spare, and here I am starving to death!' I will go back to my father and say to him, 'Father, I have sinned against God and before you. I no longer deserve to be called your son. Treat me then as one of your servants.' With that thought in mind he set off for his father's house. He was still a long way off when his father caught sight of him. His father was so deeply moved with compassion that he ran out to meet him, threw his arms around his neck and kissed him. The son said, 'Father, I have sinned against God and before you, I no longer deserve to be called your son' … But the father turned to his servants and said, 'Quick! Bring out the finest robe and put it on him. Put a ring on his finger and sandals on his feet. Take the fattened calf and kill it. We shall celebrate and have a feast, for this son of mine was dead and has come back to life. He was lost, and now is found.'"*

How many of us can relate to this parable? During Jesus' time (and still today under Jewish law), pigs and everything that was associated with them was considered of the utmost unclean, especially for Jews, who must have viewed this parable as shocking, seeing how Jesus interjects the prodigal son's thoughts of eating from the pig's sty. But He does this to show us that no matter how low we have fallen and how dirty and unclean we feel have become, there is always the hope of forgiveness. But before we can be forgiven, we must acknowledge our sins, just as the prodigal son did before God and his father, and ask for forgiveness. He felt he no longer deserved to be called his father's son. He felt unworthy of such title and would be satisfied if his father just treated him like one of his servants. But his father instead rejoiced at the sight of his son coming back home and ran to embrace and kiss him.

This is exactly how God treats all of His sons and daughters. He embraces each and everyone one of us with complete love, mercy and forgiveness. He has never stopped loving us; He is waiting for us, just like the father in the story, to see us coming back down that road toward our rightful home. "For this son of mine was dead, and has come back to life. He was lost, and is found" is the perfect quote for many of us today.

Many of us today may be physically alive but are spiritually dead. Many of us may know where we live and where we work, but we have really lost our way. We have become proud, indignant and haughty. We know we have sinned against God, our brother or sister, but continue to keep it inside and not acknowledge it. We are proud and stiff-necked and will not allow humility to come into our hearts. We do not know how to ask for forgiveness or find it, when all we have to do is ask.

Let go of that hot coal of pride that burns your hands the longer you hold on to it. Why continue to hold on to something that causes you pain? Seek and ask for forgiveness, and it shall be given to you. Humble yourself before God, and your brother or sister, and you will be exalted. Let your hearts of stone and steel be turned into flesh.

Brothers and sisters in our Lord our God, forgive, and you shall be forgiven. Ask and you shall find. That is the message the Lord wants us all to know and understand. He knows that we will wrong others, and that others will wrong us. We are only human. Things will be said and done that will hurt, humiliate and anger us, this is a given. But the key is how we in turn confront and deal with these circumstances? Do we become angry, lash out and form grudges? Or do we become angry, lash out, and then find it in our hearts to forgive or be forgiven? Remember anger by itself is not malignant, but only if we allow it to settle into our hearts, where the enemy can begin to cultivate it.

Remain strong, my brothers and sisters in the Lord. Continue to pray for me. I need many prayers of intercession from you all, and I as always continue to pray for you all. Treat each other well, and next time you say the Lord's Prayer, remember the message of forgiveness that Christ gave us.

Your brother,
horacio

Letter XVI-They That Are Not Against You Are With You

Good morning, brothers and sisters in our Lord Jesus Christ, on this beautiful morning of the 13th day of this sixth month. It is with great joy and peace that I come to you once again with another message of preparation for the coming years.

In today's world of multi-faceted options and decisions, we sometimes have a hard time discerning what is right from wrong, truth from lie. Often times we see the many religious sects and factions that have branched out throughout the world, all claiming to have the right answers. All claim to know God's true word and their interpretation of it. All claim to have God's favor, while at the same time condemning and rebuking those that do not share in their beliefs and practices. The key here, my brothers and sisters, is not whether God is on our side but whether we are on His.

Many throughout the world have confused and misinterpreted—not only today but for thousands of years—God's causes with their own self-interested causes. (If not the individual's self-interest, then their religious community's self-interest).

Many people lack the historical basis, knowledge and understanding to refute claims when being backed into a corner, and therefore take the attitude of "If you can't beat them, join them." What would have happened if Jesus had taken this stance? For surely, there was no other more famous person in history who was mocked, criticized, questioned and ultimately put to death for His beliefs than Jesus Christ.

But by the same token, we must not condemn others for their belief but rather respect them and their points of view, even if the same is not true of them. This is key to leading a good Christian life and living by example for others to see.

If anyone attacks you and your beliefs while trying to impose their beliefs on you, then you must ask yourself if they truly have God's grace. If anyone condemns you and your opinions, then you will see (if you are wise) what their true motives are. Did Jesus impose by force or verbally His will and beliefs on people?

Jesus' constant message and example to us throughout the Gospels is one of humility, selflessness and sacrifice. He led by example so that His disciples could follow and pass on the example to others. In Luke 9:48, Jesus says, *"Whoever welcomes this little child in my name welcomes me and whoever welcomes me, welcomes the one who sent me. And listen: He who is found to be the least among you all he is great indeed."* This was His message then and continues to be the message today and for tomorrow as well.

One of the many things I have learned in my thirty years of life on this earthly planet is that throughout human history on this earth, we have not been able to live without hostility and anger toward one another. Then we added our religious beliefs into the mix and created an even more volatile formula.

We see throughout history how religious fervor and fanaticism have caused violence, aggression and death. We see this happen especially with those religious members who see themselves and their communities as having special favor from God, or perhaps see their way of salvation as the only way of entering heaven. So they impose and force their beliefs on others. This is happening now and has been the case throughout.

It is clear that Jesus was not a fanatic, nor did He share in the belief of carrying out His message through violent fanaticism and fervor. He did not come to bar people, regardless of age, sex, race, ethnicity, and or illness and disease, but He came to comfort and include them in His message. He did not share in the belief of punishing those that did not accept His message but rather in living peacefully with them and conveying His message through peaceful means. If they chose not to accept Him or His message, then He would leave and look elsewhere for individuals who would openly correspond to God's call. In Mark 6:10, Jesus added, *"In whatever house you are welcomed, stay there until you leave the place. If any place does not receive you and the people refuse to listen to you, leave after shaking the dust off your feet. It will be a testimony against them."*

We also see in Luke 9:49 how John spoke up, *"Master, we saw someone who drove out demons by calling upon your name, and we tried to stop him because he doesn't follow you with us."* But Jesus said, *"Don't stop him, for He who is not against you is for you."*

It is precisely this message that He came to give and plant within all of us. The message of accepting those that do God's will, even though they may not be within our religious community or family. [Remember the wise men that came bearing gifts for Jesus? They were not part of God's people (Jews), but they served His purpose as well.]

Jesus here clearly makes the point that even those who are not within our immediate religious group can and should continue to do God's work in Jesus' name. Jesus rebukes John for trying to stop the man because John fell into the same trap that most of us fall into. That is confusing God's cause and His interest with our own.

Many of us that call ourselves Christians try to stop others that are doing God's work because we feel/believe that other people are perhaps not as enlightened as ourselves. Perhaps it is because we believe that our way is the best, and they should know better than to do God's work outside of our religious structures, mindsets and communities. Whatever the reason may be, we allow our selfish interest to cloud our spiritual vision and not see what it truly is that Jesus wants from us. "He who is not against you is for you." Who are we to stop someone from doing what is good and promotes well being within the Christian community as a whole?

As we read a little further in Luke 9:51-56, we see how Jesus reacts toward His apostles for being narrow minded and vengeful because they were rejected by the Samaritans. *"As the time drew near when Jesus would be taken up to Heaven, he made up his mind to go to Jerusalem. He had sent ahead of him some messengers who entered a Samaritan village to prepare lodging for him. But the people would not receive him because he was on his way to Jerusalem. Seeing this, James and John, his disciples said, 'Lord, do you want us to call down fire from Heaven to reduce them to ashes?' Jesus turned and rebuked them, and they went on to another village."*

Here again we see the response Jesus gave both John and James for having made such a suggestion. He rebuked them for "wanting to call down an air strike from heaven" because the people had rejected them. But Jesus prefers to accept this message of rejection from the Samaritans and move on to the next village. He does not share His disciple's thirst for retribution and pay back.

How many of us are like James and John? When someone rejects us, our faith or our religious beliefs, we become angry, defensive and vengeful. We seek to strike out immediately to ease some of the pain of hurt and rejection. We ourselves also want to call down fire from heaven to wipe the aggressors and/or rejecters. We fall into the trap that the disciples fell into. They were confusing their cause and self-interest with God's cause and His interest. And in doing so, they were also seeking to do harm instead of good for their sake but not God's. This is the danger, brothers and sisters in the Lord.

We must pray that the Lord give us eyes to see, ears to hear, and hearts to know and sense the truth. We must not allow ourselves to fall into this trap of believing that our way is the **only** way. We must not fall into the narrow-minded notion that God is with us, even though we are not with Him. For we have just seen that even though James and John were actually with God the Son, He was not with them in their thoughts and their beliefs. He did not share in their thoughts and concerns. For it was on both occasions that He rebuked them for thinking and doing the things they did.

We too, must know when God is rebuking us for doing what we do, think or say that go against His causes and concerns, and not ours. For He does knock us on the head a few times; we just have to be wise enough to know when He is doing so.

Brothers and sisters in the Lord, I continue to ask for your prayers, especially during this period in my life. I ask that you keep me in your thoughts and ask that you intercede for me. I, too, continue to pray for all of you. Everyone from California to Illinois to Kentucky and throughout Texas. You know who you all are, and I ask that you continue to spread the Good News. Be strong in the Lord, and ask that He give you wisdom and understanding. I ask this through Christ our Lord, amen.

Your brother in need,
horacio

Letter XVII-Enter Through the Narrow Gate

Good morning to you, brothers and sisters in the Lord Jesus Christ. I give thanks and praise that the good Lord has blessed me with another beautiful day of life, and I give thanks for many other intangible blessings as well. Both the seen and the unseen, the physical and the spiritual, the blessings and hardships. I, too, give thanks for you all and pray that you are doing well.

I come to you today on this twentieth day of the sixth month of this two thousand and five year of our Lord with a message of hope and work. Let us not be fooled, my brothers and sisters, into believing false teachings and theories.

Many today claim to know God and preach about God, but I tell you that even they are not yet saved. God is love and forgiveness, and He wants us to have a relationship with Him. But not many are willing to sacrifice their time, interest or other resources in order to know and listen to what He truly has to say. How can you love someone, yet never take the time to spend time with him or her, learn about him or her, or sacrifice for him or her?

Many in today's society truly believe that God should revolve around them and their lifestyle. That He should accept them just the way they are and what they do. They fall into the notion or theory that is so commonly preached today that basically says, "Do whatever you feel like doing and whenever you feel like doing it," and you will still be saved. "If it feels right do it." "This is a free country, and I can do whatever I want to!" The list goes on and on. It is this selfish mindset that has created a gap between Him and ourselves. We are the ones that have moved farther away from Him through the practice of these selfish freedoms (license) and not Him away from us. For He is like the father that welcomed back the prodigal son with open arms, but only after the son had acknowledged through a contrite heart what he had done and repented for his sins that in turn brought about his true conversion and repentance.

In today's fast-paced society, we commonly run into these theories and notions that are not only promoted and disseminated by people that have no idea of who God truly is, but, ironically enough, by people that have titles and diplomas saying they are men of God.

It is like telling a high school or college student, "Don't worry about learning and studying for your class during the semester because when it is time to take the final, you will pass it anyway; so for now, you can continue to do whatever it is you want to do." Or saying, "Do not worry about paying your bills and your taxes at the end of the month or year. Do whatever you want for now, and worry about that only when the time comes." Still yet another example, "Do not worry about teaching your kids right from wrong when they are young. Let them do what they want, and do not hinder them in any way. Just love them and accept whatever they do. But once they grow older and become headaches not only to you but to society, then worry about them." Or "Plant your garden, but do not worry yourself about watering or tending to it, for you will still reap a good harvest."

This is exactly what many supposed men of God are teaching their disciples, their flocks. Do as you please now for God will still allow you to enter His kingdom when your time comes. How can we pretend or allow ourselves to buy into these selfish doctrines? Simple: we ourselves are selfish.

We want the good grades without working for them. We want our bookkeeping and finances to be in order without having to work on them. We want good and obedient children without having to teach and train them properly. We want a good harvest without having to water or tend the seedlings. And finally, we want salvation and to enter the kingdom of God without ever having worked, learned, taught, watered, or fully understood what it is to be a good follower and servant of Christ. We cannot achieve a supernatural ends (salvation) using only natural means. We, too, need to use supernatural means in order to gain supernatural ends. This is where divine sanctifying grace helps us achieve those ends. We obtain it through prayer, penance and sacrifice.

We as a global community have bought—hook, line and sinker—the notion that is so prevalent in our society. That being, "One can obtain anything and everything without ever actually working for it." Do not take my words for it, but here are Jesus' words in Matthew 7:13: *"Enter through the narrow gate; for wide is the gate and broad is the road that leads to destruction, and many will go that way. How narrow is the gate that leads to life and how rough the road; few there are the ones who find it."*

Jesus here, by His own accord, acknowledges the width and all encompassing road that leads to destruction. He points out that many, or the majority choose that path, because it is convenient and by far the more popular one. It is the path of least resistance, and the one that offers to people what they want to hear, say or do.

But look at what He says about the road less traveled. He points out that it is the one that has a narrow gate, and how rough or difficult it is to choose that road. He further points out that few are the ones that find it, and even less, choose it. This is the path—if we choose to take it—that promotes true sacrifice, penance, and meditative and contemplative prayer.

On which road are we on? Are we on the one that flows from or toward popular opinion? The path that is the popular one to take or of least resistance? The one that provides an all encompassing message and easy way out for everyone, or are we on the latter one? The one that is hard to take but leads to everlasting life? [Also look in Acts 14:22 for added reference to what the apostles themselves viewed as the rough path to take in order to enter the Kingdom of God.]

Furthermore, look at what He says in Matthew 7:21 (Luke 13:24): *"Not everyone who says to me, 'Lord! Lord! Will enter the Kingdom of Heaven, but the one **who does the will of my Father in Heaven**. Many will say to me on that day, 'Lord, Lord, did we not speak in your name? Did we not cast out devils and perform many miracles in your name?' Then I will tell them openly, 'I have never known you, away from me you evil people!"*

Here Jesus makes a very strong point: many will come to Him at the end and will attempt to sweet talk Him into making Him believe that they knew Him, spoke of Him, and did things in His name, but He will know the truth; and the truth being that He will reject them, just like they rejected Him and His teachings on this earthly/temporal plane. He clearly states that not every one that calls His name will enter, but only those that did the will of His Father.

Jesus also sheds some light on what will happen in the kingdom of heaven through the following parable found in Matthew 25, Mark 13:35, Luke 25: *"Ten bridesmaids went out with their lamps to meet the bridegroom. Five of them were careless, while the others were sensible. The careless bridesmaids took their lamps as they were and did not bring extra oil, but those who were sensible, brought with their lamps flasks with extra oil. As the bridegroom delayed, they all grew drowsy and fell asleep. But at midnight a cry rang out: 'the bridegroom is here, come out and meet him!' All the maidens woke up at once and trimmed their lamps. Then the careless ones said to the sensible ones, 'Could you give us some oil, for our lamps are going out?' The sensible ones answered, 'There may not be enough for both you and us, you had better go to those who sell and buy for yourselves.' They were out buying oil when the bridegroom came, and those who were ready went with him to the wedding feast, and the doors were shut. Later the rest of the bridesmaids arrived and called out, 'Lord, Lord, open to us,' But he answered, 'Truly, I do not know you."*

Here again we see the comparison of those that were ready and found themselves to be truly prepared for the day they would be called to wedding feast, and those that thought they were ready, but in the end found themselves to be lacking, and therefore were left out. We see, too, how the five unprepared maidens attempted to make all the necessary adjustments at the end but were too late.

So, too, must we be careful and not allow ourselves to be careless but instead prepared. Let us not be fooled into going through the wide gate and stepping onto the path of the wide smooth road, but instead let us be wise and sensible, and enter through the narrow gate, and carry our burdens on that which is the road less traveled and of a rough nature.

Do not be fooled by those that allow for everything and anything, and lead you to believe that God, too, allows anything and everything for there are reasons for His teachings and precepts. They are not just there for decorative and superficial purposes, but rather as the cornerstone and building blocks for our foundation in the faith. There is a reason for this divine order. There is light and darkness in the world, and He came to deliver us from this darkness.

He is the true and ever living light that shines upon all of us, both good and bad. But this does not mean that both good and bad will both be allowed to enter into the banquet.

It is true that Jesus came to be with sinners and heal the spiritually and physically ill, but it is also true that those that He healed, in both senses, experienced a true conversion and repented of their sins, and then followed this up by becoming proclaimers of the Good News of Jesus Christ and living out His precepts and teachings.

Do not be fooled, brothers and sisters, that just by mere knowledge of His name, you will be saved, but rather know that by knowing Him intimately through both faith, work, loyalty to His precepts and His love.

Is it enough to know that by food and water we will be nourished and kept alive, but do nothing to obtain them? No, rather it is through both knowledge and the work of knowing how to obtain these self-nourishing needs that we live. We must work to obtain the resources that in turn allow us to obtain these needs. It is not merely enough to have knowledge of them and that by thinking about them we will satisfy our bodies' needs.

So, too, must we work at knowing who God truly is and what resources we need in order to fulfill His will and not ours that will allow us to nourish our spiritual needs.

I pray for you all, my brothers and sisters, and for your families as well. Remain strong in the in faith and works so that our Lord continues to be pleased with us.

Let us always be reminded of giving thanks and praise to Him for it is always right to give Him thanks and praise. I ask that you pray for me, especially now, I could really use some extra prayers. Be wise, and ask that the Lord continue to allow us to see, hear and know the truth when we are presented with it.

Your brother in Christ,
horacio

Letter XVIII-Nothing To Fear

Good morning, brothers and sisters in the Lord. I come to you this morning of the thirtieth day on this sixth month of the year to bring forward another message of preparation so you may continue on your path toward being spiritually prepared during these times. But, more importantly, for the coming years. Years that will prove to be challenging, lean and frightening. But if you are strong in the Lord and have faith in His will, you will be given life and see the fulfillment of His promises.

The coming years will prove to be hard, but more so for those that have never known God and don't plan to. They will show to be lean both economically speaking, as well as spiritually speaking. We already see some of the initial birth pangs of this coming time throughout, and it will continue to evolve faster and faster.

Hostility toward Christians will continue to rise, as well as a continued hostility and denunciation of God's words and precepts. Read your local newspaper, watch and hear the news on television or radio, and you will not have to wait long to see, hear or read the immense movement of anti-Christian sentiment sweeping across the world.

Brothers and sisters in the Lord, today I come with a message of hope and words that give light in darkness.

They are not my words, but the words as written in Holy Scripture that provide for this hopeful message. We currently live in a world dominated by fear and the ever-present threat of fear. Everyone has certain fears that live and are allowed to grow within each and every one of us. Whether they are substantiated or not, they are there and they have become part of our lives. They dictate what we do or don't do in life. We become, in some cases, slaves to our fears.

It doesn't help when we live in a society that perpetuates these fears through the media. Fear sells, and living in a society whose livelihood is dependent upon the sales of goods and services, it is no wonder how fear has become a very marketable and profitable commodity.

We cannot and should not allow ourselves to become dominated by fear, brothers and sisters, but instead become souls that are dominated by hope.

It has been said that the two greatest motivating forces in human nature are reward and pain/punishment. We are either motivated to action by one or the other.

In other words, we are motivated by hope and fear. One is of God's calling; the other comes from the enemies. Where one moves us by the promise of reward, hope, peace and everlasting life through the gifts of patience and humility, the other moves us through the act or threat of pain, hopelessness, war and everlasting death.

One looks forward toward the future with clear principles, morals and virtues, and the other cannot see clearly for lack of these intangible elements, and therefore lives in death and confusion.

Two of the best examples I can think of are found in the New Testament: When Jesus calms the storm [Matthew 8:23, Mark 4:35, Luke 8:22] and when Jesus walks on water [Matthew 14:24, Mark 6:45, John 6:16].

"Jesus got into the boat and his disciples followed him. Without warning a fierce storm hit the lake, with waves sweeping the boat. But Jesus was asleep. They woke him and cried, 'Lord save us! We are lost!' But Jesus answered, 'Why are you so afraid, you of little faith?' Then he stood up and ordered the wind and sea; and it became completely calm."

Then there was the time He walked on water: *"Meanwhile, the boat was very far from land, dangerously rocked by the waves for the wind was against it. At daybreak, Jesus came to them walking on the lake. When they saw him walking on the sea, they were terrified, thinking that it was a ghost. And they cried out in fear. But at once Jesus said to them, 'Courage! Don't be afraid. It's me!' Peter answered, 'Lord, if it is you, command me to come to you walking on water.' Jesus said to him, 'Come.' And Peter got out of the boat, walking on the water to go to Jesus. But, in face of the strong wind, he was afraid and begun to sink. So he cried out, 'Lord, save me!' Jesus immediately stretched out his hand and took hold of him saying, 'Man of little faith, why did you doubt?"*

In both instances, we see how Jesus' disciples were fearful and doubtful, and how Jesus in both cases always reassures them and asks them why they possessed such little faith?

In Peter's case, he began to take that leap of faith on the water, but in the face of adversity he panicked as he began to sink. Jesus, though, being the good shepherd as always, stretched out His hand and pulled him out of the water. But notice what He asks: "Man of little faith, why did you doubt?"

Brothers and sisters, how many of us are like Peter? We want to believe, and we want to have faith, and we even begin to take that scary leap of faith. But in the face of adversity, when we lose faith and begin to sink and cry out, Jesus saves us!

Some of us perhaps are like the other disciples that remain in the boat. We just prefer not to take that leap of faith. It's just too risky. What if I sink? This is precisely the fear(s) that keep us from being true faithful followers of Christ, especially in today's world of global fears. The enemy is hard at work keeping us paralyzed in fear. He wants to continue to keep us enslaved to our fears, whatever they may be.

But here is where hope begins to shine through for the Christian believer and follower. We must have strong faith and persistence in the Lord. The moment we step out of that boat, and the wind begins to try to knock us down, we must endure and persist in stepping onto the lake with Jesus so as to be able to walk with Him. When adversity strikes us in the face, we must have strong and undeniable courage and faith in Him who was sent for our sake to keep us from sinking. Never give up hope, remain steadfast, and the Lord will reward and compensate you for your faithfulness.

But how do we build strong faith? Simple: by praying, penance, praying, and knowing the Word of God.

Also, by maintaining a good and loving relationship with all of our brothers and sisters, the most and the least of them, as well as by keeping God's laws and commandments, which in today's world seems like a dying notion, on both a personal and global level. But most importantly, by being wise in knowing that the Lord will bring these storms to see if we react like the apostles did in that boat on that stormy sea. To see if we doubt or are further reinforced in our spiritual faith. The Holy Spirit will be sent to spiritually train each and every one of us as some point in our lives. Accept the challenge, and say YES to God.

The coming years are going to be very lean and challenging, my brothers and sisters, such as the world has never seen before. Do not be fooled into thinking that all is bright and rosy; for it is then that you will be caught unprepared for what is to come. There are many that paint a pretty picture of the world now, and they are the same people that see the future through rose-colored glasses. [Both they and their leaders can do no wrong and are incapable of acknowledging any wrongdoing, while the rest of Rome burns].

Do not be fooled, but rather continue your preparation in the Lord for He is the only one that can save you when you begin to sink into the waves of calamity and despair. He will extend His hand to you and save you. But there is one condition: You must be in the boat with Him to begin with.

Continue to pray, my brothers and sisters in the Lord Jesus Christ, that He continues to guide, strengthen and impart wisdom upon you all. That fear has no space in your mind and soul, and that hope and faith abound within you all. Continue to pray for me as well, for I do need your prayers.

Reject your hidden fear, and rebuke them in Jesus Christ's name. We all have them, but it is in how you deal with them that will determine if you live in hope, or live in fear.

Your brother and friend in Christ,
horacio

Letter XIX-The Fire That Purifies

Good morning to you, my brothers and sisters in the Lord our God. It is with great faith and pleasure from the good Lord that I come to you on this fifth day of the eleventh month in this 2005th year.

I come once again with another letter of preparation. This letter is actually number nineteenth in the series, but at the time I first wrote it, I left it semi finished, and therefore did not send it out. So it is today that I finally finished it and am sending it out for your discernment.

I will begin my letter with a scripture passage from I Corinthians 3:10-15, *"I, as a good architect, according to the capacity given to me, I laid the foundation, and another is to build upon it. Let each one be careful how he works upon it. No one lay a foundation other than the one, which is already laid, which is Jesus Christ. Then, if someone builds with gold upon this foundation, another with silver and precious stones, or with wood, bamboo or straw, the work of each one will be shown for what it is. The Day of Judgment will reveal it, because the fire will make everything known. The fire will test the work of everyone. If your work withstands the fire, you will be rewarded; but if your work becomes ashes, you will pay for it. You will be saved, but it will be as if passing through fire."*

Each one of us, my brothers and sisters, as we live here upon earth, are building upon this foundation. If we are Christians, regardless of denomination, we are building upon a foundation that was set as the ultimate standard by Jesus. St. Paul in this passage addresses the nature and consistency of our works. How are we building upon this foundation? Are our works made of gold, silver or other precious stones that can withstand the fires of purification? Or are they perhaps made of wood, bamboo or straw that will turn into ash when put to the ultimate test?

This question is for each one of us to answer in our own hearts and minds. Is the work that we do as Christians of any value? Will they withstand the fire of purification, or will they turn to ashes?

St. Paul goes on to remind us, *"If your work withstands the fire, you will be rewarded, but if your work turns to ashes, you will pay for it.* ***You will be saved, but it will be as if passing through fire.****"* What does St. Paul mean, you may ask?

Also in Matthew 5:25 we read, *"Don't forget this: be reconciled with your opponent quickly when you are together on the way to court. Otherwise, he will turn you over to the judge, who will hand you over to the police, who will put you in jail. There you will stay, until you have paid the last penny."*

Many today in the Christian world believe that there are only two destinations for our souls to go after we depart this physical plane. But we in the Catholic tradition believe and have faith in Purgatory. This refers to the place where souls are held *(until the last penny has been paid)* and directed toward one place or the other; if one is not of pure of heart and completely cleansed of all impurities; or still has certain debts that are owed, or were not forgiven or released. This is where the purification, or purging if you will, takes place. Similar to what St. Paul just finished describing, "You will be saved, but it will be as if passing through fire." In other words, these will be the fires of purification and/or the jail that will hold souls until the debts have been completely paid/purged.

So many people pass away on a daily basis, but can we honestly say that they were all saints or died in a state of grace? That they passed away doing only God's work? Of course not. Some perhaps yes, but the vast majority pass away with many impurities and not exactly as doing the will of God. Yet they were not completely evil people either; they were just not completely pure of heart, mind and soul

In Psalm 24:3-5, we find exactly who can ascend to stand in the presence of God, *"Who will ascend the mountain of the Lord? Who will stand in his holy place? Those with clean hands and pure heart, who desire not what is vain, and never swear to lie. They will receive blessings from the Lord, a reward from God, their savior. Such are the people who seek him, who seek the face of Jacob's God."*

These are the ones that seek and can stand in the presence of the Lord. Those with clean hands and pure hearts will be blessed and rewarded, just as St. Paul wrote. For is not our God perfect in every sense of the word? Is He not completely clean, pure and unblemished? So how could anything or anyone less than completely pure and completely clean stand in His presence?

In the past, I've heard Christian televangelists misleadingly describe how Purgatory came about. They talked about how it had its origins in pagan customs and continued in their uninterrupted description of how it basically had no foundation in modern Christianity.

The one thing they left out was how it can actually be found in the Old Testament and how it actually stems from Jewish belief. In II Maccabees 12:38-46 [Depending on the Bible you have, you may or may not have this book. In the year 384 A.D., the Decree of Pope Damasius established the canon of Scripture for the Christian Catholic Bible. They accepted some of the books that had been written in Greek that had earlier been rejected by the Jews during the council of Jamnia, held in the year 95 A.D. These books were called the deuterocanonical, or books of the second standard. When the Protestants departed from the Catholic Church, they decided to leave these second standard books out, because they considered them apocrypha, or non-authentic. But to this day, the Catholic bible remains unchanged, hence the citatation from the II Book of Maccabees.[1].],

"Judas reorganized his army, and then went to the city of Adullam. Since it was the week's end, they purified themselves and celebrated the Sabbath there. The next day the companions of Judas went to take away the bodies of the dead and buried them with their relatives in the tombs of their fathers. They found under the tunic of each of the dead men objects consecrated to the idols of Jamnia, which the Law forbade the Jews to wear. So it became clear to everyone why these men had died. Everyone blessed the intervention of the Lord, the just Judge who brings to light the most secret deeds; and they prayed to the Lord to completely pardon the sins of their dead companions. The valiant Judas urged his men to shun such sin in the future, for they had just seen with their own eyes what had happened to those who sinned. He took up a collection among his soldiers which amounted to two thousand pieces of silver and sent it to Jerusalem to be offered there as a sacrifice for sin. They did all this very well and rightly inspired by their belief in the resurrection of the dead. If they did not believe that their fallen companions would rise again, then it would have been useless and foolish thing to pray for them. But they firmly believed in a splendid reward [just as we do] for those who died as believers; therefore, their concern was holy and in keeping with faith. This is the reason why Judas had this sacrifice offered for the dead, so that the dead might be pardoned for their sin."

Brothers and sisters, especially those not of the Catholic faith, this passage describes exactly why we in the Catholic church still believe and pray for our dearly departed. It's because of our faith and belief in the resurrection of the dead and for the pardoning of sins that they may have died with. Because as we have just seen, when God decides to call us, we can be anywhere and completely unprepared to face Him. How many of us on a daily basis are completely prepared to face God, if called upon to do so? How many of us are completely clean

---

1.   http://www.newadvent.org/cathen/04613a.htm

and pure of heart, mind and spirit? We are not all saints, but by the same token, we are not all completely evil either. Most of us lie somewhere in the middle.

Last year, my brother and I decided to make wine, using the wild grapes that grow in and around our property. We gathered about twenty pounds of them and began. Throughout the whole process, the most time consuming and laborious part was sifting and purifying the juice. For several days and using several methods, we sifted the juice over and over and over until it was clean enough and without any impurities to be bottled. It wouldn't be very wise to drink wine with all its impurities and imperfections, would it? Or anything else for that matter. So how can we expect anything less from God Almighty's standard for us?

You see, my brothers and sisters in Christ, death as we know it is only the first stage of our sifting process. This first stage merely separates us from our physical world. But the second death, and after we have gone through the fires of purification, will either allow us to join God and be able to stand in His presence, or to be separated from Him for eternity. For even Christ said in Matthew 12:31-32 [also in Mark 3:22, Luke 11:15,], *"And so I tell you this: people can be forgiven any sin and any evil thing they say against God, but whoever says evil words against the Spirit will not be forgiven. He who speaks against the Son of Man, will be forgiven, but he/she who speaks against the Holy Spirit will not be forgiven, either in this age or in the age to come."*

Jesus here also refers in to the second phase of purification. He who speaks against the good works, as inspired and driven by the Holy Spirit, WILL NOT be forgiven, either in this age, or IN THE AGE TO COME; the one that will completely either join us to God, or completely separate us from Him for eternity. To live in true everlasting life, or to die the true death.

Brothers and sisters, it is with great hope, trust and faith in our loving and merciful Lord that I bring to you these letters and messages. I am merely the pen that is being used, nothing more and nothing less.

I accept my role as servant to our Lord and bring to you these Spirit-filled messages. I pray for you all continuously and ask that you all do the same for my family and my needs as well. Let us draw closer to He Who Is, and His message for each and everyone one of us.

The coming age will be one of great sorrow, pain, fear and death. This is why it is vital, my brothers and sisters in the Lord, to stand firm and not have our faith waver! We must support and look out for one another. We must acknowledge the true living Christ living among us.

The poor, the widowed, the orphaned; for it is here that we can find the Spirit of Christ dwelling among us. Let us pray for one another, and love one another, and forgive one another. Let us also pray for our dearly departed so that they, too, can have the chance to stand in the presence of God.

I wish a blessed week to you all and that God continue to strengthen and prepare you all. Amen.

Your brother,
horacio

Letter XX-He That Can Accept This, Should

Good morning, brothers and sisters in the Lord, on this beautiful twenty-sixth day of the seventh month. It is with great joy and pleasure that I come and greet you today. I pray that you and your families are doing well.

I hope that you and your friends are moving ever closer to God and His message and that your preparation is continually growing. This is the twentieth letter in a series of forty, and I deliver it to you filled with the Holy Spirit not only myself but for you as well.

Today, brothers and sisters, we live a world that is full of disposable items. Everything from cameras to dinnerware, we are surrounded by a throw-away mentality that seems to have affected one of society's core foundations—the family. We are constantly bombarded with the message from salesmen and marketers, "If it's old, get rid of it and buy a new one," whatever it may be. We seem to constantly want to hide or completely destroy that which has stood the test of time, whether they be buildings, natural gifts (trees and mountains), or even sometimes our own families. Everything is hidden or replaced by something else, all in the name of progress and prosperity.

In the case of our families, all you have to do is visit your local nursing home to see once lively and energetic people wasting away and forgotten by society and, in many cases, their own families.

Or perhaps look at the divorce rate in this country and contemplate the number of children growing up in single-parent households. We have fallen into the enemies' trap. We have become divided, and a family or country that is divided cannot stand. Remember Jesus mentioned this as well (Matthew 12:25): *"Every Kingdom that is divided by civil war will fall apart, and every town or household that is divided can not last."*

Nothing is held sacred any more, but rather only seen as useful for a desired amount of time, and then eventually replaced with something newer or better. Everything is made to break and fall apart (created obsolescence), thereby allowing for the replacement of said item, and further promoting this disposable mindset in our society. The same is true of marriages.

In today's world, people have been fooled into thinking and viewing each other as material items that can be easily thrown away and disposed of; hence, the divorce rate in this country. Basically, two out of every three marriages end in divorce, and there are millions of others that never even get married but instead have children out of wedlock. Self-control and self-discipline have given way to self-satisfying license.

This has become the new standard and the new norm. Brothers and sisters, it is up to us to create and promote a culture of life that supports, aids and preserves the family unit.

The enemy has been hard at work over the past several decades in destroying this once sacred unit. Where once families remained together and marriages were held with deep bonds and committed to sacrifices, today people grow weary of each other and look for someone else out of selfish desires with no thought of sacrifice for one another or their families.

Once families prayed together and stayed together through thick and thin, through feast and famine. Today people have lost their way and no longer know God and remain with each other only as far as it is pleasurable or convenient.

We must lead by example, brothers and sisters in the Lord. We must become the beacons of light that shine to others in the darkness to help lead them safely back to port. We must continue to pray for families, and pray often.

Selfishness, apathy, lethargy and complacency has crept into our national and cultural psyche and have permitted us to treat our spouses or each other as disposable or easily replaceable items. This has further been allowed to happen due to the lack of God in our lives.

If we have no love or knowledge of God, how can we expect to love one another? If we have no knowledge of God's mercy and forgiveness in our lives, then how can we show mercy and forgiveness to others who harm us? If we have no knowledge of God's law, rules or precepts, then how can we know that what we are doing is truly wrong and hurtful to Him?

We must also continue to pray for men and women that choose to serve God's purpose. That they may be strengthened and guided by the Holy Spirit to serve God's kingdom, for it is they that truly have the toughest challenges, especially in today's world. It is they who are the spiritual warriors and combatants that fight the good fight, along with us as support troops. The enemy works even harder on them to make them fall and stumble; that is why we should pray all the more for their protection and shielding from the enemies' attacks.

Remember, not all of us are of marriage material. Jesus said in Matthew 19:9-12, *"Therefore I say unto you: whoever divorces his wife, unless it be for infidelity, and marries another, commits adultery.' The disciples said, 'If that is the condition of a married man, it is better not to marry.' Jesus said to them, 'Not everybody can accept what I have just said, but only those who have received this gift. Some are born incapable of marriage. Others have been made that way by men. But there are others who have given up the possibility of marriage for the sake of the Kingdom of Heaven. **He who can accept this, should accept it.**"*

Notice how Jesus says, "but there are others who have given up the possibility of marriage for the sake of the Kingdom of Heaven, he who can accept this, should accept it," basically referring to today's clergy and other men and women of God.

For it is they who have given up the possibility of marriage for the sake of doing God's work, and Jesus further makes it very clear that whoever can accept this challenge, should accept it. Not maybe, or perhaps, but should.

We see something similar in St. Paul's letter to the Corinthians (I Corinthians 7:32): *"I would like you to be free from anxieties. He who is not married, is concerned about the things of the Lord and how to please the Lord. While he who is married is taken up with the things of the world and how to please his wife and he is divided in his interests. Likewise, the unmarried woman and the virgin are concerned with the service of the Lord, to be holy in body and spirit. The married woman, instead worries about the things of the world and how to please her husband. I say this for your own good. I do not wish to lay traps for you but to lead you to a beautiful life, entirely united with the Lord. If anyone is not sure whether he is behaving correctly with his fiancé because of the ardor of his passion, and considers it is better to get married, let him do so, he commits no sin. But it another, of firmer heart thinks that he can control his passion and decides not to marry so that his fiancé may remain a virgin, he does better. So then, he who marries does well, and he who does not marry does better."*

In both excerpts, we clearly see how both Jesus and Paul write about marriage in the sense that if one gets married, that's fine. But he that does not and gives it up for the sake of doing God's work, does even better. Not just anyone can serve in the Lord's army, just those that have been called to this vocation.

Perhaps not all of us are or were marriage material, but that does not mean we cannot serve a purpose. We can begin to promote and lead others to the Kingdom of God. Through both words and works, we can begin to set a new standard that will work against the current world trend of throwaway marriages, relationships and people. We can serve God's purpose in many different ways and should find the way that is best suited to us. Whether we are married or single, we (like Jesus said) should accept this responsibility. If we can accept it, then we should.

Remember, my brothers and sisters, a family that prays together stays together. If you are married and are experiencing difficulties due to the temptations this world has to offer, then I highly suggest you pray and worship together as a couple or family. A house divided cannot stand, and neither can family that has grown divisive.

I will continue to pray for you, my brothers and sisters in the Lord. But I, too, need your prayers. Please do not forget about me and continue to pray for my needs and me as well. Continue to remain strong, and be faithful to the Lord our God. Pray, pray and pray some more. Become a living prayer so others can be affected and infected by your light. Remember the P.U.S.H. principle: pray until something happens. Do not give up on God, and He will keep His promise to you and your loved ones.

Your brother,
horacio

Letter XXI-Fortunate The Poor and Humble

Good morning, brothers and sisters in our Lord Jesus Christ. It gives me great pleasure to come to you all once again with another message of preparation as we head toward a very uncertain future. The only absolute certainty is He who is, and He who is Yahweh. Who was, is and will always be.

It is in He who we should put our faith and trust during these volatile times. I do hope and pray that you all are doing well, both physically and spiritually.

It can be very hard sometimes to maintain a positive outlook, especially when we see all the destruction throughout the world. But this is when we should put our trust in the Lord, to protect and guide us through these winds of change. Turn to Him, brothers and sisters, not out of fear but out of genuine love for Him.

Brothers and sisters, today I bring forth a message of humility, which has basically become obsolete in today's fast-paced world of winners and losers. Because in today's world, no one chooses to be humble anymore. Whether we win or lose, we still opt to be sore winners or losers. We choose to be rude, brash, cocky and proudly insensitive. Whether it is on the field of play or on the field of life, we seem to get further and further away from the grace of humility. From our local town politicians to our top nation's politicians, they all opt for their proud and haughty ways. From our local priests and ministers to our religious world leaders, they, too, are guilty of this.

We must keep in mind what God does to the proud. Let us be reminded of what kind of person Jesus was and how He chose to live His life. One of the best examples to demonstrate this can be found in the Beatitudes, Matthew 5:3, Luke 6:17. For it was through the Beatitudes that He gave us the blueprint for leading a humble and selfless life and the promise of the rewards for those that keep them. *"Fortunate are those who have the spirit of the poor, for theirs is the Kingdom of Heaven. Fortunate are those who mourn, for they shall be comforted. Fortunate are the gentle, for they shall possess the land. Fortunate are those who hunger and thirst for justice, for they shall be satisfied. Fortunate are the merciful, for they shall find mercy.*

Fortunate are those with a pure heart, for they shall see God. Fortunate are those who work for peace, for they shall be called children of God. Fortunate are those who are persecuted for the cause of Justice, for theirs is the Kingdom of Heaven. Fortunate are you, when people insult you and persecute you and speak all kinds of evil against you because you are my followers. Be glad and joyful, for a great reward is kept for you in God. This is how these people persecuted the prophets who lived before you."

It is here that Jesus sets the mold for all of us that call ourselves His followers. This gives us hope. If you are poor or mourn, are gentle, thirst for justice, are merciful, pure of heart, are laborers of peace, and are doers of justice, blessed and fortunate are you all.

He is the antithesis of the proud, boastful, arrogant, rich/greedy, corrupt, merciless, and black of heart, for these would be considered the unfortunate.

In which category would you place our current society? Would we fit into the mold set by Jesus? It is not just the ignorant (of Jesus) that seem to fall into this latter category, but increasingly enough, it seems to be those that call themselves His followers that seem to be most in this category. For the former have the excuse of being ignorant of His precepts, but the latter know better and still they continue to live this way. They would be better off never knowing Jesus than to have known Him and gone back to their former ways.

It is just as it is written in II Peter 2:19-22, "*They promise freedom, when they themselves are slaves of corruption; for anyone is a slave of what dominates him. Indeed, after being freed from worldly vices through the knowledge of the Lord and Savior Jesus Christ, they returned to those vices and surrendered to them, and their present state has become worse than their first. It would have been better for them not to have known the way of holiness than, knowing it, to turn away from the sacred doctrine that they had been taught. In their case, these proverbs are relevant: ' The dog turns back to its own vomit,' and 'Hardly has the pig been washed than it again wallows in the mud.'*"

Here, too, Peter says the same thing, "It would have been better for them not have known the way of holiness, than to have known it and turned away from sacred doctrine." For many are the born again that have fallen back into the mud, and many more are the teachers, priests and ministers that have themselves fallen and taken souls with them. But this is where we should also practice mercy and forgiveness to them that fall and continue to fall. Not so much out of love for them but for God Himself. For once we understand His immense love and mercy for us, then and only then can we begin to reciprocate this love and mercy for Him to others, even our enemies.

Jesus Christ set the perfect of example of humility and servitude when He washed His apostle's feet prior to the (Last Supper) Passover meal. For it was customary in those days for Jews to have their servants wash the feet of traveling guests. Also, many of the poor did not wear sandals, and only the economically better off had the resources to buy sandals.

So it was here that Jesus gives us the perfect example of complete humility and servitude toward His apostles and creates for us this perfect example to follow. Here, too, we see how through this humble sacred act, Jesus cleanses and purifies His apostles before receiving the bread and wine. In John 13:4-15, we read, *"So he got up from the table, removed his garment and taking a towel, wrapped it around his waist. Then he poured water into a basis and began to wash the disciples' feet and to wipe them with the towel he was wearing. When he cam to Simon Peter, Simon said to him, 'Why, Lord, do you want to wash my feet?' Jesus said, 'What I am doing you cannot understand now, but afterwards you will understand it.' Peter replied, 'You shall never wash my feet.' Jesus answered him, 'If I do not wash you, you can have no part with me.' Then Simon Peter said, 'Lord, wash not only my feet, but also my hands and my head!' Jesus replied, 'whoever has taken a bath does not need to wash (except the feet), for he is clean all over. You are clean, though not all of you. Jesus knew who was to betray him; because of this he said, 'Not all of you are clean.' When Jesus finished washing their feet, he put on his garment again, went back to the table and said to them, 'Do you understand what I have done to you?' You call me master and Lord, and you are right, for so I am. If I, then, your Lord and Master have washed your feet, you must also wash one another's feet. I have just given you an example that as I have done, you must also do."*

How many of our world leaders today would follow this example? I am most certain when I venture to say that probably not one. How many of us would do this for our family members? Jesus took on the role of servant and did something that was customary of His time for servants to do. He was at the feet of His guests, His apostles. He did this to demonstrate to all of us that it is through serving and approaching as a servant to others, where true and authentic authority comes from. Come as a servant, and you will be exalted; come exalted, and you will always be humbled.

His apostles, especially Simon Peter, seemed a bit hesitant at having Jesus, who was their Lord and Master, wash their feet, but Jesus reassures him that unless He washes him, he can have no part of Him (the bread and wine) and the sharing of the Eucharist.

Humility and selflessness are two personality traits and qualities that are very seldom seen in today's modern world of being number one in everything. No one wants to be associated with someone/something that is humble, but instead with someone/something that is rude, brash and arrogant, and constantly reminding you of his/her status in the world. Perhaps this is why America has the image problem it does in the world. If we are true followers of Christ, and/or we want to become followers, then we must keep in mind what it was He came to set as the standard. If no one wants to be associated with the poor, meek and humble, perhaps this is why so many today are so lost. They have lost and/or rejected the path that leads to Christ.

In Isaiah 42:1-3, we are reminded how the prophet prophesized Jesus' nature and demeanor, *"Here is my servant whom I uphold, my chosen one in whom I delight. I have put my spirit upon him, and he will bring justice to the nations. He does not shout, or raise his voice in the streets. A broken reed he will not crush, nor will he snuff out the light of the wavering wick. He will make justice appear."*

We must study and be informed of how He lived and how He taught us to live with one another. We must remind each other of how Christ took the pain and punishment for us. In Isaiah 53:5-7, we are reminded by the prophet of the Savior's mild and humble nature, even as He was going to His death. *"Forsaken because of our sins, he was crushed for our wickedness. Through his punishment we are made whole; by his wounds we are healed. Like sheep we had all gone astray, each following his own way; but Yahweh laid upon him all our guilt. He was harshly treated, but unresisting and silent, he humbly submitted. Like a lamb led to the slaughter or sheep before the shearer, he did not open his mouth."*

Brothers and sisters in the Lord, I hope and pray that humility becomes, if not already, a life trait in all of our lives. That through humility and selflessness, we come to serve one another and become more like He that died for us and our sins. In a world that has run rampant with pride, arrogance and rudeness, that we remain steadfast in our uncompromising values and principles of selflessness and humility. I as always pray for you, and in return ask that you pray for me, and please pray that God gives me strength, guidance and wisdom. I ask this favor more than anything else. That God continue to enlighten and prepare you all, and that He do this in Christ's name. Amen.

Your brother,
horacio

Letter XXII-Do Not Worry Yourselves

Good morning, brothers and sisters in the Lord Jesus Christ. I come to you this twenty-fifth day of this eighth month of the year to bring you another message of hope and preparation for the coming lean years.

The time for preparation is now. The time to repent and bring yourself to full and true conversion is now. The time to begin a relationship with our Lord and our God is now and not after the fact. We must acknowledge our mistakes and straighten our paths. Pray that the Lord gives you strength and courage to be able to stand firm during these coming years.

Brothers and sisters, in today's fast-paced world, we oftentimes forget to treat each other with kindness, mercy and compassion. We isolate ourselves from the world around us, and modern appliances and technology have further created a nation and a world of separated, lonely and isolated individuals.

Where we once gathered outside and shared fellowship with our friends and neighbors, we now return to our homes and hurriedly go inside to our air-conditioned homes and apartments, and turn on our 150-channel cable television, and go online to sit and stare at a computer screen for hours on end.

This is currently the world in which many of us living in this country experience. We live isolated and separated from one another. We no longer commune and seek fellowship with our neighbors, but instead we seek fellowship and commune with our televisions, computers and video games. We have replaced genuine friendships and relationships with those that can only speak to us when they are turned on with the click of a button.

This is the world we live in: everyone hidden in their gated communities and isolated from one another. This becomes fertile ground for the enemy and his army, for it is here where and when he chooses to attack us. When we are alone and vulnerable, and begin to feel lonely, empty and depressed.

Depression is a very serious issue in our country and seems to be growing more every year. Suicides and the thought of suicide grow and seem to have a direct correlation with the wealthier and better off a country is. According to

W.H.O.[1] (the World Health Organization), seven of the eight major industrialized nations, otherwise known as the G8 countries [France, United States, United Kingdom, Canada, Germany, Japan, Italy and Russia] are all included in the top 12 countries with the highest suicide rates in the world, the only exception being Italy.

Yet, on the other hand, the top five happiest countries in the world[2] [There were many sources for this information, but I chose a study conducted by the University of Michigan World Values Survey] were: Nigeria, Mexico, Venezuela, El Salvador and Puerto Rico.

Notice the difference between the countries that have the some of the highest suicide rates and the countries that are considered to be the happiest in the world. These "happy countries" are all basically—at least by our government's standards—considered to be poor third-world countries. Countries that have rampant government corruption, poor infrastructure, poor economies and poor diets; yet this is where some the happiest people on the globe can be found.

This is where genuine fellowship and togetherness are still viewed as more important that individual success and material wealth. This is where family and the unity of the family core is still seen as important and treated as such. After all, when you don't have much, you value more what you do have.

These are also countries that are steeped in complete devotion and faith to God for all their needs. For they truly abide by what Jesus said in Matthew 6:24-27, Luke 12:23, 16:13: *"No one can serve two masters; for he will either hate one and love another, or he will be loyal to the first and look down on the second. You cannot at the same time serve God and money. This is why I tell you not to be worried about food and drink for yourself, or about clothes for your body. Is not life more important than food and is not the body more important than clothes? Look at the birds of the air, they do not sow, the do not harvest and do not store food in barns and yet your heavenly Father feeds them. Are you not worth much more than birds?* **Which of you can add a day to his life by worrying about it?"**

If we read on a little further, we also see how Jesus addresses the pagans, or those that had no knowledge or relationship with God (Matthew 6:31), *"Do not worry and say, 'what are we going to eat? What are we going to drink? Or, what shall we wear? The pagans busy themselves with such things, but your heavenly Father knows that you need them all.* **Set your heart first on the Kingdom and justice of God and all these things will also be given to you. Do not worry about tomor-**

---

1.   http://www.fathersforlife.org/health/who_suicide_rates.htm
2.   http://thehappinessshow.com/HappiestCountries.htm

row, for tomorrow will worry about itself. Each day has enough troubles of its own."

In Luke 12:29, Jesus adds, *"Do not set your heart on what you are to eat and drink; stop worrying. Let all nations of the world run after these things; your Father knows you need them. Seek rather the Kingdom, and these things will be given to you as well."*

If we truly acknowledge and see what it was Jesus told His disciples, we can truly begin to reflect how His teachings are relevant in today's world.

Let us look at the countries that have the highest suicide rates and their level of genuine joy and happiness. Can we truly say that having more material wealth and higher standard of living is the cause and source of their happiness? These countries are similar to what Jesus referred to as trying to serve two masters but ended up finding out that one cannot serve two, but only one.

On the other hand, let us look at the countries seen as the happiest and coincidently have basically a non-existent suicide rate. These countries may not have a higher standard of living, or excess material wealth and goods, but they have an excess of faith and devotion that what they need will be provided. They, too, found out that they could not serve two masters so they ended up serving the one that could provide internal peace and happiness. They do not depend on their governments or corporate leaders for this, but rather they depend on God.

Jesus points out to all of us that we should not focus on the material aspects of life or over concern ourselves with those things that we want or need, but instead focus on the Kingdom, **and then** everything else will follow. For who but God knows what we truly need or perhaps want? He searches our hearts and knows our true motives and necessities.

Brothers and sisters in the Lord, living in today's world, especially in a society that has opted to serve wealth and the pursuit of wealth, instead of God, can be very challenging for us. We often find ourselves lonely and isolated in a world full of material distractions and illusions that are offered by the master of this world. This is where we as followers of Christ must support and encourage one another. For it is when we try to fulfill, satisfy and zealously seek for that which is temporally created (manmade goods, items, relationships), that we end up feeling empty, alone and unfulfilled. It is when we live solely by the flesh, and for the flesh, that our spiritual waters dry up and become empty, broken vessels of clay.

Suicides in this country and throughout other industrialized first world nations have become very common and tragic events. For a person to feel so isolated, depressed and lonely enough that the only recourse they feel or believe they have is to end their life is a complete tragedy. Hope in every sense of the word has disappeared for them.

We must encourage fellowship and reach out to all those who may need a helping hand or encouraging word. The Bible refers to them as the widowed and the orphaned. These are all those that either have become the lonely, isolated, withdrawn or ostracized either by choice or by an act of God.

In today's world and in this society, it has become extremely easy to be apathetic and unconcerned about our fellow man. Whether they are our neighbors, our family members or a complete stranger, we must and should extend our support and encouragement to them. We are the ones that should go against the tide of apathy and cynicism. We are the ones that should proudly proclaim from the rooftops who it is we serve. We are the ones who should not stand by and let the enemy take hold of our friends or neighbors but instead rebuke the spirit of the enemy and save them from falling into that trap. The enemy sees an opportunity and takes it whenever he can. We should be careful not to fall into those traps ourselves. Loneliness and depression are the enemy's fertile grounds for planting the seeds of doubt and contemplations of suicide. We must be strong and hold onto Jesus' robe and have complete faith in He who died for us, that He will save us from the enemy's grasp.

Brothers and sisters in the Lord, I hope and pray that this letter reaches all of you in good spirits and strong health. Let us continue preparing ourselves for the lean years that are to come and are all ready beginning to show themselves now. We must hold strong to our Christian faith and beliefs and know with certainty that God will Shield us, Protect us, Enlighten us, Guide us, Provide us, and always love and accept us, if we turn to Him. So let us pray that He give us the eyes, ears and hearts to see, hear and feel the truth, so that we may grow in love, knowledge and preparation in His name.

Your brother,
horacio

Letter XXIII-The Good Samaritans

Greetings to you, brothers and sisters in our Lord our God, and well wishes upon all of you, my friends and family members throughout that receive this letter today.

I come to you in good physical, emotional and spiritual health this first day of the seventh month, thanks to our Lord Jesus Christ.

It is a very warm and dry Texas morning here, and we continue to pray for rain, and ask that you continue to pray for rain as well. I also ask that all of us continue to pray for those souls that have been affected and continue to be affected throughout the Gulf Coast.

It is during these lean times, my brothers and sisters, that we must support one another as good followers of Christ and demonstrate to the world what good Christian principles can accomplish when put into practice. It is during these lean years, and the ones that are to come, that we must be prepared to encounter and endure many sufferings, trials and tribulations.

It is during these lean years that we will be reminded how much we truly need and are dependent upon our Creator for comfort, protection, providence and mercy.

Brothers and sisters, let us pull together in synchronicity and not apart during these times of widespread suffering and conflict. Whether it's here, in Africa, the Middle East, Europe, South America or Asia, the times of suffering are upon us and will continue through the following years. That is why in each and every letter, I keep reminding you to be prepared. Be prepared when you yourself will have to face these tribulations. Be prepared spiritually and faithfully more so than physically, although physical preparation is important as well.

Let us be self assured and confident that when those times come upon us or our loved ones, we will be strong in our faith and love of God to overcome these periods of suffering and hardships. If it is in within our personal power to help those that are suffering, then let us extend our hands and help them, brothers and sisters. With what little we can do or give, let us be generous, my brothers and sisters.

Let us recall the story of the good in the good Samaritan (Luke 10:29, Matthew 22:34, Mark 12:28), *"The man (a teacher of Jewish Law) wanted to keep appearances, so he replied, 'Who is my neighbor?' Jesus then said, 'There was a man going down from Jerusalem to Jericho, and he fell into the hands of robbers. They stripped him, beat him and went off leaving him half dead. It happened that a priest was going along that road and saw the man, but passed by on the other side. Likewise, a Levite saw the man and passed by on the other side too. But a Samaritan, too, was going that way, and when he came upon the man, he was moved to compassion. He went over to him and treated his wounds with oil and wine and wrapped them with bandages. Then he put him on his own mount and brought him to an inn where he took care of him. The next day, he had to set off, but he gave two silver coins to the innkeeper and told him: 'Take care of him and whatever you spend on him, I will repay when I come back."*

This example in the Bible was given by Jesus when He was asked by one of the teachers of Jewish Law the question of **"Who is my neighbor?"** In other words, whom should I love? Who should I look after, or help, just as I would myself? Jesus answered the way He did to demonstrate to this man, and anyone else who would listen and understand, because He wanted to show that it is not always those who we think of or assume that will love and aid someone in need. But perhaps it is those we consider as unbelievers, pagans or non-Christians that will.

In His example, He first describes how a Jewish priest was the first man to come along and see the wounded man, but instead of stopping to help, he walked to the other side of the road and on by. Perhaps it was because he didn't want to burden himself, or maybe get dirty (seeing how the Jews were always obsessed with cleanliness and purification) that he decided not to get involved, and therefore walked by and left the wounded man. The Levite (a religious official), too, saw the wounded man lying there in pain and in agony, but he, too, decided to walk by and not deal with the situation. It was not until the last man, a Samaritan, someone they (Jews) considered as heretical and a pagan, came along, saw the dying man and aided him. He treated his wounds, took him to an inn, and even made arrangements with the innkeeper to make sure that whatever the injured man needed or wanted, he would cover all expenses incurred.

After telling this story to the man, Jesus then asked, *"Which of these three do you think made himself neighbor to the man who fell into the hands of the robbers? The teacher of the Law answered, "The one who had mercy on him" and Jesus said, 'Go then and do the same."*

It is today and tomorrow, and the day after, my brothers and sisters, that not just one man was robbed, but thousands of people that were robbed and killed by this natural disaster in the Gulf states. Will we be like the priest and Levite? Will we be like the people that believe in God and go through all the motions of being religious, but when confronted with the dying man on the road, step over to the other side and keep walking?

Or will we be more like the Samaritan? Someone that was not seen as religious or practicing in faith, but had mercy and compassion on his fellow man, and therefore helped and saved that dying man's life?

Brothers and sisters, let us continue to pray for not only they who were affected by this natural disaster, but for people throughout the world. Those in Africa, Asia, Europe, and the Middle East. Let us grow in love and mercy for those that were/are affected, and let us show this through our generosity to them.

Our prayers are helpful, but so is our generosity to them. Whether it is through the Red Cross or countless other organizations that will help in this relief effort, let us inform ourselves of how to better help these poor souls that are suffering and in pain.

Continue to pray for me as well, just as I continue to pray for you on a daily basis. Let us grow in love and fear of the Lord, so that we become His people. Let us pray that He leads, guides, protects, provides and has mercy on us when the time comes for us to go through our own pain and suffering.

The world will continue to grow more and more volatile and uneasy. By the hand of both Mother Nature and man will the earth continue to be slowly destroyed. The coming years will be hard and lean. Let us pray that God has mercy on us.

Your brother,
horacio

Letter XXIV-Persistence Makes Perfect

Greetings, my brothers and sisters in the Lord our God. It is again, as always, with great pleasure and hope that I bring you another message of preparation for the coming years.

I come to you on this beautiful Wednesday morning on this seventh day of this seventh month. I would at this time like to thank all of you who pray for me and continue to do so. May God Almighty continue to give you strength, courage and fortitude to stand in the face of adversity, or perhaps temptation, and blaze a path across to the other side and not fall into the potholes or traps as set by the enemy.

Today, my good friends and family, I write to you in good spirits and encourage you to pray, and pray in full faith and confidence. The power of prayer, if said or meditated upon, in complete and utmost faith, can be very awesome. I know there are many nay sayers out there who would have you believe that prayer doesn't work, or that perhaps it is all superstition. But I assure you with an attitude like that, it is no wonder that their prayers were never answered. They perhaps are the ones that need the power of prayer to work in their lives so they may see for themselves this awesome gift. It was once said by St. Augustine, "We must believe in order to understand," and not the other way around, which is how so many today approach faith, prayer and religion. For it is the modern mind of modern man when it comes to issues of spirituality that is unbelieving, unknowing, and undiscerning.

Let us be reminded how Jesus explained how we, too, should pray (Luke 11:1-8, Matthew 6:9, 7:7): *"One day Jesus was praying in a certain place and when he had finished, one of his disciples said to him, 'Lord teach us to pray, just as John taught his disciples.' And Jesus said to them, 'When you pray, say this: Father, hallowed be your name, may your Kingdom come, give us each day the kind of bread we need, and forgive us our sins, for we also forgive all who do us wrong, and do not let us fall into temptation.' Jesus said to them, 'Suppose one of you has a friend and goes to his house in the middle of the night and says, 'Friend, lend me three loaves, for a*

friend of mine who is traveling has just arrived and I have nothing to offer him.
Maybe your friend will answer from inside, 'Don't bother me now, the door is locked
and my children and I are in bed, so I can't get up and give you anything.' But I tell
you, even though he will not get up and attend to him because he is a friend, yet he
will get up because the other is a bother to him and he will give him all his needs. And
so I say to you, 'Ask and it will be given to you; seek and you will find; knock and it
will be opened to you; For the one who asks receives, and the one who searches finds,
and to him who knocks it will be opened."

Here it is written for us, my brothers and sisters, how God Almighty, even though He may not grant our request or our petition immediately, is like the friend who was tired in bed and did not want to get up but ultimately did. We must keep being persistent with our prayers, almost to the point of being a bother to Him.

This is why it is important to not give up hope, but rather know and be confident that your persistent prayers will pay off and be compensated in the end. He said, "Ask and you shall receive, seek and you shall find, knock and it will be opened."

Further in Luke 18:1-5, Jesus adds to His teaching of "Persistence makes perfect." *"Jesus told them a parable to show them that they should pray continually and not lose heart. He said, 'in a certain town, there was a judge who neither feared God nor people. In the same town was a widow who kept coming to him, saying, 'Defend my rights against my opponent.' For a time he refused, but finally he thought, 'Even though I neither fear God nor care about people, this widow bothers me so much, that I will see that she gets justice, then maybe she will stop coming and wearing me out."*

In both parables, we clearly see how Jesus demonstrates how we should pray. We should remain persistent and faithful that justice will done. We should remain confident that what we seek will be found and what has been asked for will be given. We must work around His will and His timetable, and not expect Him to work around ours.

I believe this is one of the biggest reasons why people may not pray with faith and persistence: because we all live in a world of instant gratification. If something isn't done or taken care of in five minutes or less, we lose patience and decide to find something or someone that can provide this service for us in the time span we have allotted. So whenever we take this type of attitude or mindset and apply it to prayer, it is no wonder so many end up giving up on prayer and perhaps even their faith.

We turn to every and anything but God's help. Not only should we pray for our needs and ourselves, but we should also pray for others, both friends and enemies.

In Luke 22:31-32, we see how Jesus demonstrates this as well, *"Simon, Simon, Satan has demanded to sift you like grain, but I have prayed for you that your faith may not fail. And when you have recovered, **you shall strengthen your brothers.**"*

Jesus tells Peter how the enemy had demanded to have access to Peter, but that He (Jesus) had prayed for his steadfastness in his faith so it would not fail when the time came to remain strong. He would in turn pray for and strengthen his brothers.

We, too, must pray for one another, my brothers and sisters, so that we, too, can remain strong in the face of adversity, trials and temptations. The enemy is constantly seeking to make us trip and fall into his traps, and many of us do from time to time. But that is why it is so important that we pray for one another so that each time we fall and trip, we can have the strength, fortitude and steadfastness that we need to remain strong.

We must intercede for one another as well as ask for prayers of intercessions, too, from the Virgin and the Saints. Who better to be praying for us than the Mother of God and the Saints.

I know I continually ask for prayers from you all, but I do it out of necessity and not out of routine action. I can truly feel when people have been praying for me and when they have not. When I request these prayers, I am doing it as a request for a favor. I keep being persistent with you all in hopes that some of you may begin to pray for me. I keep applying the principle that Jesus taught us of being persistent and never ceasing. You will be amazed at the power of prayer and what it can do in your lives, if you just believe.

One thing we should keep in mind when praying is also whether we are full of and in the state of God's good grace (obtained through/with living a virtuous life, penitent life and prayerful life), or whether due to sin we have in fact become indebted. Because it is sin that ruptures our relationship with God. God through His bountiful mercy and sacrifice on the cross made us all free, brothers and sisters. It is this divine freedom that allows and further promotes us to do that which is good. But it is the abuse of this great gift, through sin, that weakens our freedom, our charity, our grace and our virtue. We trade that which is genuine freedom for that which is slavery to sin, and therefore become indebted to sin. For it is sin which creates a proclivity to keep sinning and thereby keeps us from true freedom. We must remember who it was that purchased our true freedom and at what price it was purchased. Because it is when we forget, or lose sight of this great gift that was purchased for us, that we begin to abuse, corrupt and become indebted not to God, but to sin itself.

If we are not aware of this debt, then every time we pray, but keep doing that which promotes sin, it is almost as if going to a bank and asking for a loan, but being told that we are out of credit and profoundly in debt. We must keep in mind that the more we take out of our account that God has set up for each and everyone of us, the more we indebted we become.

It is also like the following example: imagine that every time you sin either against another or yourself, you are sticking a 2-inch nail into some part of your body. Regardless of whether or not the sin is grave or light, the nail is still inserted either a little or a lot. After having confessed and repented of your sin, the nail is removed, but the wound remains. The more nails, the more wounds, and therefore the longer time it will take for you to heal. But if after a week or two, you again insert a nail into the same wounds, those wounds will never be healed, and the cycle continues once again. The doctor will not allow you to practice or eat certain things until you are fully healed. But how can that ever be accomplished when we ourselves keep re injuring the unhealed wounds every time we fall? Even though we ask for permission for certain things and/or favors from the doctor, he will not allow for certain requests and/or favors. This is further complicated when two wounded individuals, or two deeply indebted individuals (i.e. relationship couples or marriages), ask for a loan (prayer, favor or blessing from God) or petition from the all powerful doctor, and after having taken inventory of their joint or single account/file, find out to their dismay that they have no credit for the requested loan, or are not fully healed or recuperated for said health request.

What then follows is what we have today—failed marriages and relationships of a massive scale because people have yet to realize that they have accrued an immense debt, or are extremely injured or wounded, yet continue to abuse, neglect and corrupt that which God almighty gave us through His son.

Many people today never take the time to make deposits into their account, only baseless withdrawals. It is no wonder why so many people today continue to follow their wounded and indebted lives down a path of servitude to the wrong creditor, and yet cannot figure out why their prayers, for whatever reason, are never answered. How can you ever be healthy if all you eat is junk food? How can you ever be healthy if you never exercise your spiritual muscles? How can people ever have access to God's grace and true freedom, when they constantly live in sin's vices and true slavery? The answer is simple, my brothers and sisters. Repent of your sins and turn to He that is our Lord and savior, and He will redeem you and your freedom. Because we have all been bought by Him, but through our own choices, have chosen to leave our Father and true family.

St. Paul said in Galations 6:6, *"He who receives the teaching of the Word ought to share the good things he has with the one who instructs him. Do not be fooled. God cannot be deceived. You reap what you sow. The person who sows for the benefit of his own flesh shall reap corruption and death from the flesh. He who sows in the spirit shall reap eternal life from the spirit. Let us do good without being discouraged; in due time we shall reap the reward of our constancy. So while there is time, let us do good to all and especially to our family in the faith."*

So let us go forth with confidence in His great mercy and love for us. It is at times that we attempt to deceive others by what we do, but we can never deceive God. For God cannot deceive, nor can He be deceived. He knows what we truly deserve by the level of deposits or withdrawals we have made in our lives. Will we receive rewards and compensations, or will we be placed in jail as a consequence until the last penny of our personally incurred debt through sin is paid?

Let us also refer to Matthew 5:25, *"Don't forget this: be reconciled with your opponent quickly when you are together on the way to court. Otherwise, he will turn you over to the judge, who will hand you over to the police, who will put you in jail. There you will stay until you have paid the last penny."*

Let us instead lead a life of servitude in God, always keeping a balanced account. Remember, the more you take, the longer it will take for that debt to be paid off. The more wounded you are from sin, the longer the healing process. God will answer our prayers, but only if we have a healthy state of grace account. We all reap what we have sown, even though we may not like the fruit that we are to harvest. This is why we should sow good fruit, so as to reap good fruit, and do not incur a debt that you will sooner or later have to pay off.

To some, it is as if I was preaching to the choir, but to others, I encourage and support your conversion to a life full of prayer, faith and confidence in Him. I continue to pray for you all, my brothers and sisters, and ask that you PLEASE pray for me. I need your prayers and your well wishes.

Let us be strong, and encourage those that need help and prayers. If anyone of you all out there needs prayers, please let me know, and we will form a prayer chain.

As always, your loving brother in Christ,
horacio

Letter XXV-Modern Day Rome

Good day, brothers and sisters in Christ. I truly hope that your families and loved ones are doing well today, this 12th day of this ninth month. I come with a message for reflection and contemplation.

Brothers and sisters in Christ, what I present to you today is the following: Is history in the process of repeating itself, and if so, is the U.S. a modern-day Roman civilization?

Many have been the people throughout that have made this comparison. But is there any relevance in the comparisons, and if so, what are they? Is there, after all, a reason for us to study and become aware of history and past failures in order to perhaps prevent us from going through the same?

If we recall, or perhaps some of us may not even be aware of this, but Rome and all its might were at one time the most powerful—militarily and economically—empire in the known world. Roman influence spread throughout and quickly became the world's dominant power in basically every aspect of human civilization. But just as quickly as it rose, Rome fell, and most of the world thought or felt that this was the end of the world, at least as how they knew it. And they were correct to some extent.

There was not one single event or reason that caused this mighty empire's downfall, but rather it was a combination of several factors that caused this world power to come crumbling down.

Scholars and historians throughout history have studied these factors and have come up with a list of varying factors for its demise. Some of the most prominent factors are[1]: A decline in morals and values throughout society, political corruption, high inflation and high trade deficits, inefficient military planning and spending, and public health issues. Do any of these topics of concern sound familiar in today's American society?

At its height, the Roman Empire became blinded with greed and over indulgence. Roman citizens as well as wealthy politicians gave into their lustful desires and became slaves to their baser instincts. Orgies and solicitation of prostitutes

---

1.   http://www.roman-empire.net/articles/article-018.html

became a common practice. Homosexual behavior was condoned and accepted as being normal and healthy. The family unit was attacked and eventually beaten to the point of no return. Selfishness, greed, over indulgence and sexual promiscuity became the norm, and traditional family units became obsolete. Is there any relevance to today's modern U.S. society?

Violence became a very sought after commodity and was promoted as "family entertainment." Families throughout Rome and the rest of the empire watched all sorts of violent-filled events in the great arenas. Christians were fed to lions, and gladiators fought to the death. Blood soaked the arena floor so much that sometimes it was necessary to pause events so a new layer of sand could be poured. Then activities continued.

In today's world, I am reminded of this practice every time I see or hear of television's popular "Extreme Fighting" competitions. Or when I see so much money paid to view violent and sex-filled programs on both the small and big screens. Is there any relevance to today's modern U.S. culture?

Political corruption became so rampant in Rome during its heyday that the position of emperor eventually was obtained by whoever had the most money. If I'm not mistaken, wasn't it during last year's presidential campaign that a record was set as far as the amount of money spent on a U.S. presidential campaign? Was the best man truly selected for this great position of leadership, or was he just the biggest contributors? Any similarity here?

During the might of Rome days, the empire became so dependent on foreign goods (mainly from the Orient as is the case today with the U.S. and its trade deficits with China; today China is the U.S.'s largest creditor) that it began to import more than what it exported, thereby creating huge trade deficits (most of which were deficits with the Orient). This triggered other economic financial problems and woes to its citizens. Coupled with high inflation, the scarcity of gold as a commodity, hoarding by Roman citizens, and theft by roaming barbarians, not enough money was in circulation and the money that was had little or no value. This led people to barter for goods and services.

Where they once had in excess, they had been reduced to bartering for their basic needs. We have not yet come to this, but does any of this ring with a semblance of truth for today?

It was also during this time that Rome's military started to crumble. With outposts all over the known world at the time, it became almost impossible to keep those posts properly supplied with goods and men. Therefore, they had to cut back on military spending because it was too costly. A lot of people during this time had also stopped volunteering for the Roman army. Having become complacent and indifferent to Rome's overall military objectives at the time, they did not view joining the army as a viable or noble career choice any more. Where once the Roman legions had been served with loyal and traditionalist men, now the army had been reduced to trying to hire mercenaries, slaves and foreigners to fight for the good of Rome. The latter fighting force probably did not have had that same desire, loyalty or common goals for the good of Rome.

During the earlier centuries of the empire, Roman citizenship was given to those who served in the fighting force, but after several years, it could be obtained either by purchase or having a Roman father. Another cause that further depleted the military was the constant and ongoing battles with outlying barbarians (terrorist?). Whether they were the Huns, Vandals, Visigoths or any other group of barbarian tribes, this further depleted not only the forces, but also Rome's ability to fund and support these outlying skirmishes and battles while also trying to support other domestic public policies and infrastructure.

These ancient battles sound eerily familiar to our current war on terrorism. Look at the outposts, or military bases if you will, that the current U.S. government has throughout the world—in Europe, the Middle East, the Far East, Central and South America. Look at the current problems facing the armed forces; not many people sign up voluntarily any more. Look at the base closings and realignment the military has to implement in order to keep supplies sent to all these places, and the current fighting against our modern day barbarians (the terrorists). These fighting bands of Islamic tribesman are just beyond the reach of the U.S arm of justice. Is there any similarity here? Also today, just as back then, the U.S. government has sent paid mercenaries [2](contractors), just as Rome was forced to do back then.

The factors that I have just mentioned are all part of but not solely the reason that mighty Rome fell. One more reason is: it was also during this time that Christianity took root within its mighty walls and structure, and began to spread. Initially Rome and its might came down hard on Christians. They killed Christians in an assortment of ways and most of the time in a way that amused them. But for every one Christian killed, twenty more joined the new movement. The fallen became martyrs and—whether directly or indirectly—became the cause for a new major movement that in the end would signal the demise of an empire and the rise of a religion.

---

2.   http://slate.msn.com/id/2098571/

Christianity was born and would rise and spread. But here is the relevant point I want to offer: the more the might of Rome suppressed these Christian martyrs, the more they grew in numbers.

In today's world, the U.S. government is currently involved in this massive worldwide war on terror, to use their terms. But let's look at it from a historical point of view. If history is correct, and logic inevitably follows, then are we to surmise that this war on terrorism will truly be successful?

Or, are we to gather, as history teaches so often, that perhaps these manhunts and killings of Islamic martyrs will only help to strengthen and increase their base? Al Qaeda after all means just that, the base.

It is clear to me that Osama Bin Ladin got just what he wanted from the after effects of 9-11. We went into what is turning out to be the next world war. For the more his movement and his men are killed and hunted down, the more his organization will grow and strengthen. Just like the Christian movement grew in strength and numbers during the persecution of Christians, so, too, will his movement grow in support against the might of modern-day Rome and its allies. [Throughout history, it has been demonstrated and clearly shown that the more you suppress and oppress a particular group of people, whether in a religious, social, ethnic/racial context, the more that groups draws strength, conviction, fervor and resiliency. This is further the case when it is against a religious group of people, because religion is what people live and die for. Whether it was the Jews in ancient Egypt, the Christians in ancient Rome, or the modern day Muslims, the bigger and mightier the empire, the more resilient the movement became against the super power of that particular time in history. Let us also contemplate on which group of people outlived the other. Is mighty Egypt still around? Is the mighty Roman Empire still around? Or did those religious groups outlive them?]

This is why, brothers and sisters in the Lord, we must continue to prepare ourselves in all aspects, especially the spiritual and faith-filled sense. This war on terrorism will never be won, but instead will grow in number, danger, and destruction throughout the world. All we have to do is look at history for the answers.

For the past fifteen to twenty years, it is as if we have become aware at a subconscious level of what perhaps is coming.

It is very similar to the analogy of a school of fish or a flock of birds that turn left, right, up and down all in unison and in synchronous motion. Not one of them is responsible for the movement of the whole, but rather it is almost as if through a collective conscious thought that they all move in unison. Before the action occurs, they in a sense have collectively pre-thought the next movements. Their collective actions are reflections of their collective thoughts.

We, too, have in a way sensed what perhaps may be coming. As a collective society/culture, we, too, have been visualizing and collectively thinking of what perhaps may be the next collective movement or action in our world. All you have to do is look at the movies and TV programs that have been created in the last 15 to 20 years—end of the world scenario type movies.

Are our collective thoughts a sign of what perhaps may be the coming collective actions? So is there any good news in any of this? Yes, there is, my brothers and sisters. The good news is that just as Jesus came during the times of the first Roman empire (pantheistic, non Judeo/Christian power), so, too, are the chances high that He will come during and under the next world empire that will be atheistic and communist in nature.

Also, let us not only look at the negative aspects of our current or most recent negative collective thoughts, but let us also look at the heightened focus and attention that the Gospel and Jesus himself have started to receive. Let us acknowledge that the Gospel now is being taught and spread throughout the world in every country. Also, just as there have been dark end-of-days movies, books, and music being spread and promoted throughout the world over the last several years, there, too, has been the focus on Jesus' return.

This letter is a bit of a departure from my usual letters, but I wrote it so that you all would become aware of what we face and what is to come. We must continue to pray, pray and pray. Let our hearts and our minds be filled with the Holy Spirit, and let us continue to pray for one another. I have one last thing to ask for. One of my good very good friends is in need of prayers, Grace A. I ask that we all pray for her and her family so that God Almighty may guide and help her through her personal trials. Let us ask this in full faith and confidence to our Lord our God. Let us pray that He give us the eyes to see, the ears to hear, and the heart to know and feel the truth.

horacio

Letter XXVI-Let the Children Come to Me

Good morning to you, brothers and sisters in the Lord our God. May you, your family and loved ones be in good health and spirits. I come to you this beautiful twentieth day of this ninth month of the year 2005 to bring another in a series of messages of preparation for the coming lean years.

In today's world, we are faced with many controversial issues that divide and create animosity between us. It is far easier to have hate and hold anger and resentment in our selves than it is to have love and show mercy and forgiveness to those who transgress against us.

No where do we see this more evident than when it comes to the abortion issue in this country. On the one hand, you have a group that believes it is their right to do whatever they wish to do with their bodies and all that pertains to their bodies; and on the other hand, you have those that wish to do away with it completely, yet they resolve the problem through violent or hurtful means.

They maintain that they are Christians who are concerned for the unborn, yet they carry out their acts in a very un-Christian manner. We all realize this is the current law in this country, regardless of whether we are for or against it. Did not Jesus say, "Give to Cesaer what is Cesaer's, and give to God what is God's?" Respect the rule of the land, and respect the laws of God as well. (Even though it is a law of the land currently, any and every law that subverts or undermines both natural and divine law is not a morally licit law, regardless of man's decision to formulate, pass and enact laws that allow this. For man's law throughout most of history hasn't necessarily reflected God's laws. We must, as disciples of Christ, serve as watchmen/women, and be clear with our conscience and stand firmly and objectively against this intrinsic evil that has been allowed to legally invade many nations of the world.)

Let us be reminded of how many thought that Jesus would be the warrior-like messiah, similar to David, who would come and defeat the Roman oppressors. That He would gather and assemble armies that would help the Jewish nation regain prosperity through violence. That He would overturn the oppressive institutions that held their nation down.

But was this what He did? Wasn't it because of His prayer, sacrifice, selflessness, compassion and hope that Rome and its institutions accepted Christianity and eventually converted?

In the same way today, my brothers and sisters, we must pray, sacrifice, be selfless, compassionate and hopeful that these current world trends will be reversed. Not through violence or merciless attacks, whether verbal or physical, but always through prayer, love, mercy and penance as well as through a morally formed and defined conscience to the objective truth of God and His precepts.

Our brethren that practice these acts of abortion do so out of the ignorance of God's laws. They do so out of the ignorance of God's power and might to always be with them and help them. Many do so out of both ignorance and selfishness. For if they truly knew what they were doing, they would be filled with much pain, remorse and anguish; for whether they believe in karma (you get what you give) or in the Scripture (you reap what you sow), they will truly receive what they have sown through their act of abortion.

It will be through their own fruits that they will harvest from what they have sown without the need of further condemning or judging them from our part. For God knows what each one of us deserves, and He and He alone will provide justice, even if the law of man does not. He knows what we do, say or think, and will either reward or reprimand us accordingly to His objective and divine justice. He knows what we have done in our past and will someday call us to account for these thoughts or acts whether in the present life or in the after life.

Let us look at what Jesus says to a Samaritan woman in John 4:5-24, *"He came to a Samaritan town called Sychar, near the land that Jacob had given to his son Joseph. Jacob's well is there. Tired from his journey, Jesus sat down by the well; it was about noon. Now a Samaritan woman came to draw water and Jesus said to her, 'Give me a drink.' His disciples had just gone into town to buy some food. The Samaritan woman said to him, 'How is it that you, a Jew, ask me, a Samaritan and a woman for a drink?' (For Jews, in fact, have no dealings with Samaritans; it would almost be as if a Jewish man today asked for a drink today from a Palestinian woman.) Jesus replied, 'If you only knew the Gift of God! If you knew who it is that asks you for a drink you yourself would have asked me and I would have given you living water.' The woman answered, 'Sir, you have no bucket and this well is deep; where is your living water?' Are you greater than our ancestor Jacob, who gave us this well after he drank from it himself, together with his sons and his cattle?' Jesus said to her, 'Whoever drinks of this water will be thirsty again; but whoever drinks of the water that I shall give, will never be thirsty again; for the water that I shall give will become in him a spring of water welling up to eternal life.' The woman said to him, 'Give me this water, so that I may never be thirsty and never have to come here to draw water.' Jesus said, 'Go, call you husband and come back here.' The woman answered, 'I have no husband,' and Jesus replied, 'You are right to say, 'I have no husband, for you have had five husbands and the one you have now is not your husband. What you said is true.' The woman then said to him, 'I see you are a prophet; tell me this, our fathers used to come this mountain to worship God, but you Jews, do you not claim that Jerusalem is the only place to worship God?' Jesus said to her, 'Believe me woman, the hour is coming when you shall worship the father, but that will not be on this mountain or in Jerusalem. You Samaritans worship without knowledge, while we Jews worship with knowledge, for salvation comes from the Jews. But the hour is coming and is now here, when the true worshipers will worship the Father in Spirit and truth: for that is the kind of worship the Father wants. God is spirit and those who worship God must worship in spirit and truth.' The woman said to him, 'I know the Messiah, that is the Christ, is coming, when he comes he will tell us everything.' Jesus said, 'I who am talking to you, I am he.'"*

Here we see how this Samaritan woman is taken aback by the request that Jesus makes of her. Samaritans and Jews did not get along too well. Regardless, Jesus asks her for a drink in hopes of eliciting the response that He got. Jesus then says to her, "If you only knew the gift of God! If you knew who it is that asks you for a drink, you yourself would have asked me, and I would have given you living water." The woman is clearly ignorant of who it is that she is addressing, but even so, Jesus offered her living water. The woman was still somewhat hesitant and a bit weary of the stranger, but something that Jesus said had captured her attention. Jesus then told her that that all who drank from that well would experience thirst again, but that whoever **would drink from the water that He was offering would never experience thirst again**.

This quenching water refers to the spiritual nourishment that quenches our thirst when we finally know Him and begin to have a relationship with Him. The woman became interested and requested some of this water. Jesus then tells her to go, call her husband, and then return. But the woman answers that she has no husband. Jesus here confirms that what she is saying is true and even goes further by stating her own past to her. She had had five different men she called husbands, and the one she was currently with was not her husband either. The woman was surprised by this response and believed Jesus was a prophet. Jesus continued speaking to her and told her, *'The hour would be coming, and is now here, when true worshipers would worship the Father in spirit and truth; for that is the kind of worship the Father wants,'* and after He said this the woman acknowledged that she, too, knew the Messiah would be coming and expected Him to reveal everything to them. It was after this that Jesus told her that He was just that person.

The woman then went into the city and began to spread this news. Because of her, many more believed and converted. She became a disciple that day and helped to spread the message so that others like her could also have their thirst be satisfied through the living waters that Jesus provides each and every one of us.

In many ways, many people today are like this Samaritan woman. They probably would not recognize Jesus if they met Him and might even have contempt for Him. They are ignorant as far as what it means to have spiritual nourishment and are in many ways not satisfied with what their lives offer them. But they continue to drink from the well of physical sustenance without ever realizing that there is living water to be had. The fact that this woman had been with a total of six different men she called husbands is a clear indication of her search for something meaningful yet elusive in her life. She had been searching all her life for what Jesus was now offering to her—that forever quenching drink of living water that leads to eternal life.

Many people today are like this Samaritan woman, my brothers and sisters, and it is up to us to offer them a drink from our canteen of living water. In a society of broken families and crippled souls, it is our duty to help them find the source of this water. Once they have found their way to the well, it is up them to want to drink from this water, for as the old saying goes, "You can lead a horse to water, but you can't make him drink."

In another example, we see how Jesus has compassion for a woman who had been caught in the act of adultery. In John 8:3-11, *"Then the teachers of the law and the Pharisees brought in a woman who had been caught in the act of adultery. They made her stand in front of everyone. 'Master,' they said, 'this woman has been caught in the act of adultery. Now the Law of Moses orders that such women be stoned to death; but you, what do you say?' They said this to test Jesus, in order to have some charge against him. Jesus bent down and started writing on the ground with his finger. And as they continued to ask him, he straightened up and said to them, 'Let the man among you who has no sin be the first to throw a stone at her.' And he bent down again, writing on the ground. As a result of these words, they went away, one by one, starting with the oldest, and Jesus was left alone with the woman standing before him. Then Jesus stood up and said to her, 'Woman, where are they? Has no one condemned you?' She replied, 'No one.' And Jesus said, "Neither do I condemn you, go away and don't sin again."*

In many ways, I believe this is very relevant to today's world. How would Jesus address the following question: *"Master, this woman has just had an abortion, what do you say we do to her?"* I have no doubt in my mind of how Jesus would answer this question. He would not condemn her, attack her, or berate her. He would show her the same compassion He showed the adulteress. But, just as He did with the adulteress, He would also tell her, "Do not sin again."

Let us be reminded that by the measure that we measure, so, too, will we be measured. Brothers and sisters in the Lord, let us be reminded of how God comforts and reassures all us who have a deep concern and become distressed every time a child's life is taken by abortion (Isaiah 49:15): *"Can a woman forget the baby at her breast and have no compassion on the child of her womb? THOUGH SHE MAY FORGET, I WILL NOT FORGET YOU."*

Our Lord reminds us through these words that even though human mothers can forget, abandon, or show no compassion toward their own children, He that is, will not. [For even throughout most of the animal kingdom, we see how the females take care of their young and defend their right to life. Even the alligator, a cold-blooded reptile, defends her young and creates/sustains an environment for their young's safety. Animals do this out of their natural God-given instinct. But it is we humans who have free will and can decide whether to do what is good or bad. To sustain life or to end it.

Many times I question if animals are really not more humane and humans are really not more wild and savage. For animals live and die based on their instincts, and we humans have a choice. Do we kill or do we defend life? Do we knowingly do what is good or knowingly do what is bad? Let us reflect and pray on what is the right choice.

For in many cases throughout the world today, animals have been given more rights than humans. Endangered sea turtles are one example. You cannot eat them or even their eggs because there is a federal law (http://ecos.fws.gov) protecting them and their unborn. Yet the same cannot be said of unborn humans. This is the case throughout the world—more protection is given to animals and their unborn than it is to the unborn human. What is worth more—human life or animal life? Who did Jesus come for? Whether you call it a fetus or a human life, is there any doubt that what is taking place inside a womb is called life? Life is the process of growth and maturation. Is there any doubt that what will be brought forth to light in a matter of month's time is anything short of or less than a human infant?

After all, if we follow this line of logic, we then can infer that by the mere act or process of wanting to end this life is the acknowledgment and understanding that what will be brought forth, if unimpeded, will be human life. So by their own account, even if unaware of it, they are acknowledging this life in the womb, by wanting to abort it.

Something similar can be found in Mark 10:13-16, *"People were bringing their little children to him to have him touch them, and the disciples rebuked them for this. When Jesus noticed it, he was very angry and said, 'Let the children come to me and don't stop them, for the Kingdom of God belongs to such as these. Truly, I say to you, whoever does not receive the Kingdom of God like a child will not enter it.' Then he took the children in his arms and laying his hands on them, blessed them."*

Let us be confident that even when women can forget their babies and have no compassion on them, God is there. When human cruelty and selfishness shun and rebuke children, God is there to reassure us that the Kingdom of God truly belongs to the young and innocent. For it is when we become childlike that we begin to be more dependent on He that created us. For it is when we become childlike that we begin to have hope in the future. For it is when we become childlike that we begin to forget past offenses more easily and let go of those things that have prevented us from moving forward.

Let us also be reminded, brothers and sisters, that Jesus, too, died innocently and without guilt, similar to thousands of unborn babies that die each and every year throughout the world. But just as Jesus endured this painful death and ultimately ascended up to heaven, we must be confident that these millions of innocent lives are in heaven with God. For no matter the schemes of the enemy, he will not be able to stifle the message of the Gospel and those that spread the Good News.

Brothers and sisters in our Lord Jesus Christ, let us go forward and offer others this living water that can only be found in He that was sent for us and for our salvation. We must not condemn those that live in ignorance or selfishness, but rather let us offer them a drink from this everlasting spring. Let us bring them to conversion through the spirit and the truth, not by what we demand or impose on them, but instead by how we live through Christ. Even if they reject our offer, let us continue to pray for them with all the more reason.

Many today are slaves to societal and cultural norms that dictate to us what we need, want, must have, or must do. But through it all, many become like that Samaritan woman that have searched throughout life, doing what she thought she wanted, and having what she believed she needed, but in the end was still left parched and thirsty for something else.

Living in ignorance can only be justified when you have no access to other knowledge or information and have not been exposed to the truth. But if after living in darkness for years someone with a lantern comes to your home and offers you the gift of light and you reject it, then ignorance stops being out of circumstances and starts being out of choice.

Let us be the ones to introduce this light of truth, this living, giving water. For just as the Samaritan woman partook of this water and led others to this life giving water, so, too, will others be encouraged and led to help others find their way.

For the times are changing, my brothers and sisters, and we will continue to see and hear more frightful things. Let us not be worried or fearful because these things must pass, as it is written. Let us instead be hopeful in what is to come. For He that is in the truth, knows of everlasting life. Continue to pray for me, my brothers and sisters, and I, too, as always continue to pray for you. May you have a blessed and safe weekend, and may you continue to strengthen yourselves spiritually for the coming times.

Your brother,
horacio

Letter XXVII-Slave No More

Brothers and sisters in Christ, it is with great pleasure and hope that I come to you this morning on this eighth day of this tenth month.

I truly hope and pray that each one of you and your loved ones are doing well. I continue to pray for you as I wish that you continue to pray for me as well. Again, I emphasize that if anyone one of you, or someone whom you know, is in need of prayers, please let me know.

Brothers and sisters, truly we are living today in a modern world in which slavery has once again come back. For hundreds and thousands of years, slavery was seen as being an acceptable means to an end. Slaves were usually brought from conquered lands to work and serve their masters in the conquering nations. Later slavery evolved into taking people from certain regions of the world and taking them back to a particular location to be sold to the highest bidder. All in all, slavery has been around for thousands of years and continues to rule our world today.

Slavery may not seem as obvious to the undiscerning eye as it once did. Where chains, shackles and cuffs were once the most obvious physical methods of controlling and containing a slave, today it is not as obvious but rather more subtle. For today it not only affects the poor and uneducated, but, ironically enough, I believe it affects the well off more than the former. For today's slavery is not one of physical chains, shackles and cuffs, but rather it is one that remains unseen but yet is truly felt.

In today's world, my brothers and sisters, we have entered a new age of slavery. It has morphed into a new form, but it's the same slave master that controls not hundreds or even thousands but millions on a global basis. Today's slave master is not as obvious as he once was, though. Where once the slave master required and commanded work, today's slave master is far more evil and insidious. For today's slaves don't even realize the shackles and chains that wrap around their bodies and keep them tied to their masters.

Today's slaves are still a means to an end, not through temporally constructive means but rather through eternally destructive ones. Today's slaves in many cases are proud of their slavery and even promote it as a freedom (license) to do what they please. Yet they are completely unaware of the ultimate ends to their voluntary servitude. If you were to ask anyone in today's world whether or not they would voluntarily choose to be a slave to anything or anyone, the answer most (not all) would give would be a resounding no (due to arrogant pride). Yet many are exactly this and are completely unaware that they are at the control of their possessive and oppressive masters. Who are these masters, you may ask?

Today's masters are more cleverly disguised and harder to distinguish, but if you have a discerning eye to see and an ear to hear, you will see and hear who they are. Do not be fooled, my brothers and sisters, into believing all that feels, looks and sounds good is, for it is here that the true slave master begins to tempt and entice you right before he begins to place the shackles around your legs, neck and arms, even as you sit and enjoy the tempting treats.

For today's slaves do not come in the form of laborers or working servants in far and distant lands, but rather they come as your next-door neighbor. Or perhaps they come as your political or religious leaders. They come in every shape, form and color. They come from all levels of the socio-economic spectrum. They are the poor, rich and wealthy. Today we live in a world with two main slave masters. One is God almighty, maker of Heaven and earth, and the other is the ruler of this world and all that remains and pertains to this earthly temporal plane. Who do you serve and have obedience to?

Look around and see how people voluntarily seek and serve to do the work of this earthly slave master. See how they do things that they think and feel derives from their personal freedoms but are really helping to fulfill the objectives of the master that helps drive/fuel their choices? The choices of sexual freedom and perversions, alcohol and drug abuse, violence, murders, thefts, deceit, and the biggest one of all—love of money.

All these slave masters have one sole slave master that they serve, but they make sure that through their influence, they help retain and create new willing and obedient servants. For even though they may serve a destructive slave master, individuals still need to fulfill the first and by far the most important rule in slavery, that of obedience. Obedience to their flesh, obedience to money, obedience to drugs and alcohol, obedience to being disobedient to God's laws and precepts. These are by far the most important rules that they live by and sometimes even encourage others by. It is through these laws that the enemy and ultimate earthly slave master has recruited and kept millions of souls, both living and dead. He lures us by tempting us to disobedience. He lures us by allowing us to see what we can have if we just take short cuts. He lures us by offering us more money and power. He lures us by presenting us beautiful bodies that are like whitewashed tombstones, appealing to the eyes, but full of death and decay underneath. He lures us by allowing us to believe through our pride that we should be the ones in control and not God (like Adam and Eve).

Brothers and sisters, he lures us in so many ways that it would be impossible to name them all. That is why we must pray and acknowledge that we need and depend on God to let us properly discern and know when it is we who are faced with these temptations by the enemy, and pray that He give us strength and steadfast faith. We alone cannot defeat him, but with the help of our heavenly Father, we are unstoppable.

Let us recall what Jesus said in John 8:34: *"Truly I say to you, **whoever commits sin is a slave**. But the slave doesn't stay in the house forever; the **son stays forever**. So, if the son makes you free, you will really be free."*

Here Jesus clearly demonstrates that it is not the slave or the servant that remains in the father's house or inherits the father's house, but rather it is the son who stays forever. It is the children who inherit the property and all that belongs to it, not the hired help.

In today's world, who, after spending a lifetime working and sacrificing to build a home and purchasing land, would leave everything to the hired help instead of their own children? I would venture to say no one.

In the same way, my brothers and sisters, how can we expect to receive any inheritance from God the Father if we ourselves are the slaves and/or hired help of the house instead of His children? Adam and Eve were also God's children, but after they disobeyed, did they remain in the garden? Moses was one of God's greatest prophets and leaders of his people, but after he disobeyed, was he allowed to go into the promised land? Lucifer and his fallen angles were once angels in heaven, but after they rebelled and disobeyed, did they remain in heaven?

We, too, must not assume anything but rather continue to strive to be one of God's **obedient** children, and not one of his hired helpers (slaves) that continue to do the work of sin.

Let us crucify the slave masters that hold us in bondage to their every whim and desire. Let us crucify the flesh, my brothers and sisters. Let us through prayer and sacrifices, crucify once and for all the earthly desires and all that they bring with them. Let us respect one another and see each other as brothers and sisters instead of lusting after one another. Let us break the chains of bondage from money that has kept so many of us as slaves and servants to that which drives so many away from God and His laws. Remember what Jesus said, "One cannot serve two masters." Let us throw away the shackles and handcuffs that have kept us paralyzed from serving the one that calls us **His children**.

Brothers and sisters, the enemy is strong and powerful, and we must acknowledge that in order for us or for those close to us who may need to break away from this slavery, it is vital that we begin to strengthen our love, our prayers, and our faith in He who was sent and died for our salvation. Let us first begin by surrendering ourselves to His will, and, secondly, by striving for obedience to His will.

Brothers and sisters, let us be aware that this type of slavery has been around forever. But in today's world, it is becoming increasingly clear that the prevalence of this slavery is clearly increasing and becoming a very dominant force.

Let us be reminded that even Paul wrote about this in his letters, and describes the following in Romans 1:18-32: *"God is now ready to condemn the wickedness and any kind of injustice of those who have silenced the truth by the wicked ways. For everything that could have been known about God was clear to them: God himself made it plain. For, though we cannot see him, we can at least discover him through his works, for he created the world and through his works we understand him to be eternal and all-powerful, and to be God. So they have no excuse, for they knew God and did not glorify him as was fitting, nor did they give thanks to him. On the contrary, they lost themselves in their reasoning (in today's modern world science and technology are viewed as more important by many) and darkness filled their minds. Believing themselves wise, they became foolish; they exchanged the Glory of the immortal God for the likes of mortal men, birds, animals and reptiles. Because of this, God gave them up to their inner cravings, they did shameful things and dishonored their bodies. They **exchanged God's truth for a lie**; they honored and worshiped (slaves to money, the flesh, drugs, political power) created things instead of the Creator, to whom be praise forever, Amen! Because of that, God gave them up to their shameful passions: their women exchanged natural sexual relations for unnatural ones. Similarly, the men giving up natural with women, were lustful of each other, they did men with men, shameful things, bringing upon themselves the punishment they deserve for their wickedness. And since they did not think that God was worth knowing, he gave them up to their senseless minds so that they committed all kinds of obscenities. And so they are full of injustice, perversity, greed, evil, they are full of jealousy, murder, strife, deceit, bad will and gossip. They commit calumny, offend God, are haughty; they are proud, liars, clever in doing evil. They are rebellious towards their parents, senseless, disloyal, cold-hearted and merciless. They know of God's judgment which declares worthy of death anyone living in this way; yet not only do they do all these things, they even applaud anyone who does the same."*

Brothers and sisters, does this not describe our current and modern civilized society? Does it not clearly point out that in a country or countries where there is abundance and freedoms of all sorts (like there was in the Garden of Eden), it becomes increasingly tempting to deviate from God's laws and precepts and instead go after those things that fulfill our selfish desires instead? Just like the apple was used to represent the tempting offer of sin, so, too, does money, sex, alcohol and power offer the same to millions today. It is not enough to acknowledge God and believe in Him, but **we must also obey Him**. Just like St. Paul said, "For everything that could have been known about God was clear and available to them. God himself made it plain." So there was no excuse back them, and even less so today, there is absolutely no excuse to not know, obey and follow God's laws and His will.

Brothers and sisters, let us rip the chains of slavery that hold us in bondage. Let us decide today to cease being a slave to sin and begin to fulfill our true roles as children of God. Let us, through strength that is appropriated to us from God, begin to crucify the desires that drive us away from Him and into the bondage of slavery to the master of this world. If you or anyone of you need help and feel you can't do it alone, that is why I, and many others out there, are here to help you and your loved ones regain your rightful place in the family of God and not as the hired help. We will pray for you and continue to provide support and comfort to you as well.

Jesus sent out His disciples in two for a reason—so that when one felt weak or vulnerable, he would be strengthened by the other. So, too, my brothers and sisters, let us support and comfort one another when one of us comes under attack from the enemy and begins to feel weak and vulnerable to temptation.

Continue praying for me as I continue to pray for you all. The time to prepare is now, and the coming years will show just who truly was prepared, and who truly was not. We are beginning to experience some of the birth pangs throughout the world, but that is only the beginning of what is to come. Many will be caught off guard, and due to their slavery, and will not inherit what rightfully belongs to the family of God. The events that are coming to pass and those that have yet to pass will truly be like a furnace testing the value of gold and silver. For those that do not survive the purification process of the furnace will be those that presented themselves as being or having value, but under the heat of purification became charred and quickly destroyed. But those that are truly created and contain the precious material of true faith and hope in He that is will survive the purification of the furnace no matter the heat. The coming years will prove who exactly has true faith, even when everything around them is being burned in the furnace. Will their faith withstand? Will they be confident in their faith that God almighty has included them in His family? Will they show to be obedient and repent with a contrite heart for their sins? Only time will tell. For it is in these coming times of distress that the worth of each will be tested through their faith. Only they and they alone will be to blame if it does not survive the furnace that is to be.

As always, your brother in Christ,
Horacio.

Letter XXVIII-Woe To You Pharisees!

Good morning, brothers and sisters in our Lord Jesus Christ. It is with great honor and pleasure that I come to you this morning on this twentieth day of the tenth month of this 2005th year.

I truly hope you are all doing well wherever you may find yourselves. That you, your families, and your loved ones are well and healthy. If you or anyone of you is in need of prayer, please let me know. I, thank God, am doing well and praise God for all that He has given me, especially the wisdom and strength needed to carry on His mission in my life. I also give thanks and praise for the gift of my mother who just turned a few years younger on the eighteenth of this month.

Brothers and sisters in Christ, over the past few years I have come across many individuals from different cultural and socio-economic backgrounds that have relayed to me a very similar message. That message being, "I am no longer a member of the Church due to my falling out with a certain priest." Or perhaps it was scandals in churches throughout the country that caused many people to lose faith and leave. Whatever the reason, it almost always had something to do with a member of the clergy and/or their words or actions that caused them to take these decisive matters [In reference to those I have encountered].

I, too, have encountered certain church leaders who perhaps I didn't like but that does not mean I am willing to renounce my faith in the church. Nor does it mean that I condone what they did or said. My faith sustains me through these dark periods and allows me to have hope for what is to be. I, too, may have had differences of opinion, whether written or said, with the leadership; but my faith in the leadership of Christ and the church as established through the apostles sustains me.

For I am not here to practice external religion, but rather internal religion. For it is those that focus and practice on the external aspects of religion and man-made rites and rituals, that waver through these periods of instability. For they are more concerned with practicing the rite of external circumcision than with having circumcision of the heart. That which is internal. This is why their faith flounders like a fish out of water when they experience conflicts or confrontations with the leadership of the church, and therefore decide to leave or change religions.

Rites and traditions within the church are going to always be the tools and instruments that help us focus our faith, similar to a Stradivarius violin. The violin itself, although a very well built and a traditionally well-known instrument, in and on its own accord is nothing if not for the virtuoso (very good player) that can pick it up and play a symphonic melody on it. The violin itself is merely the means to the harmonic end, not the end in and of its own. So, too, are the focus on rites and traditions. They are nothing, if not for our faithful living of the faith on a day to day basis, and the light that is emitted from within us, that find their source in God, that shine to those around us.

It these individuals (those focused on the external aspects of religion) that find more comfort and stability in having knowledge of the temple, rather than knowing who the temple is for. It is these individuals that find more love and security in the social aspects of a gathering, rather than the host of the banquet. It is these individuals that find more peace and serenity in their beliefs of God, rather than in His truths and those that speak and promote His truths.

Jesus himself made it known to us, brothers and sisters, that it was truly love and mercy that pleased God and not merely sacrifice and the external practices of worship, but rather things those that come from the heart and work in unity and harmony with the latter. (Matthew 12:6-7, Hosea 6:6)

Brothers and sisters, let us not be so weak of heart, but rather pray that God strengthens your spirit, and you will begin to experience religion from the inside out, and not from the outside in.

I myself realize that not all of God's shepherds have God's goals in mind, but perhaps have their own. Or that perhaps not all speak God's truth, but the truth as they see it.

We must realize that the Church is in constant attack by the enemy and his forces, and just like nations do, so, too, does the enemy send in spies and other faithful followers of his to disrupt and corrupt the Church from the inside out. This is why it is vital, my brothers and sisters, that we know, study and meditate upon God's word to realize when someone speaks contrary to the Word. For it is through His Word in union with apostolic tradition (2 Thess. 2:15) and magisterial teaching (Galatians 2:2-10), that we measure what is truth and what is not. What is true and authentic doctrine. All three of these will always give light and support the other, similar to the Father, the Son and the Holy Spirit. No one of these can ever be in direct opposition or contradiction of one another. They all give light and support to the other.

In John 8:45-47, Jesus says, *"Now I speak the Truth and you don't believe me. Which of you could find anything false in me? Then, if I speak the Truth, why do you not believe me? He who is of God hears the Words of God; you don't hear because you are not of God."* Also in John 14:5-7, in response to a question made by Thomas, Jesus answers him, *"Thomas said to him, 'Lord, we don't know where you are going; how can we know the way?' Jesus said, 'I am the way, the truth and the life; no one comes to the Father but through me. If you know me, you will know the Father also; indeed you know him and you have seen him."*

Let us be reassured of our relationship to God almighty through our relationship with Christ and His Words of truth, not through external forms of worship and routine acts. Just as Thomas asked Him, **"How can we know the way?"**

So, too, many in today's world ask the same question. But let us be certain of our faith and not be like so many that flounder out of simple and trivial confrontations with church leaders.

For let us recall how the leaders of the faith treated Christ in His life of missionary work. They, too, were constantly attacking Him and His teaching because it was a new form of preaching and message that was attracting multitudes of followers. This, of course, didn't sit well with the institution of the time and the keepers of that institutional hierarchy. It was this new form of preaching to the lowly ones that threatened in some form or fashion their livelihoods. [We see a perfect example of this in Matthew 21:12, Mark 11:11, Luke 13:35, John 2:14, when He expels the dealers in the temple.] It was they that had power that didn't want to cede this power and authority to anyone or anything else. It was they that had the knowledge that kept themselves, their fixed paradigms and their closed mindsets from being open to anything or anyone else, even if it meant rejecting God himself! It was they who felt were God's chosen, and, therefore, made every attempt to be pure, spotless and clean. But the only problem with this is who needs God if you're perfect? Who needs a doctor, if you never get sick? Did not Jesus himself say that He came for the sick? For knowledge truly is power, my brothers and sisters, and just as it was then, so, too, today.

But let us be reminded of how Jesus addresses this issue of the teachers of the law (Matthew 23:2, Luke 20:45, Mark 12:38): *"The teachers of the Law and the Pharisees occupy the seat of Moses (or St. Peter's/or any other seat of religious authoritative power whether Catholic or Protestant, for modern times),* **Listen and do all they say, but do not imitate what they do, for they themselves do not practice what they teach.** *They prepare heavy burdens that are very difficult to carry, and lay* *them on the shoulders of the people. But they do not even raise a finger to move them. They do everything in order to be seen by people; so they wear very wide bands of the Law around their foreheads and robes with large tassels. They like to occupy the first places at feast and reserved seats in the synagogues/churches; they also enjoy being greeted in the marketplace and being called master by the people.*"

It is here where Jesus reminds us of how to treat this issue. He tells us not to do as they do, but to listen to them, for they are knowledgeable in the Word of God, but oftentimes are themselves their own worst enemy.

Let us be reminded of how Christ as our first and perfect priest came to teach us so that we may begin to follow His example, and not those of power motivated teachers of the law. It was through servitude and humility that He enabled us to see how the head should be servant to all and not the other way around. It was through love and mercy that He laid the groundwork for us and not only through the practice of rites or rituals. [To him that has been given more, more shall be expected.] It is also precisely because of their roles as leaders in Christ's army, that their self awareness should have prepared them for additional duties and responsibilities in fulfillment of their roles and not less.

If a higher-ranking officer in God's army is derelict in his duties, then he's more responsible for the loss of men/women under his command, or under his protection. If a private is derelict in his duties, then his errors and mistakes still have consequences, but not as severe as a general's or higher-ranking officer's.

Let us be reminded of how He addressed the priest of His time (Luke 11:37, Matthew 23:13): *"As Jesus was speaking, a Pharisee asked him to have a meal with him. So he went and sat at a table. The Pharisee then wondered why Jesus did not first wash his hands before dinner. But the Lord said to him, 'so then, you Pharisees, you clean the outside of the cup and dish, but inside yourselves you are full of greed and evil. Fools! He who made the outside, also made the inside. **But according to you, by the mere giving of alms (sacrifices/rituals), everything is made clean.**"*

Is this not how so many people today, including church leaders are? There is more concern placed on the outside, or external facade of worship, than what is true praise and worship from the inside. Clean the inside first, then you can begin to clean the outside.

Let us not be taken in or taken out by what the pastor or priest of one church says or does. For if you put your trust in them, they may disappoint/hurt you tomorrow. You may be lead into or out of your faith by them, only to be left alone and in despair. For whom you like and trust today, you may not tomorrow.

You can, however, choose to select a different shepherd or flock, if you believe that your current leader/community does not, or is not currently pursuing/promoting a spiritual/evangelizing/social services message or agenda. How closely does your current community or leader live by or focus on the Beattitudinal precepts?

Let us rather put our trust in He who is the true Shepherd, for He cannot disappoint you. He cannot mislead you. He will not abandon you. He is the good shepherd and he reminds us of this in John 10:11-13, *"I am the good shepherd. The good shepherd gives his life for the sheep. Not so the hired man or any other person who is not the shepherd and to whom the sheep do not belong. He abandons the sheep as soon as he sees the wolf (the enemy) coming; then the wolf snatches and scatters the sheep. He is only a hired man (false teacher) and he cares nothing for the sheep."* In John 10:27 He continues, *"My sheep hear my voice and I know them; they follow me and I give them eternal life. They shall never perish and now one will ever steal them from me. What the Father has given me is stronger than everything and no one can snatch it from the Father's hand. I and the Father are one."*

Brothers and sisters, this is the twenty-eighth letter in a series that I bring to you all as a message of preparation for the coming years. Let us be internally clean first, then we can begin to focus on the other aspects of religion or faith. Do not be intimated by those who possess power whether through knowledge or financial means, but rather mindful of them, and pray for them. Do not let your anger or your pride be the source of having an unforgiving spirit, whether it is toward a friend, family member, or church leader, but rather forgive and release that person from both yours and their bondage. Do not allow condescending or sarcastic remarks from those in leadership positions affect your faith, but rather let your faith be strengthened by it. For if you find yourself being affected by them, then you should know just how deep your faith really is. Also, keep in mind, that you, too, are being treated just as disciples of Jesus throughout have always been treated by those that are the proud, powerful, arrogant and critical. Hence the reason for your rejoicing when times such as these come upon you. Rejoice and know that He who is sees all, and always keep in mind that the proud shall be humbled and the humble exalted.

Continue to pray for me, my brothers and sisters, as I always pray for you. I pray that God give you eyes to see, ears to hear, and a heart to know and feel the Truth, when/where ever you encounter it.

As always, your brother in Christ,
horacio

Letter XXIX-Get Behind Me Satan

Greetings to you once again, brothers and sisters in Christ our Lord. It is with great pleasure and hope that I come to you once again. On this cool twenty-ninth day of the tenth month, I bring another message of preparation for the coming lean and very challenging years that lie ahead.

I truly hope and pray that you have been led by the Holy Spirit to become stronger, wiser and more discerning in what you see, hear and feel. For it is through Him that we are guided, but only if we allow ourselves to be. We must be open and willingly submit and correspond to the call that God makes to each and every one of us. For no two people are called through the same channels but each one through particular means.

Brothers and sisters, today I write to you about evil and the source of it. It tempts us, it confuses us, it leads us astray, lies to us, gives us false illusions and ultimately leads us to death, both in the spiritual and physical sense.

Yet today there are some ministers, pastors and other leaders of the faith that lead us to believe there is no such thing as evil, and some have even gone as far as stating that there is no such thing as Satan! (Satan in its literal sense meant opponent or adversary, but through the years it has become synonymous with the name of God's main adversary). If there is no such thing as Satan, then I would ask these false teachers of the law if they even believe in God?

Why do you think these wolves in sheep's clothing, which profess to be leaders and teachers in the law of God, promote or even agree to this growing worldview that there is no Satan? Simply because if there is no Satan, then there are no boundaries or consequences to what we do. We can fulfill our hearts' desire in every which way we choose without any feelings of guilt, **fear** or consequences. We can do whatever we please and believe whatever we want because if there is no hell for us and only a heaven, then what is the point of only doing good and not bad? What is the point of only doing God's will and following His precepts and His law? Modern man has completely done away with **His precepts, laws**

and commandments for us, further promoting a culture and society with no moral, ethical and value driven precepts.

They say to us, "Go on and please and satisfy your every desire on earth today, and tomorrow you will still be on your way to the eternal paradise." "Live according to your needs, wants, desires, temptations because there are no consequences." They teach us to become blind to what will devour us.

Imagine if every gazelle or antelope on the African plain was blind or had been deprived of its life-sustaining senses by a total neglect of them. How would they know their predators were near? How would they know when to run or when to have fear for their lives? They wouldn't, and the same thing is currently happening now. When you don't use something, it goes to waste. When we don't use our conscience, it becomes blind, death and mute. In a sense, we forget how to use it. Or perhaps it has been overly abused, and hence the reason for the numbness and senseless non-feeling state.

I'm sorry to the bearer of bad news, my brothers and sisters, but I would do you and myself a great disservice if I didn't stand in stark contrast to this growing worldview. Let us be reminded that the worldview is not God's view, but rather that of His great adversary. This is why the enemy chooses to tempt and mislead us, sometimes through leaders of the faith, into believing he doesn't exist. For he is crafty, cunning, deceptive, and tempting. Let us recall this in Genesis 3:1-5, *"Now the serpent was the most crafty of all the wild creatures that Yahweh God had made. He said to the woman, 'Did God really say, 'you must not eat from any tree in the Garden?' The woman said to the serpent, 'We may eat the fruit of the trees in the garden, but of the fruit of the tree that is in the middle of the garden God said, 'You must not eat and you must not touch it or you will die.' The serpent said to the woman, 'You will not die, but God knows that the day you eat it, your eyes will be opened and **you will be like gods**, knowing good and evil."*

We see how from the very beginning, Satan has always been a deceiver. He lures and tempts us through soothing words into being disobedient to God through our selfish and proud natures. He nurtures our desires, and we can either follow and be deceived like Eve, who like so many today want to be like gods, either through our knowledge, power, or wealth, or stand our ground and rebuke him. But to rebuke him, we must be strong in the Word of God, strong in grace and strong in a prayer. We must also be careful because he can even tempt and deceive us through the Word, if we do not receive it in a state of humility, state of grace, and, most importantly, in complete surrender and openness to the will of God.

In Matthew 4:1-11 (also in Luke 4:1, Mark 1:12), we see how he tries to tempt our Lord Jesus Christ. The enemy knew that he could not tempt the Son of God with just any words, so he tried to deceive him through Scripture. *"Then the spirit led Jesus into the desert to be tempted by the devil. After spending forty days and nights without food, Jesus was hungry. Then the devil came to him and said, 'if you are the Son of God, order these stones to turn into bread.' But Jesus answered, 'Scripture says: People cannot live on bread alone, but on every word that comes from the mouth of God (Deuteronomy 8:3).' Then the devil took Jesus to the holy city, set him on the highest wall of the temple, and said to him, 'If you are Son of God, throw yourself down, for scripture says, 'God will charge his angels to rescue you. They will carry you lest you hurt your foot against a stone (Psalm 91:11).' Jesus answered, 'But scripture also says, 'You shall not challenge the Lord you God (Deuteronomy 6:16.)' Then the devil took Jesus to a very high mountain and showed him all the nations of the world in all greatness and splendor, and he said, 'all this I will give you, if you kneel and worship me.' Then Jesus answered, **'Be off Satan**! The Scripture says, 'Worship the Lord your God and serve him alone.' Then the devil left him, and the angels came to serve him."*

We see how the enemy came to tempt and mislead Jesus by trying to deceive him through Scripture. This is why, my brothers and sisters, we must be wary of wolves in sheep's clothing that come preaching the Word of God but deep down have hidden motives and intentions. We ourselves must be strong in the **Word** so as to not be misled. But in addition to this, we must also test the message with **apostolic tradition** and **magisterial teaching** as our reference points. For it is when we have all three in union and in support of each other that we can truly know we are abiding in truth. For it is these three that serve as the lighthouse that guides us safely to home port through the fog of confusion the devil stirs up in hopes of making us crash and sink in the waves of universal salvation (message of salvation currently being preached globally).

We see how Jesus confronts the enemy, and in the end rebukes him and commands him to, "Be off, Satan!" So, too, must we rebuke and do so forcefully so as to banish him and his influence with the help of God and His army of saints and mighty angels that serve Him.

The enemy blurs the lines of Truth and tempts us into believing we should be the ones in control. After all, isn't this the exact way he tempted and deceived Eve? By luring her into wanting to know more. By allowing her to believe that she and not God should be in control. By allowing her to believe that she would be like a god. Let us look at how the enemy tempted Jesus.

He first tempted Him in trying to prove His divine nature by trying to make Him perform a miracle. But Jesus refused to fall into that trap by stating, *"Man shall not live on bread alone, but on every word that comes from the mouth of God."*

Here Jesus clearly shows not only the enemy, but us as well, that man cannot and should not live by only the physical sustenance that the world provides but rather through the knowledge and understanding of God's Word. For it is God's Word that brings eternal life, true sustenance and wisdom to our lives. For we are not only temporal beings but spiritual ones as well. Physical sustenance must be accompanied by spiritual sustenance as well.

He was then taken to the top of a wall, and Satan again tried to get Jesus to prove his divine nature by challenging Jesus to throw himself down from the wall and quoting Psalm 91:11, *"God will send his angels to save you, lest you hurt your foot on a stone."* But Jesus knew the enemy's motives and told him, ***"You will not put the Lord your God to the test."***

How many times are we tempted to put the Lord our God to the test, instead of just knowing and having faith in His will and purpose for us? The enemy tempts us by leading us astray and feeds our anger, our disillusionment, or our sadness and creates in us feelings or thoughts that lead us to put our God to the test. We become bitter, cynical and unbelieving in His Word and His purpose and question God, "If you are so great, then why didn't you do this for me?" Or vice-versa. We begin to doubt God's will and begin to be led by that cunning serpent that feeds our anger, our remorse, our hatred, our jealousy and our loneliness.

But this why we must be strong in our faith and lead others to be strong as well. If I see my brother who is thirsty or hungry for the truth, will I not share my life-giving water with him or life-giving bread with him? For I am my brother's keeper.

Let us recall God's strong advice to Cain in Genesis 4:6-7, *"Then Yahweh said to Cain, 'Why are you angry and downcast? If you do right, why do you not look up? But if you are not doing what is right, sin is lurking at your door. **It is striving to get you, but you must control it.**"*

We, too, must control it (sin), my brothers and sisters. We must be strong, and strength stems from prayer, and prayer from faith, and faith from hope. Hope in He who is. We must not allow it to come in through the door, but remain strong and rebuke it. Cain did not, but we must.

The third time Jesus was tempted, the enemy took Him high atop a mountain and showed him all the nations of the world. As he did this, he tried to tempt Jesus with great power, influence and wealth. All Jesus would have to do is kneel and worship him. But here Jesus had finally had enough of Satan's evil temptations and rebuked him with a stern "Be off, Satan!"

It is here, too, we see how the enemy tries to tempt us, my brothers and sisters. He tempts us through fame, power, glory, and, of course, none of these three previous things has any merit if not for money. For it is money that all three have as a common denominator.

Many in today's world, and throughout history, have knelt and are kneeling to the master of this world in exchange for these three items. What Jesus rebuked, man scavenges for and agrees to abide by. Woe to them on their day of judgment!

Brothers and sisters, be aware that the enemy is going after souls with a vengeance right now and taking many throughout. It is always disheartening for me to see so many lost and wandering souls that have no need for the truth, yet they themselves continue to lead others astray and lead others to stumble. Ironically, many are religious leaders.

Two days ago, I was listening to a radio program where a Jewish rabbi and a Christian preacher were talking about certain issues of the day. One of the issues that caught my attention and led me further to confirm the enemy's grasp on religious leaders of today was what they said about homosexuality. Basically, both agreed that it was an acceptable lifestyle choice, and if it was up to them, marriages and families raised by homosexual couples should not only be promoted but also accepted. Both mind you, both claim to be men of God's laws and precepts. Both continued by claiming how throughout the Bible, homosexuality was never really condemned, and how Christians, today, should basically be accepting, not only of homosexuality but of abortion too!

Brothers and sisters, I don't know what Bible both of them were reading from, but the Bible as I know it has always had black and white, right and wrong, clear cut laws and precepts. The Bible was not meant to conform to any of man's ideologies or fleeting philosophies. It was meant to be set as a standard for all times, for all peoples. It was not meant to be amended like a Constitution, where things can be taken out and inserted depending on the century and mindset of the times.

Let us be reminded of two of the most well known examples in the Bible where God reprimands and unleashes His fury due to the sinfulness and wickedness of people and one of the sins that is most grievous to Him.

Genesis 18:20-22, *"Then Yahweh said, 'How great is the cry for justice against Sodom and Gomorrah! And how grievous is their sin! I am going down to see if they have done all that they are charged with in the outcry that has reached me. If it is not so, I will know. The men with him turned away and went towards Sodom, but Yah-weh remained standing before Abraham."*

Genesis 19:1-13, *"When the two angels reached Sodom in the evening, Lot was sitting at the gate of the town. As soon as he saw them, he rose to meet them, bowed with his face to the ground, and said, 'My lords (Father, Son, Holy Spirit), I pray you come to your servant's house to stay the night. Wash your feet, and then in the morning you may rise early and go on your way.' They said, 'No, we will spend the night in the square.' But so strongly did he insist that they went with him to his house; there he prepared a meal for them, baking bread without yeast. This they ate. They had not yet gone to bed when men from town surrounded the house; they were the men of Sodom, young and old, the entire population. They called Lot and said to him, 'Where are the men who arrived here tonight? Send them out so that we may have sex with them."* Lot went out to meet them, shut the door behind him and said, 'I beg you, my broth-ers, don't do such a wicked thing. I have two daughters who are still virgins, let me bring them out to you please, but don't do anything to them men, for they have come to shelter under my roof.' But they replied, 'Get out of the way! This fellow is a for-eigner and he wants to play the judge! Now we will do worse with you than with them.' But the men inside (The Father, Son, Holy Spirit) the house stretched out their hands to bring Lot inside and shut the door. As for those at the entrance to the house, they were struck with blindness, from the smallest to the largest so that they were unable to find the door. The two men said to Lot, 'Who is still here with you?' Your sons in law? Get them out of the place; your sons, your daughters and all your people in the town. The cry for retribution against it is great before Yahweh who has sent us to destroy it."*

The other example is in Genesis 6:5, *"Yahweh saw how great was the **wicked-ness of man on the earth** and that evil was always the only thought of his heart. Yahweh regretted having created man on the earth and his heart grieved. He said, 'I will destroy man, whom I created and blot him out from the face of the earth, as well as the beasts, creeping creatures and birds, for I am sorry I made them.' But Noah was pleasing to God."*

Brothers and sisters in Christ, we have crystal clear examples of what is accept-able to God and clearly what is NOT. Many today, though, like that Christian minister and Jewish rabbi who have become blinded by the influence of man and man's precepts. Or perhaps it is through their pride and the flattery of that pride that has led them to compromise their faith.

Let us remember that the enemy fooled Eve in the very same way, by allowing her to believe that through her knowledge, she would be in control and she would know what was right and wrong. So, too, has the enemy fooled, tempted, enticed and trapped many today, like that minister and rabbi. No longer is it God's interpretation of the Law, but rather man's selfish concepts of what is right and wrong. For man decides what is convenient to him now, and what is not, with no thought of tomorrow and his eternal salvation. For remember what Jesus said, Matthew 7:13-14, *"Enter through the narrow gate, for wide is the gate and broad is the road that leads to destruction, and many go that way. How narrow is the gate that leads to life and how rough the road. Few there are who find it."*

In Matthew 24:9-14, *"Then they will arrest you, and they will torture and kill you. All nations will hate you, for you bear my name. In those days, many will stumble and fall; they will betray one another and become enemies. False prophets will appear and mislead many people, and because of such **great wickedness**, love will grow cold in many people. But the one who holds out to the end will be saved. The Good News of the Kingdom will be proclaimed throughout the world for all nations to know, then the end will come."*

Jesus lets us know clearly the path we should take as well as the Christian teaching and proclamation will come under attack, as it currently is. He also tells us of the false prophets who will mislead many, similar to the many so called men of God that preach God's law as they see it and how it should conform to the new modern world and its so called progressive views.

But hope is also given to us by Christ when He says, "**But the one who holds out to the end will be saved**." Whoever stands strong in their faith and in their acts or deeds, will be saved. For many today do not realize the importance of Scripture and how it being fulfilled. Many give it no importance and see it as a hindrance to their selfish needs and desires. But I tell you this, God's words and his promises are always fulfilled. Jesus confirms this in Luke 16:17, *"It is easier for Heaven and earth to pass away, **than for a single letter of Scripture not to be fulfilled**."*

What is written will come to pass and be fulfilled. We must not stand in the way of God's will, although there are many that believe they should, or can. Whatever thoughts, words or deeds we may encounter that would be a hindrance to His will come not from God but from man. For just as Peter attempted to try to otherwise convince Jesus that He shouldn't fulfill His destiny, Jesus turned to him and said (Matthew 16:23), *"Get behind me Satan! You would have me stumble. Your thoughts are not from God, but from man."*

So, too, us, my brothers and sisters, should be obedient to the will of God not only for our personal selves, but for what will come to pass in our world. We can perhaps intercede for a while and hold off God's cleansing of the world for a bit, but only for a bit.

The cleansing has just begun, and in the following letters I will address this issue in depth. Let us pray, my brothers and sisters, that God gives us strength and shields us from the enemy's attacks. The enemy attacks us in many different ways, and we must rebuke him, as Christ did in the desert.

The enemy does exist, regardless of what many say. This is why we should become strong in our faith through prayer and penance, and pray that God Almighty give us eyes to see, hears to hear, and a heart to feel the Truth. The enemy can only affect us if we allow him to enter into us. This is similar to what God told Cain: *"Sin is at your doorstep, striving to get to us, but we must control it!"*

We are the ones in charge, and we are the ones that can either open that door and allow it to tempt us and live in us, or we can rebuke it and stand firm in our faith. The enemy cannot make us do anything we don't decide to do first. He nurtures our desires, and it is then up to us to fall into the trap, or jump over it. Even though most of us fall at one point or other, we have the faith and hope of knowing that if we repent and have true conversion of body and soul, then we will be reconciled with God. But we must first acknowledge our sinful ways, ask for forgiveness, and repent. Many will be called to do this, but few will be chosen, for the majority will not ask for forgiveness, much less repent.

Continue praying, my brothers and sisters, for me as I always pray for you all. Remain strong in the Lord, and He will give you eternal life. Take care, and please, spread the message.

Your brother,
Horacio.

Letter XXX-The True Bread and Wine of Life

It is with great pleasure and hope that I come to you this morning, my brothers and sisters in Christ. On this morning of the ninth day of this eleventh month, I thank God for the gift of life that He imparted on me thirty one years ago today in a small adobe brick house with dirt floors on my grandfather's ranch down in the central Mexican state of Zacatecas. It was there in a humble home, born to humble people, that the good Lord allowed me to see the light of day for the first time, and for this I am forever grateful to Him and indebted to He who is eternal.

On this day, I also pray a special prayer for you, my brothers and sisters in Christ, that He keep you protected, guided, comforted and loved today and for the rest of your days upon this earth. For it is with great joy and thanksgiving that I am grateful to our good Lord for having met and crossed paths with each and everyone one of you at some phase in my life. Whether it was in second grade or just last month that the good Lord brought us together, I thank God for the gift of each one of your friendships.

Today, my brothers and sisters, I come to you with the message of Christ. The message that He gave us to follow and promote to others that are still in darkness. For it takes nothing to fall into darkness, but it takes sacrifice and selfless giving of oneself to follow and be in the light. Sin and darkness go hand in hand, just like weeds and the bitter fruits that those weed plants produce. One gives fruit to the other.

But grace and light are like good crops that farmers plant and tend. It takes nothing for weeds to grow and give their bitter fruit, but it takes careful preparation, tending and sacrifice to keep a good garden/field in order.

But in today's modern world, my brothers and sisters, we are bombarded everywhere, whether through print, air waves, motion pictures or Internet, of how weeds and the bitter fruit that they give are actually good for us. There are many that pretend to be the bearers of God's light, yet promote what the current world trends are, culturally, politically and socially speaking. They are full of pride and arrogance and are not only attempting to instill and impose their attitudes, beliefs and lifestyles on us, but on God's will as well; and some even use God's word to promote their causes!

Let us plainly recall that Jesus was NOT in favor nor did He promote what the world promoted. Because the world, and all that it promotes, influences, accepts and tolerates as truth, is NOT in line with God's truths. This is why Jesus was killed: Because He was not a spokesperson for the world and all of its sinful attitudes and beliefs. **Just remember this, my brothers and sisters, if the worldview accepts it, promotes it and views it with tolerable eyes, chances are it is not of God. Same is true vice-versa, if it is promoted, accepted and strengthened by the Word of God and His disciples, chances are it WON'T be accepted by the world.**

How is it that a true Christian and follower of Christ and His rules and precepts is supposed to influence others to become Christian and followers of Christ? Through selfish prideful words or deeds? Or rather through selfless, humble and obedient words and acts?

Did Christ teach us to impose our attitudes, beliefs or lifestyles on others? Or to accept with an open heart and complete surrender to the Will of God so others would see the truth/light in our words and deeds and be encouraged to believe and hope?

Do not be fooled, my brothers and sisters, into believing you can have you cake and eat it, too. For many in today's modern societies have been fooled into believing this and are now leading others to believe the same foolishness! I do not write or speak to please the eyes of people or their ears but rather to please the eyes and ears of God.

But many today, including many that call themselves Christians, do the exact opposite. They want to be admired, accepted and praised by the masses that follow and adhere to the world's agenda. They want to be praised and flattered by those on the left for their understanding and compassion. Or perhaps by those on the right for their apparent virtue and their selfish and money-driven values.

But what about God? Where does He fit into their agenda? Who speaks for Him? Who speaks and/or writes to please Him and not mortal ears? Answer that question, if you can.

In Luke 13:1-5, Jesus says, *"One day some persons told Jesus what had occurred in the Temple: Pilate had Galileans killed and their blood mingled with the blood of their sacrifices. Jesus replied, 'Do you think that these Galileans were worse sinners than all the other Galileans because they suffered this? I tell you no. But, unless you change your ways, you will all perish as they did. And those eighteen persons in Siloah who were crushed when the tower fell, do you think they were more guilty than all the others in Jerusalem? I tell you no. But unless you change your ways, you will all perish as they did."*

Here we see how Jesus responds to a statement that was relayed to Him in reference to fellow Galilean compatriots, who had just been killed by the Romans. For it was in those days that Jewish rebels would try to conspire and revolt against their Roman oppressors. But Jesus does not get caught up in the politics of the times, the acts committed by the rebels or the Roman authority. Both carried out their violent agendas in the same way. Both were wrong. Instead Jesus says to them, ***"But unless you change your ways, you will all perish as they did."***

Similar to today, people on both sides of many issues are wrong. Pride, selfishness and arrogance cloud their vision, then they try to impose their will on others through violent or destructive means. The righteous, proud and boastful religious condemn, attack and persecute the sinners (abortion activists and homosexuals for example). They speak of being pro-life on the one hand but are gleeful when a person is given a death sentence.

On the other hand, you have those that are ignorant of God's laws, precepts and mercy that attempt to promote and influence others with their lifestyles and call what is good, bad, and what is bad, good. Both are wrong; unless they change their ways, they will all perish (in a spiritual/physical sense), just as Jesus said.

It is true that Jesus came to us to find the lost sheep, and that we, as His disciples should continue this mission. In Luke 15:1-7, we read, *"Meanwhile, tax collectors and sinners were seeking the company of Jesus, all of them eager to hear what he had to say. But the Pharisees and the scribes frowned at this, muttering, 'This man welcomes sinners and eats with them,' so Jesus told them this parable: 'Who among you, if he has a hundred sheep and loses one of them, will not leave the ninety-nine in the wilderness and seek out the lost one till he finds it? And finding it, will he not joyfully carry it home on his shoulders? Then he will call his friends and neighbors together and say, 'Celebrate with me for I have found my lost sheep.' I tell you, just so, there will be more rejoicing in heaven over one REPENTANT sinner, than over ninety-nine upright who do not need to repent."*

We clearly see the parable describes how joyful an event it will be in heaven when one repentant sinner has been found and converted. The key word in this parable is repentant, which means that someone has acknowledged his sinfulness, asked for forgiveness, and ***changed his ways***. This does not mean someone that acknowledges and/or believes in God, but selfishly and proudly continues to do that which is hurtful and shameful to God. These people are agnostic, and in many cases atheist, if they completely deny God.

Yet today the world is filled with these people. The people that proclaim not only to us, but even to God, this is how I am, accept it. Their ignorance stems from the selfish cultural and societal trends that have now come to characterize this morally depraved and darkened current age. [For in this age, we have been taught by modern thinking that there are no consequences for our actions. We have a right to do whatever we want. I have a right to fulfill my every heart's desire and not feel any guilt. Because after all, who wants to feel guilty, when there is so much to indulge in. Whether it's money, sex or political/religious power. Not only do they want to continue doing this for themselves, but they encourage others to do so too.] Whose philosophy or way of thinking does this sound like? Does it sound like God's or someone else's?

In John 3:19-21, we see how Jesus describes the reason why people prefer to remain in sin and darkness: *"This is how the Judgment is made: Light has come into the world and people loved darkness rather than light, because their deeds were evil. For whoever does wrong hates the light and doesn't come to the light for fear that his/her deeds will be shown as evil. But whoever lives according to the truth, comes into the light so that it can be clearly seen that his works have been done in God."*

Those that prefer the darkness do so because they fear the light. The light that shines on everything and everyone, and makes known what our words and deeds truly are. Those that are offended by the light, or those that carry the light within, many times are an inconvenience to those that prefer darkness. Fire and water do not mix. Those that carry the fires of sin within them are careful to stay away from those that carry the **life-giving waters** inside for fear that they may be put out. But as God's obedient disciples, we must seek those that carry within them those sinful fires and help to put them out. We must help lead them to conversion and **full repentance** so they do not face the eternal fires. We must lead them by prayer and example, not by condemnation and violence.

Brothers and sisters, we must help lead them to Christ, and in Christ they will find eternal peace and salvation. We must offer them the body and blood of Christ, and lead them to the life-giving bread and wine that is the Eucharist. For it was in John 6:53-58 that Jesus tells us, *"Truly, I say to you, if you do not eat the flesh of the Son of Man and drink his blood, you have no life in you. He who eats my flesh and drinks my blood lives with eternal life and I will raise him up on the last day. My flesh is really food and my blood is drink. He who eats my flesh and drinks my blood, lives in me, and I in him. Just as the Father, who is life, sent me and I have life from the Father, so he who eats me will have life from me. This is the bread which came from Heaven; unlike that of you ancestors, who ate and later died, he who eats this bread will live forever."*

It is here in this sacrament that we as Catholics come to share and have Christ become part of us, and we become grafted more so into the image and likeness of Christ. For it is by faith that the truly faithful live by, and not just by sight, or sound or any other of the senses. We are transformed and come to share life in the risen Christ through this intimate encounter of the Eucharist and the wine.

The word sacrament itself is described as something material that symbolizes and brings about a spiritual reality. It was through this act that Jesus, our Lord and Savior, brought us closer to Him and allows us to share that intimacy with Him every time we gather in memory of him and the last supper until His glorious return. Through the Eucharist, He helps us grow and mature in faith and understanding of our spiritual and religious life.

Each and every one of us needs food for physical sustenance each and every day. Yet they the day we go without food, for whatever reason, begin to have hunger pangs and feel deprived of a basic daily need. So if we can't go for more than one or two days without physical sustaining needs, why do some of us go for weeks, months, years and sometimes a lifetime without spiritual sustaining food and drink, which are those of the Eucharist and the wine; the body and blood of Christ.

But just as it was then, so too many today cannot and will not accept this concept. In John 6:60-69, we see how many of his followers stopped following Him after He relayed the message of His body and blood, *"After hearing this, many of Jesus' followers said, 'This sort of teaching is very hard! Who can accept this?' Jesus was aware that his disciples were murmuring about this and so he said to them, 'Does this offend you?' Then how will you react when you see the Son of Man ascending to where he was before? It is the spirit that gives life; the flesh cannot help. The words that I have spoken to you are spirit and they are life. But among you there are some who do not believe. From the beginning, Jesus knew who would betray him. So he added, 'As I have told you, no one can come to me, unless it is given to him by the Father.' After this many disciples withdrew and no longer followed him. Jesus asked the Twelve, 'Will you also go away?' Peter answered him, 'Lord, to whom shall we go? You have the words of eternal life. We believe and know that you are the Holy One of God."*

So, too, today, and throughout the past two thousand years, my brothers and sisters, many that could not and would not accept this concept have continued to deny the Eucharist as the actual body and blood of Christ. But who is losing out on this intimate experience?

On the other hand, we see how Peter remains faithful and loyal to Jesus when he says, "Lord, to whom shall we go? You have the words of eternal life." My brothers and sisters, we, too, must not withdraw from Him due to His strong words and strong message but rather remain loyal and faithful just as St. Peter did.

This is why, my brothers and sisters, we must draw closer to Him and become His intimate followers and obedient disciples. Let us celebrate the finding and repentance of wayward sheep, and let us remember that the world and all its tendencies, trends, and culturally acceptable attitudes are not of God's. For it is another that rules and influences the whims of this earth, and His followers have never accepted nor will they, the truth and the light that is God.

I give thanks and praise for your love, prayers and friendships, and pray to God Almighty that He continue to guide, protect, shield, comfort, restore and give peace to you, my beloved brothers and sisters in Christ. I ask this through Christ our Lord, amen.

Your brother,
Horacio.

Letter XXXI-Prophet Isaiah's
First Message

Good evening, my brothers and sisters in the Lord Jesus Christ. I come to you on this thirteenth day of this eleventh month with a message of what's to come.

This is Letter XXXI in a series that have all been meant for preparation for what is to come. The letters I have written up to this point have all been meant to elicit a spirit of awareness and preparation. Wake up, my brothers and sisters, for the Lord and His hand are poised to strike the earth and its inhabitants. Awake from your slumbers of apathy and conformity, and listen and pay attention to what the Lord is telling you. Awake and be poised and internally prepared: for what is coming will not be for the spiritually and faithfully weak of heart.

To those who continue to do what pleases their selfish hearts' desires, I merely pray that you will not be caught in the middle of one of your escapades when the Lord calls your name and takes you from the land of mortality. To those who continue to live and abide by their sinful natures, those of hate, selfishness, greed, lust, lying tongues, adultery and other sexually immoral lifestyles, I pray that the Lord shows mercy to you when the hands of time give way to eternity.

The following letters I write will be about what is to come. Not through my words do I write these messages, but through the Bible's own prophets do I bring you the warnings and messages that the Lord has written through His prophets for us and for our salvation.

For if we study that which has been written before and applied to the First Covenant, then we will find the answers we need to know for what we are currently experiencing in the world today and what will occur in the world tomorrow. For if we truly study and look at how the Lord punished those that broke his first covenant (the Jewish people), then we will begin to look at what is in store for all of us who are currently living within the second covenant (us Christians) and its precepts.

How quickly we humans forget our past errors and the history of those errors, and the consequences those errors brought not only us but also the earth itself. How foolish we are when we begin to proclaim ourselves masters of the earth and the universe. Do you forget that there is but one being that is responsible for all creation? Do you forget that before there was any science and technology, He is? The Alpha and the Omega, the Beginning and the End.

Now the earth is poised once again and on the fringes of a major cleansing. A cleansing that will bring about renewed life, hope and faith, but as is with any cleansing, will first bring about the destruction of all that is of no use. Just like a fire in a forest that burns out of control. After all has been burned, torched and destroyed, the following spring new life appears, and the forest begins to regenerate itself with new growth and life. So, too, the earth is begging to renew itself, and God almighty will allow for this cleansing to take place. But not all will be destroyed; a remnant must be left to ensure the future growth of His people.

Today, just like it was in the times of the prophets, there are two nations of the same religion that are divided. The two then were Israel and Judah. Today these two names can also be applied to the modern Christian church and its division, Catholicism and Protestant/Evangelicalism. Just as Judah branched off from the main branch of Israel, so, too, did the Protestant church branch off from Catholicism. Back then there was a visible and central head for the followers of the first covenant, which was the walled off city of Jerusalem. Today, the same visible/central head as established through the second covenant of Jesus Christ and His apostles is nestled among the hills of Rome: the walled off city of the Vatican. But on a more optimistic level, just as the two branches of Israel (Israel and Judah) reconciled and united shortly after World War II, so, too, will the two branches of Christianity once again unite for a common good, after what is to come in the future.

Brothers and sisters in the Lord, I will present for your discernment what and how the Lord tells us today was not just for His people of the First covenant, 4,000 plus years ago, but for us as well (His people of the second covenant/Christians).

We must first see how, if we overlap the second covenant and its nations, its peoples, its errors and mistakes, they fit into a perfect mold over that which was the first covenant and its references. For if you study the past, you will know the future. The mistakes and consequences of the past are and will once again be committed and the same consequences endured. Just as God reprimanded the people for breaking His first covenant, so too will we, the people of his second covenant (Christians) be reprimanded and dealt with in a severe manner for the decisions, we as a society and culture are promoting, not only to our nation, but to nations throughout the world. [The following scripture passages will all be in bold face, and the italics will be my commentary.]

I will begin within the book of Isaiah, but first I will take a Scripture passage from Ezekiel 19:1-9: **"As for you, son of man, intone a lamentation for the princes of Israel. Say: A lioness among lions was your mother! Crouching among the cubs she nursed her whelps. One of these she pushed forward and he grew to be a young lion, able to tear his prey and become a man-eater. But the nations heard about him and he was trapped in their pit; and they brought him with hooks to the land of Egypt. When she saw that her hope had come to nothing, she took another of her cubs and made him a young lion. He strutted among the others for he had become a strong lion, able to tear his prey and be a man-eater, too. He destroyed their strongholds and ravaged their towns. The country and its inhabitants were alarmed at the sound of his roar. But the nations came against him from regions round about. They spread their net over him, and caught him in their pit. They put him in a cage with hooks and brought him to the king of Babylon. There he was put in custody so that his roar was no longer heard in the mountains of Israel."**

Perhaps you may not understand too well, but let me shed some light on this parable.

You see, my brothers and sisters, the first lion, in whom the lioness had so much hope in, was first elected by the mother to grow and mature into something good and meaningful. But as he matured, he became a man-eater and eventually became rebellious and wicked. So it came to pass that he was allowed to be trapped and led into captivity to Egypt.

So, too, was the first covenant (the first cub), the hope and pride of God, but he soon saw that as the religion matured and people became apathetic, complacent, disobedient and evil in their thoughts and actions, he (God) allowed for their capture and eventual enslavement by other nations that served His purpose and His will in allowing the downfall to take place. Let us be reminded that these other nations that have come to punish and enslave His people were oftentimes nations that did not believe in Him, know Him, or obedient to Him (Yahweh). Yet they, too, served His purpose in punishing those that were/are His disobedient children.

We then come to the second cub (the second covenant). Here, too, the parable talks about the hope and promise the lioness had in pushing out this second cub, but just like the first cub, he, too, matured (as the religion matured) and eventually became a proud and boastful lion (we see how it describes him as strutting around). He, too, became good at doing evil, and therefore God had to allow him to be trapped and captured by the King of Babylon.

Brothers and sisters, let us reflect on how Christianity has matured and evolved over the past 2,000 years, and where it is today. Let us clearly see who all are the countries that are currently involved in present day Iraq (or Babylon as it was know then), and how they are all basically Judeo-Christian countries in this coalition. Let us recall how in this parable we just read that God is going to allow for the capture and entrapment of this second cub (or the Judeo-Christian countries) to take place in the land of Babylon (modern day Iraq and the surrounding Middle East region).

The prophets wrote not only for their times, my brothers and sisters, but they were writing to us as well. They warned not only those of the first covenant of what was to come, but they are warning us now!

In the Book of Revelation 11:3-13, we see here how God talks about His two witnesses, similar to the comparison of the two lion cubs. For here we also see who exactly these two witnesses are, what their mission was, what God will allow to happen to them, and afterward, the hope that comes after the cleansing has taken place. [In the following paragraphs, all that is written in bold is Scripture, and the italics are my commentaries.]

"Meanwhile, I will entrust my Word (God's Word and message), to my two witnesses (Judaism & Christianity) who will proclaim it for one thousand two hundred and sixty days, dressed in sackcloth. These are the two olive trees and the two lamps which are before the Lord of the earth. If anyone intends to harm them, fire will come out of their mouths to devour their enemies; this is how whoever intends to harm them will perish. They will have the power to close the sky and hold back the rain (*the prophets and the men of God were all given these powers by God*) **during their prophetic mission: they will also have the power to change water into blood, and punish the earth with a thousand plagues, any time they wish.** [*This is a perfect illustration of how Moses and the other prophets throughout biblical history, first had to fulfill their missions and how they were given power from above to fulfill their missions from God. Also, the two olive trees, symbolize Judaism and Christianity (in Judaism/ Catholicism, olive oil has always had a reference to either the spirit of God, and/or the charisms), as does the image of the two lamps, or the two religions that gave light to God's Word and his truth, which was Jesus Christ.*] **But when my witnesses have fulfilled their mission** [*after both Judaism and Christianity have both matured and fulfilled God's mission, after both Covenants have run there course and fulfilled God's plan*], **the beast that comes up from the abyss will make war upon them, and will conquer and kill them.** [*Just like the parable of the cubs and their entrapment, God will strengthen the hand of the foreign powers, in order to use them as the rod* *that corrects the spoiled and proud nations that proclaim his name. The beast, meaning the enemy, will be allowed to defeat, conquer and kill the nations of the two witnesses, Judaism & Christianity.*] **Their dead bodies will lie in the square of the Great City which believers figuratively call Sodom or Egypt** [*the two cities here are both literal and symbolic because Sodom on the one hand was a very sinful city that had been punished for disobedience and wickedness. Egypt, on the other hand, had been the powerful nation of ancient modern civilization. Which nations today have the mindsets of Sodom and the power, wealth, and prestige of Egypt?*], **where the Lord was crucified. And their dead bodies will be exposed for three days and a half** [*this number is not to be taken literally, but rather symbolically, for this period will last several years. In ancient Jewish traditions, the number 3 1/2 always represented the imperfect, or that which is evil or wicked. Because it is half of seven, the perfect number, representative of God himself. So 3 1/2 here, too, stands for this period of evil, dark, and wicked years that humanity will live and suffer through. Nostradamus has written that this third conflict with Mohammedans (Muslims)/Russians/Chinese would last for thirty years. Let us reflect on these nations and how they are not of Judeo/Christian origins.*] **To people of all tribes, races, languages and nations who will be ordered not to have them buried. Then the inhabitants of the earth will rejoice** [*the earth, or the world and its whims, are not of God's, that is why they will rejoice, but their rejoicing is short lived*] **congratulate one another and exchange gifts among themselves because these two prophets [Judaism and Christianity] were a torment to them.** [*Let us reflect on which religion has always been at odds with both Judaism and Christianity over the past two thousand years, and still is as we speak. So we see here how God will use the hand of Islam with help from the Far East and Russia to strike the nations of his two witnesses down.*]

Brothers and sisters, are we seeing any of this now?

I will now present—starting with the book of Isaiah and ending with Ezekiel—of what exactly we, as the holders and keepers of the second covenant, are accused of and exactly how this cleansing will come about. The prophets wrote so people could repent and change their ways. Noah, too, warned people before the first great cleansing, but did anyone listen? Did anyone listen to the prophets and their message? Will anyone listen now?

"This is what Isaiah, son of Amoz foretold concerning Judah (modern day Protestant/Evangelical countries-primarily western Europe and America) and Jerusalem (modern day Vatican City; Israel can be seen, in the Second Covenant context, as the Catholic Church, or those countries that at one time were primarily Catholic, basically most of Western Europe) in the

days of Uzziah, Jotham, Ahaz, and Hezekiah, kings of Judah (political/religious leaders). Listen, O heaven! Give heed O earth! For the lord speaks: 'I raised Children, I brought them up, but they have risen against me [*the rebelliousness of both Jews and Christians, and their stubbornness in wanting to follow their personal and selfish desires*]. The ox knows its master, and the ass its owner's manger, but Israel [*the Second covenant church-the Catholic Church and/ or the countries where it is/was the primary religion-can refer to most of, if not all of Western Europe*] does not know me, my people do not understand. A sinful nation, a people weighed down with iniquity, a wicked race, perverted children! They have turned away from Yahweh and despised the Holy one of Israel. Shall I strike you again and again? You will only rebel more, for your whole head is diseased and your whole heart afflicted. From the soles of your feet to the top of your head, wounds and bruises, sores: unclean and unbound, not eased with soothing ointment. Your country lies desolate, your cities razed by fire. Raped and sacked is your land, laid waste before your very eyes, as when besieged by alien hordes [*these will be the Muslim invaders and the consequences of their invasion into, not only Rome, but most, if not all of Western Europe*]. The Daughter of Zion [*in the Second Covenant context, this will always refer to the Church. For it was Judaism that gave birth to the Christian Church*] is abandoned like a shanty in a vineyard, like a hut in a melon field, like a hamleted town. Had not Yahweh, Lord of host left us a small remnant [*the small group that will remain protected during and after the great cleansing, which will ensure the continuation of God's people; although it does not refer to or mean a raptured church.*], we would be like Sodom, we would be like Gomorrah [*no remnant was left of these evil peoples and towns after God's fire from Heaven wiped them out*]. Hear the warning of Yahweh, rulers of Sodom. Listen to the word of God, people of Gomorrah [*this basically applies to most of the industrialized countries throughout the world that have accepted and promoted these lifestyles and societal/cultural norms as acceptable*] Your endless sacrifices-What do I care about them? Says the Lord. I have had more than enough of whole-burnt offerings of rams and the fat of fatlings; the blood of bulls and lambs and he goats does not delight me anymore [*no longer will God almighty be satisfied with meaningless sacrifices and/or heartless religion. Where people foolishly think that going to church, or practicing external religion is enough to please God, but carry inside all that is abominable to God*]. When you come to trample on my courts, who asked you to visit me? I do not need your oblations. Your incense is an abomination. Your new moons and Sabbaths and meetings, evil with holy assemblies, I can bear no longer [*This is all that involves the external facets of practicing a religion externally. Focusing more on the social and external aspects of ones faith*]. **New moons and appointed feasts have become a burden. When you stretch out your hands, I will close my eyes; the more you pray, the more I will refuse to listen. Your hands are bloody; wash them and make yourselves clean.** [*The blood that cries out for justice from the millions of unborn that are taken every year through abortion. Also the blood of innocent victims throughout the world that die each and every day from starvation, war, famine, while the powerful, and wealthy countries turn a blind eye.*] **Remove from my sight the evil of your deeds. Put an end to your wickedness and learn to do good. Seek justice, and give hope to the oppressed; give to the fatherless their rights and defend the widow. 'Come' says the Lord, let us reason together. Though your sins be like scarlet, they will be white as snow; though they be crimson red, they will be white as wool. If you are willing and obedient, you will eat the good things of the earth. But if you resist and rebel, the sword will eat you instead. Truly the Lord has spoken** [*Even if our sins have tainted us in pure crimson red, we can be reconciliated with God, but only through genuine repentance and with a genuine change of attitude and heart. But if we resist and rebel, the sword will destroy us instead.*]

Zion, the faithful city, has a become a harlot! She who abounded in justice, in whom righteousness lodged, has become a hideout of murderers! Your silver has become dross, your best wine diluted with water. Your rulers are tyrants, partners and thieves. They love a bribe and look around for gifts. No one protects the orphan, or listen to the claims of the widow [*to all those that belong to the church and countries that are primarily Judeo-Christian, where has true justice gone? Who stands up for the vulnerable, the unprotected, the poor, the oppressed? Religion has become diluted and been allowed to be influenced by the whims and trends of the world.*] **This is why the Lord speaks, Yahweh Sabaoth, the Mighty One of Israel: 'I will take vengeance on my foes and exact payment from my enemies. I will turn my hand against you, and I will smelt away your dross and remove your impurities** [*the cleansing will accomplish this, as well as I have mentioned before, one cannot stand in the presence of the Lord with impurities*]. **I will restore your judges, I will give back your counselors, as it was in the beginning. Then you will be called the City of Righteousness, the Faithful City** [*We as a people of God, will be restored, as well as have renewed faith, hope, and justice after the cleansing*]. **Zion will be redeemed when I come to judge. There will be a remnant: The just ones** [*Jesus also speaks of this remnant, as does the Virgin in her various apparitions throughout history. Jesus refers to this in*

Matthew 24:22] But **the rebels and sinners alike will be destroyed, and those who desert the Lord will likewise perish.**"

In Isaiah 2:1, we continue, "**The vision of Isaiah, son of Amoz, concerning Judah and Jerusalem. In the last days, the mountain of Yahweh's house shall be set over the highest mountains and shall tower over the hills. All nations shall stream to it, saying, 'Come, let us go to the mountain of the Lord, to the house of God of Jacob, that he may teach us his ways and we may walk in his paths. For the teaching comes from Zion and from Jerusalem the word of Yahweh. He will rule over the nations, and settle disputes for many people. They will beat their swords into plowshares and their spears into pruning hooks. Nation will not raise sword against nation, they will train for war no more. Oh nation of Jacob, come, let us walk in the light of the Lord!**"
[*This describes the ultimate victory of God, his power, might and majesty in their full and everlasting reign after having defeated the enemy and his forces. If we recall in Revelation, in reference to the two witnesses, we see how God will allow the enemy a short and brief victory over his two witnesses, but if we read a little further, we see just how God will ultimately overcome and victoriously triumph over the enemy's forces. In Revelation 11:11-13,* '**But after those three and a half days, a spirit of life coming from God entered them. They then stood up, and those who looked at them were seized with great fear. A loud voice from Heaven called them, 'Come up here.' So they went up to heaven in the midst of clouds in sight of their enemies. At that moment, there was a violent earthquake, which destroyed a tenth of the city and claimed seven thousand victims. The rest were overcome with fear, and acknowledged the God of Heaven.**"]

"**You have forsaken your people, the land of Jacob, for it was full of diviners. They have become soothsayers like the Philistines, and they have clasped hands with pagans** [*in today's world, there are thousands of psychics, spiritualist, and others whose livelihoods depend upon these either real or made up abilities and millions of people are mislead by them and their influences*]. **Their land is full of silver and gold, there is no end to their treasures. Their land is full of horses and there is no end to their chariots. Their land is full of idols, and they bow down before the work of their hands, before the things their fingers have made**" [*today's modernity and capitalistic systems have allowed for an excess of wealth in the land of some countries, but the vast majority of the world lives in a state poverty. The horses and chariots refer to war ready arsenal, personnel, and/ or vehicles. Let us be reminded of the potency of the U.S. arsenal. The idols here refer to anything we allow ourselves to be enslaved by; whether they be sex, money, material possessions and/or drugs*].

"Man will be humbled and the mortal fallen, forgive them not! Get behind the rocks, hide in the dust, and fear the Lord and the splendor of his majesty! The haughty looks of man will be humbled; the pride of the mortal will be brought low. Yahweh alone will be exalted on that day [*we are headed towards a major humbling by God himself, who will humble the proud and arrogant nations and peoples*].

"Yahweh will stand up on that day against all the proud and arrogant, against all that is lifted up or great, against all the cedars of Lebanon and all the oaks of Bashan, against all the lofty mountains, and all the soaring hills, against every high tower and every fortified citadel, against all the ships of Tarshish and their cargoes of luxuries [*Everything and everyone that stands proud and erect, will be humbled by the might of the Lord*].

"The arrogance of man will be humbled; the pride of mortal will be brought low. Yahweh alone will be exalted on that day, and all the idols will pass away."

"Men will flee into the hollow of rocks, into the caverns of the earth, from the terror of Yahweh, from the splendor of his majesty, when he arises to terrify the earth. On that day, men will throw to the moles and to the bats their idols of silver and gold, which they made for themselves to worship." [*On this day, humanity will rid themselves of all they came to serve and worship, whether it was money, sex, drugs, etc., and will come to know who their true master was*].

Letter XXXII-Second Part of Isaiah's Message

Good evening brothers and sisters in the Lord. I come to you this evening on this fourteenth day of this eleventh month of the year, to bring the continuation of the Letter of Isaiah, which will include chapters three through five. This is letter XXXII in a series of forty. The following is meant for your discerning eyes and mind, and pray that the Lord give you the gifts to see what it is we are facing. But this is no reason to be saddened or heartbroken, instead let your faith be strengthened by what the Lord has promised each and every one of us, if we would only listen, obey, believe and trust in him.

Ch3 "See how the Lord Yahweh Sabaoth, takes away provisions and men from Judah and Jerusalem [*from both Protestant/Catholic, or once Catholic countries; primarily Western Europe and the Americas, will God take away from*]. **The hero and soldier, the judge and the prophet, the diviner and the elder, the captain and the man of rank, the counselor, the sorcerer, and the enchanter** [*men/woman, from all levels of society, and of all class, social standings, and professions will be taken by the Lord in the coming years*]."

"**I will make striplings their princes and raw lads their rulers. People will oppress each other, every man his fellowman, every neighbor his neighbor; the young will bully the old and the base will insult the honorable. When that day comes, so be our leader and rule over this heap of ruins. But he will cry out in protest: I cannot undertake to be a healer of all this, when in my own house there is neither food nor clothing. See how Jerusalem crumbles and Judah falls, for their words and deeds have been in defiance of the Lord, a provocation in his glorious presence**" [*the Lord will humble the proud men, and their proud nations. For in these nations there is no longer any respect or love of God and his precepts. For it is love of God that will precedes love of self and love of neighbor. But how can we have love and respect of the latter two, when there is no love and respect of the former??*].

"The look on their faces denounces them: they do not hide their sin; instead, they parade it, like Sodom: Woe to them! They bring about their own downfall! [*This too is currently occurring on a worldwide basis. Never have we seen such an acceptance and promotion of homosexuality and sexual immorality on a worldwide level. Not only do they not hide their sinful nature, but 'they parade it, like Sodom' as Isaiah announces*]. But woe to the wicked: the evil that their hands have done shall be done to them" [*we all reap what we sow*].

"O my people, spoiled by your rulers, dominated by your creditors! [*The whole basis of capitalism is to rule the masses through debt, and no where do we see this more than in our own country, where both huge personal and national debt is/has become the acceptable norm of doing business; both domestically and abroad*]. O my people, your leaders mislead you and confuse the path you walk on" [*The current political leadership and leadership in the Church are misleading many. It is far easier to rule people, when the fog of confusion is upon them.*].

"Yahweh takes his place in court and stands to try his people. Yahweh calls to judgment the elders and the princes" [*God will hold accountable those he has given more to, such as the leaders in the church (clergy) and those in political office*].

"You have devoured my vineyard. The spoil of the poor is in your houses. What right have you to crush the people and to grind down the poor? declares Yahweh" [*both the church and political powers will have a lot to answer for. For it is they that have devoured the vineyard, which always stands for the earth, or the world. Nowhere do we see this more than in the polluting and contaminating of our planet, and the legislation that allows this to keep happening. Also we see today the spoil of the poor 3rd world countries, such as oil, diamonds, and other rich and valuable resources, in the homes of the rich and powerful exploiter industrialized countries.*]

"Yahweh says, 'Haughty are the women of Zion walking with their heads held high, with mincing steps, flirting with their eyes, ornaments tinkling on their ankles [*just as it was then, so too today, both women and men, parade around in their excesses of materialistic indulgences. Indulgences that spread from personal beauty to even indulging and spoiling their animals, while millions of poor starve to death each day*]. But Yahweh will cover the heads of Zion's women with scabs and make their scalps bald. On that day, the Lord will take away the ankle ornaments, the headbands and crescents, the pendants, the bracelets, and the scarves, the headdresses, the armlets, the sashes, the perfume bottles and the amulets, the signet rings and nose rings, the festal robes, the mantels, the cloaks and the handbags, the garments, the turbans and the veils" [*the Lord will take away all of people's prized materialistic possessions*].

"Instead of Fragrance, there will be stench; instead of girdle, rope; instead of well set hair, baldness; instead of jeweled gown, sackcloth; and instead of beauty, shame" [*the Lord will humble all of the proud, ignorant, and superficially materialistic*].

"Your men will fall by the sword; your heroes in battle. The city gates will lament and mourn as Zion, ravaged, sits on the ground."

Ch4. "On that day, the shoot of Yahweh (Christ and the true Christian Church), will be beautiful and glorious; and the fruit of the earth will be honor and splendor for the survivors of Israel. Those who are left in Zion and remain in Jerusalem will be Holy-all who are recorded among the living in Jerusalem [*these will be the remnant of the church, or those who remain during and after the great cleansing that is to come. All those followers of God that have hearts of gold and speak with tongues of silver while proclaiming the truth*]. When Yahweh washes away the filth of the women of Zion and purges Jerusalem [*purging of the church will come to pass*] of the bloodstains in its midst with the blast of searing judgment and the blast of destruction. Then will Yahweh create over the whole site of Mount Zion and over its assemblies a cloud of smoke by day and a glow of fire by night."

"For over all the Glory of the Lord will be a canopy and a pavilion, a shade from the scorching heat by day, a refuge by night from the storm and rain [*the Lord will always keep safe and protect those that are close to him, and obey his ordinances*].

Ch.5 "Let me sing for my beloved a song about his vineyard. My beloved had a vineyard on a fertile hillside [*my beloved here refers to God almighty, and his vineyard, is the earth/world as he created it*]. He dug it up, cleared the stones, and planted it with the choicest vines. He built there a watchtower and hewed out a winepress as well. Then he looked for a crop of good grapes [*after having tended to the earth and all that it would have on it, God began to cultivate the vines, and expected good grapes, or good obedient children*] but it yielded only wild grapes. Now inhabitants of Jerusalem and men of Judah [*men and nations of both Christianity and Judaism, Catholicism and Protestant/Evangelicalism*] judge between me and my vineyard [*choose if you will follow God, or will you follow the world*]. What more was there to do that I have not done for my vineyard? Good grapes were the yield I expected, so why did it only yield sour grapes [*God fearing and obedient children was what he expected, but to his dismay got only the opposite, fearless and rebellious people that know not when to stop pursuing their selfish and sinful natures*]. **Now I will let you know what I am going to do with my vineyard:"** [*This is the key to understanding what we are on the verge of facing my brothers and sisters. God himself, through the words of Isaiah will let us exactly know what he is going to do to the earth, or his vineyard in other words*].

"I will remove its hedge and it will be burned; I will break down its wall and it will be trampled on. I will make it a wasteland, I will neither prune nor hoe it, and briers and thorns will grow there. I command the clouds as well, not to send any rain on it" [*God will allow his vineyard to be completely destroyed and become overgrown with weeds and thorns, and rain will also cease to fall*].

"The vineyard of Yahweh Sabaoth is the people of Israel (the Catholic Church), and the men of Judah (the other half of the Church, Protestant) are his pleasant vine. He looked for justice, but found bloodshed; He looked for righteousness, but heard only cries of distress."

"Woe to you who join house to house, who add field to field, till no room remains and you are left to dwell alone in the midst of the land. Yahweh Sabaoth has sworn in my hearing: 'many houses will remain in ruins, beautiful mansions without occupants. Ten acres of vineyard will yield only a barrel of wine; ten bushels of seed only a bushel of grain.'

"Woe to those who rise early in the morning to run after strong drink, and tarry late in the evening till they are inflamed with wine. They have lyres and harps, timbrels and flutes, and wine at their banquets; but they have no thought for the deeds of the Lord, nor do they see what he is planning [*so many today brothers and sisters fall into this category. They are completely ignorant of God and his laws, and will be caught completely unprepared in the coming storm. They live their selfish lives thinking only of amusing themselves and following after their own selfish passions and desires, but have no knowledge of the tidal wave that is headed their way*].

"Thus my people, go into exile for want of understanding, their dignitaries dying of hunger, their masses parched with thirst. Therefore the grave has enlarged its throat and opened its mouth immeasurably; into it descend both masses and nobility, their throngs and their revelry. Man shall be humbled and the mortal fallen, and the eyes of the haughty cast down. But Yahweh Sabaoth (God of hosts) will be exalted when he comes in judgment (Christ); and the holy God will show himself holy in his righteousness. Then will the lambs graze as at pasture, fatlings and kids will browse among the ruins."

"Woe to those who draw iniquity with cords of deceit, to those who draw sin as with cart ropes, to those who say, 'Let God hurry, let him speed up his work so that we may see it. Let the plans of the Holy One of Israel draw near and come true so that we may know what they are.'"

"Woe to those who call evil good, and good evil [*this is basically the majority of the modern world today, that is currently being very heavily influenced by the hand of the enemy*]. Who put darkness for light and light for darkness; who put bitter for sweet and sweet for bitter. Woe to those who are wise in their own eyes and cunning in their own sight. Woe to those that are valiant in mixing drinks and heroes at drinking bouts, but acquit the guilty for a bribe and deprive the innocent of his right."

"There as the tongues of fire lick up stubble, as dry grass sinks down in the flames, so their roots will rot, and their flowers be blown away like dust, for they have rejected the law of Yahweh Lord of Host and scorned the Word of the Holy One of Israel."

"Therefore the Lord, his wrath burning against his people, raised his hand against them and struck them down. The mountains quaked; the corpses are like refuse in the streets. Yet for all this, his anger does not subside, his hand is still raised, ready to strike [*The Lord will exhaust his anger on the wicked people of the earth, and his anger will not easily be calmed*].

"He gives a signal to nations afar [*These are the nations that will come to be the rod that strikes the nations of his people. For he will strengthen their hand, and they will come from afar to do the Lords will, just like the two lions that were caught and trapped by the nations that came to subdue them, so too will these nations come to subdue modern day Judah and Israel, the modern day Judeo Christian nations. The current war on terror is only the beginning, and it will not be won*], he whistles to them from the ends of the earth; speedily and swiftly they come."

"None of them [the invading powers] is weary, none stumbles none slumbers or sleeps; not a waist belt is loosened, not a sandal-thong broken. Their arrows are sharp all their bows are strong; their horses' hooves seem like flint, their chariot wheels like the whirlwind. They roar like young lions; they growl as they seize their prey, no one to rescue it as they carry it off" [*the incoming enemy will be strong and resilient and nothing will stop his growing power. In Western Europe it will be one force that subdues it, in America it will be another. Let us recall, the proud, rebellious, wicked and disobedient will be humbled.*]

"On that day, they [*not the nations or peoples of God*] will roar over their prey like the roaring of the sea. Just look at the land-darkness and distress, the light flickering out in the shadows, darkened finally by the clouds."

Brothers and sisters, this concludes letters XXXI and XXXII, over which the Book of Isaiah, chapters one through five were interpreted for the coming years. I lay this on the table, and it is your option to discern and accept or reject the former. Just bear in mind the message I have relayed to you when world events begin to mold and shape themselves in ways most were not expecting. Let us be wise, and let us keep in mind that the prophets knew of both the First and the Second Covenant and the breaking of both, by God's people. His first of course were the Jews, the second includes all of us Christians today and tomorrow.

The message cannot be more clear my brothers and sisters, this is why I began writing these letters of preparation not only for my sake, but for any and all that will listen, not to what I have to say, but to what God calls us to be prepared for. I am merely the messenger. It is up to you to either accept or reject the message. I have done my part by presenting it to you; the rest is up to you.

Continue to pray, pray, and pray my brothers and sisters in Christ. Have faith and hope in he that died and shed his blood for us. He will not lead you astray, but will lighten your burden and comfort you when you feel you cannot go on. Call upon, and pray that the Holy Spirit give you eyes to see, ears to hear, and a heart to know, see, and hear the truth. For truly he is the way, the truth and the life, but we must accept this in full faith and confidence. We must not doubt. Be assured in Him, and He will raise you to everlasting life. Amen.

your brother Horacio.

Letter XXXIII-First Letter of Jeremiah

Good evening my brothers and sisters in Christ our Lord. I come to you all this evening, as has become customary now, with another message of preparation, on this twenty-fifth day on this eleventh month of the year. This is letter XXXIII in a series of XL. This letter is a continuation of the prophet's messages of preparation for all of us, of what's to come.

Let the Holy Spirit guide your thoughts, and your ability to understand, that which is not for all ears, eyes or hearts. For not all can eat hard food if they have just been born into life of being a Christian. They must first eat that which is soft, before they can eat that which is hard.

The food I am giving to you all this evening for your discerning minds is that which is hard, and therefore not palatable to all, not understood by all. But the message must still be delivered.

Tonight I will continue with the message as delivered through the prophet Jeremiah, another one of God's messengers that spoke to us all. Not just to the people of the First Covenant, but to those of the Second as well: to us Christians. Let us continue to keep this in mind as we read through Jeremiah, and later through the prophet Ezekiel.

We will begin in Jeremiah ch.2, where Yahweh, through Jeremiah, speaks and thinks through his prophet to his people. His first being the Jews through the First Covenant, and now to his people the Christians, through the Second Covenant.

"A word of Yahweh came to me, 'Go and shout this in the hearing of Jerusalem. This is Yahweh's word: I remember your kindness as a youth, the love of your bridal days, when you followed me in the wilderness, through a land not sown [*In the beginning God's people always start out with kindness and a humble heart, following those that have been designated as leaders through God. So too was Israel, as well as the early Christian Church. Here God almighty compares his people to that of a young, kind, loyal and faithful bride*]. **Israel was holy to Yahweh, the first fruits of his harvest. All who ate of it had to pay and misfor-**

tune fell on them, it is Yahweh who speaks *[to all those nations, or peoples that persecuted and oppressed God's people like the power of Egypt and the Jews in the First Covenant, or the power of Rome and the Christians. To those nations that took from his people, God took the power from them]*. **Hear the word of Yahweh, people of Jacob, all you families of the nation of Israel. What wrong did your fathers find in me that they strayed far from me? Why did they pursue what is worthless and become worthless themselves?** *[We are all people of Jacob my brothers and sisters. For if not for the Jewish people, we would not have had our Jewish saviour. Here the question God poses to all of us, is 'What wrong did your elders, or the leaders of the faith, find in me, that they strayed far from me?' This question has never been more relevant to the times we live in]*. **And they did not say, 'Where is Yahweh, who brought us out of Egypt and led us in the wilderness, through a land of deserts and pits, a land of drought and darkness, a land still untrodden and without inhabitants?** *[How quickly we forget the goodness that God appropriates to his people while they are young and helpless as nation. But once they mature, become disrespectful, arrogant, selfish, greedy, and proud]*. **I brought you to a fertile land to eat of the choicest fruit. As soon as you came you defiled my land and dishonored my heritage!** *[God always guides his people to fertile, open and choice lands because he wants the best for us. Just as he did for his First Covenant people, so too were Christians and Christianity brought into Western Europe, and later to the New World. But as soon as they arrived, they began defiling and dishonoring God's heritage]*. **The priest did not ask, 'Where is Yahweh?' The masters of my teaching did not know me; the pastors of my people betrayed me; the prophets followed worthless idols and spoke in the of Baal** *[The leaders of the faith, the ones who were supposed to keep and guard the Word of God, are the ones who have abandoned both his Word and He that is. Also, many follow worthless and meaningless desires and speak/act in a way that pleases the enemy and offends God today]*.

Therefore I contend with you-it is Yahweh who speaks-and I will contend with the sons of your sons! Cross to the coasts of Cyprus and see, or send to Kedar and observe with care if there has ever been such a thing! Has a nation exchanged its gods, false though they be? But my people have exchanged their Glory for what is worthless! *[Throughout history and throughout the world, many are the nations and cultures that revere and worship idols or animals, but even they are loyal to their gods, even though they may be false. But we as the people of the one true God, we the people that should know better, are often times found to be lagging in praise and worship of the one True God, behind other peoples and cultures who take their prayer and worship far more seriously, albeit misguided]*. **Be aghast at**

that, O heavens! Shudder, be utterly appalled-it is Yahweh who speaks-for my people have done two evils: they have forsaken me, the fountain of living water, to dig themselves leaking cisterns that hold no water! Did I make Israel a slave or was he born in bondage? How then did you become the spoil of others? The lions have roared against you, loudly indeed have they roared, making your country a wasteland, your cities a ruin without inhabitants. Even the Egyptians of Memphis and Tahpanhes have humbled you! Didn't you bring this on yourself, by forsaking Yahweh, your God, even as he led you in the way? *[The message here does not get more clear. As we saw in the last two letters in reference to Isaiah's message, so too here do we begin to see the message Jeremiah brings to us. God will allow this humbling to occur due to our forsakenness of his will and his precepts].* Your own wickedness chastises you and your unfaithfulness punishes you! Know, and see that it is bitter and evil to forsake Yahweh your God and no longer fear me-It is Yahweh, the God of hosts, who speaks! *[Many Christians today no longer fear God. Let us be reminded that to fear God also means to love and respect his ordinances and precepts, not just ask of him and expect of him without putting in our part.]*

Ch2:26-37 "As a thief is shamed when caught, so is the house of Israel, they, their kings, their princes, their priests and their prophets! To a tree they say: 'You are my father!' and to a stone: 'You gave me birth!' For they have turned their back on me instead of their face! In the day of misfortune they will call me: 'Rise and save us!' Where, then, are the gods of your own making? *[To nations and peoples that serve their financial, materialistic, and other interests in their hearts. Material things and possessions have taken the place of God and his worship and his interest. But on days of misfortune and upheaval, that's the day suddenly everyone becomes a believer and will run back to him. But God will ask, 'Where then are the gods of your making? Can't they save you?? There are no atheists in foxholes.]* Let them rise and save you if they can, in the time of your distress, for your gods, O Judah! Are as many as your cities. *[The cities of Judah, or modern day Judah, i.e. the Protestant/Evangelical nations, have and serve many gods. That's why Jeremiah compares them to their multiple cities. Most, primarily Protestant nations, are also very financially well off nations in the world today. The more they have economically, the more gods they have come to serve, whether they be money, material items, their own bodies and their bodies desires, i.e. sex, drugs and any other diversion or pleasure that pleases the flesh].* Why argue with me? You have all betrayed me-It is Yahweh who speaks. In vain did I strike your sons; they did not learn a lesson! And your sword, like a destroying lion devoured your prophets! All you of this generation, hear what Yahweh says: Have I been a desert for Israel, a land of darkness? Why do people say: We will depart from you and no more return to you?' Does a virgin forget her ornaments, or a bride her sash? But my people have forgotten me for days without number! How well you direct your steps in your search for lovers, even to walking along with crime! *[Here God inquires of us, what bad or wrong has he done to us, or to our nation that he deserves this treatment from us?? Does a bride forget and neglect the vestments she wore on her wedding day? Yet, we as people of God, have forgotten our groom. We neglect Him, after he has blessed us with so much. Whether it was land, health, good fortune, etc.]* Look at your garments stained with blood of the innocent poor, although you did not catch them breaking in! I know you say: 'I am innocent. Why does his anger not turn away from me?' I will accuse you: yes, you have sinned! How lightly do you change your way! You will be put to shame by Egypt as you were by Assyria. *[These will be powerful nations and peoples not open to the Word of God, but they will serve a purpose for Him. The purpose of being the rod that corrects the disobedient child. What nations in today's world are not Christian, but quickly gaining power and influence??].* You will also leave that place with your hands on your head, for Yahweh has rejected those you trust, and they will not help you!"

Ch3:11-18, "And Yahweh continued, 'Faithless Israel *[in Second Covenant context it refers to the Catholic peoples and nations]* has been less guilty than false Judah *[Protestant/Evangelical peoples and nations in Second Covenant context].* Go and shout this message to the north: Come back, unfaithful Israel-it is Yahweh who speaks-I will not let my anger fall on you for I am merciful, I will not be angry forever. *[The following is very important, because God is telling us he will not let his anger fall upon us, but we must do the following in order to be spared the rod of correction]* Only acknowledge your guilt; you have rebelled against Yahweh your God, and have scattered your favors among strangers under every green tree, and you have not obeyed my voice-it is the word of Yahweh *[it is so simple, yet so difficult for people to do. That being repenting of ones sins. This entails admitting ones guilt, asking for forgiveness, and changing ones ways. This is the only condition God ask of each and every one of us, and our nations as well. But I fear we as a people are far too stubborn and selfish even now, at the edge of destruction to admit our faults, our guilt and our sinful ways through a repentant and contrite heart.]*

"Come back faithless people-it is Yahweh who speaks-for I am you master. I will choose one from a city and two from a family and bring you to Zion. Then I will give you shepherds after my own heart, who will feed you with knowledge and prudence. And when you have increased and multiplied in the land in those days-it is Yahweh who speaks-men will no longer speak of the ark of the covenant of Yahweh; it will not be remembered or missed, nor shall it be made again! *[After we as a people, have repented and changed our ways, He that is, will once again be with us, and through his hands, select leaders in the faith that will be true, honest, humble and faithful leaders that will stand for God's intentions and not those of their own with arrogance, pride, neglect and selfish desires. We will no longer seek or be comforted by that which is only the external and material aspects of religion, but rather that which comes from inside.]* **Then they will call Jerusalem 'The Throne of Yahweh' and all the nations will gather there to honor the name of Yahweh and no longer will they follow the stubbornness of their evil hearts. In those days the people of Judah will unite with the people of Israel and together they will come back from the north to the land that I gave in heritage to their fathers.** *[Here my brothers and sisters is one of the most optimistic messages that the prophet foretells. For just as the literal Israel and Judah united and came together after so many years of being divided in the last century, so too does this apply to the current split in the Christian church between Catholics and Protestants in the Second Covenant context. But notice first how certain events must first take place, including the cleansing (unless repentance on a global scale occurs which is highly doubtful) before this uniting of the two Christian branches occurs. It will occur, just as it has been prophesied. Already we are seeing this occur throughout.]*

I do not know if we will see the uniting of both Christian branches in our lifetime brothers and sisters, but I do know that it will happen in the future, it is merely a matter of time. But both will unite together as a means of keeping the flame of Christianity lit during the coming years of darkness in which we will truly be dependent upon our brothers and sisters as never before. Our faith will be tested and many will fail for lack of it. This is why I come to you to prepare you all for the coming trials that will sway many and engulf the majority.

Letter XXXIV-Jeremiah's Second Message

Good evening brothers and sisters in our Lord Jesus Christ. I come to you all this evening on this twenty-eighth day of this eleventh month of the year, with another message of preparation for the coming years. This letter is a continuation of the message the prophet Jeremiah has for all of us today and tomorrow.

I pray that all of you are continuing your preparation, and more importantly continue to pray. Pray continuously and pray incessantly, as to tire God's ears from so much prayer. We must and shall continue to be the beacons that call and bring others to the truth. Let us stand up for what we believe in, and cease to be dormant doormats on societies front door. Let us be proud to be who we are, and who we proclaim to be followers of the one true God, through Jesus Christ, amen.

Ch4. **"If you return to me, O Israel-it is Yahweh who speaks-if you convert to me and put your monstrous idols out of my sight, you will have no need to hide from me; if you swear by Yahweh's life in truth, justice and honesty, then in him all nations will bless themselves and in him they will glory.** *[If we would just repent, as an individual, as a town, as a nation, as a world, and put away all that separates us and keeps us away from God, i.e. all that we convert into idols; our bodies, money, fame, power, etc, then we wouldn't have any need to hide from him or separate ourselves from knowing Him and having a true relationship with him. We see here a resemblance to what occurred in the Book of Genesis, when after Adam and Eve disobeyed, the first thing they did was not to come out and face God and admit to their guilt, but rather they hid; just like some many of us do today and have always done.]*

For thus says Yahweh to the people of Judah and Jerusalem *[reference to the two divisions of Christianity in Second Covenant context]* **break up deeply your fallow land and do not sow among the thorns. O men of Judah and Jerusalem! Circumcise yourselves for Yahweh and purify your hearts, lest my wrath spread like a fire that cannot be quenched because of the evil of your actions.** *[Here we are called to practice true circumcision of the heart, and not only practice the*

168

external act, but rather practice that which is internal. Just like in Christianity, many are baptized through the external and physical act of the pouring of the water, but how many truly practice internal baptism of the heart? Baptism replaced circumcision through the Second Covenant, as the sacramental act that make us children of God, but the act itself does not guarantee we will all do the work of God, nor be allowed to enter into his Kingdom.]

"Announce this in Judah, proclaim it in Jerusalem. Sound the trumpet through the land; cry aloud and say: Assemble and go to the fortified cities! Raise a standard towards Zion! Flee for safety, do not delay, for from the north I will bring evil and great disaster. *[Here Jeremiah announces to all what God is transmitting to him. Be ready nations of Christianity, regardless of denomination, sects, or creeds, the day is coming when God will allow the cleansing to begin.]*

"The lion has gone up from his thicket and a destroyer of nations has set out to make your country a wasteland and your cities a ruins without inhabitant! Because of this, wrap yourselves in sackcloth; lament and groan, for the fury of Yahweh's anger has not turned away from us. *[Brothers and sisters, here Jeremiah is very clear with his message. Just like Isaiah was, so too is Jeremiah very clear on the message that a destroyer of nations will be allowed to wreak havoc on the nations of God for their disobedience and rebelliousness to his Word. Also, that once this begins to occur, we should wrap ourselves in sackcloth and lament, meaning we should become humble and repent for the sinfulness of our deeds]*. In that day-it is Yahweh who speaks-the courage of the king and leaders will fail, the priests will be terrified and the prophets amazed. People will say, 'Ah! Lord Yahweh, you have truly deceived these people and Jerusalem, saying: 'You will have peace even as the sword is at our throat.' *[Just like it was then, so to now, do we have thousands of so called men and women of God telling us only what we want to hear, but this does not always benefit us. For if we are always only told the good, then how can we ever know what the bad is, so as to avoid doing that?? Or if we've done wrong, to know that we have done so, but learn not to do it again. But there are many men and women of God today, that only preach one side of God's nature, and therefore you get what we have an abundance of today; lost misguided and foolish people that think everything they do is pleasing to God, with no shame. Just as Jeremiah here alludes to the fact that they are always saying 'peace, peace,' everywhere, yet the sword is at our throats. Sound familiar to any people today?? That is why these false prophets, priests, kings and other leaders, will be so awe struck and dumbfounded, when they see God contradict the word of these charlatans.]* When the time comes it will be said to the people of Jerusalem: 'A hot wind from the heights in the desert is coming to the daughter of my people, not to winnow* or cleanse! A strong wind comes from there. *[This too could not be more clear. Where is it that the current war on terror is being fought? Where is it that Muslims for centuries have derived from? The hot wind that comes from the desert against the daughter of my people, are the Muslim forces coming against the Christian countries. Remember, the daughter of Judaism is always the Christian church, this was the off-spring, and today these are the forces at work.]* **A strong wind comes from there. See! Someone comes like the clouds, his chariots are like whirlwind, his horses swifter than eagles! Woe to us for we are ruined!** *[These are the forces of the Muslim invaders that will triumph against Gods people, because He that is will allow it.]*

"**Cleanse your hearts of every evil, Jerusalem, that you may be saved! How long will you nurse wicked thoughts within your breast?** *[The call is for repentance! Repent and be saved! Turn from your evil ways!]* **A voice comes from Dan and tells of disaster from Mount Ephraim! 'Give warning to the nations. Let all know in Jerusalem and Judah** *[again the two branches of Christianity]* **that enemies are coming from a distant land.' They surround Jerusalem like men guarding a field, because she rebelled against me-it is Yahweh who speaks.** *[Just like during the First Covenant sieges that were held against the walled city of Jerusalem, so too will the invaders surround the Second Covenant city symbolizing Jerusalem; the Vatican. The Vatican too is a walled off city, and is the visible and central head of the Church today.]* **Your own conduct and actions have brought this upon you. How bitter is your punishment and how it touches your heart because you rebelled against me!"**

"**I am in anguish! I tremble in the depths of my being; my heart beats wildly. I cannot remain silent for I hear the sound of the trumpet and the clamor of war!** *[Just like Jeremiah, I too cannot remain silent about what I see and know what is coming. This is precisely why I have taken upon myself to write this series of forty letters of preparation for all to be prepared for what is coming eventually. Something inside won't let me rest until this message is brought forth and to the light. Once there, it is up to people to accept or reject the message. I will have done my part.]* **Disaster after disaster; all the land is laid waste; my tents are suddenly destroyed and in a moment all that shelters me is gone. For how long must I see the standard raised and hear the sound of the trumpet?** *[All that provides security and protection will suddenly be gone and the ever continues sound of the trumpet of war continues with no end.]* **This happens because you are foolish and do not know me. You are wayward sons without intelligence, shrewd in doing evil, but not knowing how to do good! I looked at the earth and found it formless and void, and then at the sky but it was without light. I looked at** the mountains and they were quaking, and all the hills were swaying. I looked and saw that there were no people and that all the birds had fled. I looked and saw that the fruitful land was a desert and that all the towns were in ruins because of Yahweh and his anger. Yes, thus speaks Yahweh, 'The whole land may be desolate but I will not destroy it completely! This is why the earth shall mourn and the skies be darkened: because I have spoken and will not relent; it is my decision and I will not go back on it." *[Just as it was described in Isaiah, here too we see that God will allow for the destruction of his vineyard and his prized vines. His people and his nations, but here too we see the reference to his remnant that he will protect. He says, 'I will not destroy it completely!' There will be places and people that will be spared and protected during this great tribulation period here on earth, not in a raptured state.]*

"At the sound of the horseman and archer, every town takes flight; some go to the thickets and climb among the rocks. All the towns are deserted and no one is left. *[I can't help but reflect on something very similar that is found in Native American prophecy that states the same thing during this very same period. That being that all cities and towns will be deserted. This is also found in the Quatrains of Nostradamus.]* And you desolate one, what will you do? Even if you dress in scarlet and wear jewels of gold and put make-up on your eyes, in vain do you beautify yourself, for your admirers despise you and you are ready to take your life. *[What will these proud nations and people do once they have been humbled?? Even if they try and attempt to make themselves in vain to beautify themselves, they will do so to no avail].* For I hear a cry as a woman in labor, anguish as of one giving birth to a first child. It is the cry of the daughter of Zion *[the Church and its nations and peoples, Western Europe and America]*, gasping for breathe with outstretched hands: 'Woe is me! I am fainting away surrounded by murderers!"

Ch.5 "Go through the streets of Jerusalem; observe carefully and take note. Search throughout her squares to find, if you can, even one man who is honest and seeks the truth. Then I will pardon this city. Even though they say, 'As surely as Yahweh lives' their swearing is false.' *[Here we see something that is basically the same thing that happened right before God destroyed the cities of Sodom and Gomorrah. When He and Abraham exchanged a very similar dialog concerning the destruction of that city. Yahweh just wanted to find one decent, honest, obedient person, and he would spare it. But he didn't, and therefore the destruction ensued.]* Do not your eyes, Yahweh, look for truth? You struck them but they did not feel it; you crushed them but they refused correction. They set their faces harder than a rock and refused to repent."

"Then I thought: Only poor people are foolish, because they know nothing of the way of Yahweh or of the law of their God! So I will go to the cultured people and speak to them for they know Yahweh and the law of their God. But they too, have broken their yoke and burst their bonds!" *[People all across the cultural and socio-economic status levels have abandoned their relationship with God. Poor and wealthy, intelligent and slow. They are all ignorant of his laws and precepts that give eternal life.]*

"That is why the lion of the forest will slay them and the wolf from the desert will destroy them, while the leopard lurks around their cities. Whoever ventures out is torn to pieces, for great is their sin and their rebellions are without number! Why should I pardon you? Your sons have forsaken me and sworn by false gods. I gave them all they needed and yet they became adulterers trooping to the harlot's house. They are well-fed lusty stallions, each one neighing for his neighbor's wife. *[Let us reflect on the infidelity and the divorce rate throughout our country, as well as other industrialized nations as well. Seems the more we have, the more we want, in every sense of the word. Notice the words 'well fed lusty stallions,' not only are we well fed, well educated, well off, but we still want more, more and more, till our lusty filled hearts obtain never ending satisfaction.]* Shall I not severely punish them for that-it is Yahweh who speaks-should I not avenge myself on such a nation?"

"Go up, nations, through her vineyards and ravage them, and entirely destroy my vine. Tear away her branches for they are not Yahweh's. For truly the people of Judah and Israel *[both branches of Christianity]* have been utterly unfaithful to me-it is Yahweh who speaks. They have spoken falsely of Yahweh, saying, 'He does not exist; misfortunes will not come our way; we shall see neither the sword nor famine! As for the prophets, let the wind carry them. God doesn't speak to them. Let their threats fall upon themselves!" *[Here we clearly see modern age thinking in all its glory. 'He does not exist! Misfortunes will not come upon us! We won't be affected by wars, or famines or plagues! Let us reflect on the modern world and their beliefs and mindsets. Truly most people live as if there wasn't a God. They have all been fooled into thinking this through new age philosophy, science and even religion!]*

"But Yahweh the God of hosts speaks to me, 'because these people have said this, I will place words in your mouth which will be like fire, and these people will be the wood it devours."

"People of Israel *[the present Catholic, former Catholic Countries, mainly Western Europe]* against you I will bring a nation from afar-it is Yahweh who speaks-an invincible and ancient nation, whose language you do not know.

Their arrows sow death; they are valiant! They will devour your sons and daughters, devour your flocks and herds, devour your vines and fig trees. They will destroy with the sword the fortified cities in which you trust." *[This will come to pass, and is already in the initial phases. The foreign power here is Islam.]*

"But even in those days-it is Yahweh who speaks-I will not completely destroy them. *[The remnant on earth once again]*. And when they say, 'Why has Yahweh done all this to us??' You shall say, 'Just as you have forsaken me and served foreign gods (money, sex, drugs, material possessions) in your land, so shall you serve strangers in a land that is not your own.' *[Reference here is to being under control of the foreign or conquering power]*.

Declare this to the people of Jacob and make it known in Judah *[Protestant/Evangelical nations, U.S. included]*, saying, hear this, foolish and thoughtless people! Who have eyes and do not see, who have ears and do not hear! Do you not fear me? It is Yahweh who speaks-Will you not tremble in my presence? I who set the sand as a limit to the sea, and everlasting barrier it may never pass; its waves toss but cannot prevail; they roar but are unable to go beyond it."

"But these people whose heart is rebellious and stubborn, have turned aside and gone astray! They do not say in their hearts, 'Let us fear Yahweh our God who sends in season the spring rain and the autumn rain, and keeps for us weeks appointed for the harvest. Your crimes have put disorder in all this *[do any of the mixed up season, weather and climatic changes running rampant throughout the earth now sound familiar in reference to this disorder that we have caused???]* Your sins have deprived you of these blessings, for among my people are wicked men; they watch like fowlers and place snares, but it is men they catch. Like a cage full of birds, so are their houses full of booty. It has made them rich and powerful; they are fat and sleek. There is no limit to their evil; there is no justice in their judgment, for they do not uphold the rights of the orphan or plead the cause of the poor! Should I not severely punish them for such things? It is Yahweh who speaks-Will I not avenge myself on such a people? *[In a land where only the rich and powerful have a voice, how can the poor ever receive fair and honest representation? God's people throughout history have always been those with little or no voice. The defenseless, the poor, the innocent, the foreigner/immigrant. Do any of these groups have a voice today? If so, where does it come from?? Especially the innocent victims of abortion. Is God not in the right when he speaks of avenging and being the voice that speaks and acts for them?? He does, and he will. His justice is great!]* Something terrible and abomi-

nable has taken place in the land, prophets prophesy lies and priests teach
what pleases them, and my people like it to be so. But what will you do
soon? *[Here too, we see the similarities today, just as in Jeremiah's time. For today we
too have many priests and other ministers of God, that preach and teach what pleases
them, or their congregation, but who speaks for God? With today's multimember
churches, where thousands go to hear a syrupy, water downed message of God's Word.
They all preach a message for the masses, but is the message being preached shed light
on both the good and the bad?? Or just the good?]*

Letter XXXV-Jeremiah's Third Message

Good evening brothers and sisters in Christ on this twenty-first day of the twelfth month (2005). I come to you all once again with the continuation of the message the prophet Jeremiah has for us all today. I hope and pray that you and your families are all doing well this evening and that during this time of the year, we truly remember what it is this season truly symbolizes, and not just that which the corporate world has fooled so many into believing.

I come to you all my brothers and sisters in Christ as a humble servant to you all, and most importantly of the Lord our God. Let us continue to pray in full faith of the Spirit of God and that he lead us to full actualization of not only ourselves, but of He that is, and his will for us.

I will begin tonight's message where I left of with the last letter: In the Book of Jeremiah chapter six.

Ch.6 **"Sons of Benjamin! Seek safety beyond Jerusalem. Sound the trumpet in Tekoa, raise a signal in Beth-hacherem, for from the north comes misfortune and an immense disaster** [*the message is for all of us brothers and sisters living currently within his Second Covenant. Let us be prepared, for from the north shall come this disaster. The disaster here refers to the Muslim invaders that will pour into Western Europe. Most though, already live within these countries. Reinforcements to the Muslim rebellions in many Western European countries will pour into these countries.*] **Shall I not compare you, daughter of Zion, to a delicious pasture? Shepherds with their flocks are coming to her, pitching their tents around her, each one pasturing in his own part. Declare a Holy war against her, attack her at midday. Woe to us! For the day declines and the shadow of evening lengthens! Rise up in the night and destroy her palaces!** [*Here Daughter of Zion, or the Christian Church and/or Christian nations, is being compared to a delicious green pasture that is about to be devoured by shepherds and their flocks which are heading towards her. The holy war has already been declared my brothers and sisters, even as we speak, the echo of Jihad sounds through the voices of Muslim countries throughout the world. The years that are to come will be as if the day is*

175

declining into dusk, and the shadow of evening will lengthen. The years to come will be years of darkness and not of light. Hence the reason these letters, 31-38, are all being written in the evening. Let us be prepared. Jeremiah is warning us today.] **For Yahweh the God of hosts has spoken; Cut down trees and build a siege-ramp against Jerusalem, the city that is full of lies and oppression. Evil springs from her as water from a well. In her you hear only of violence and destruction, and my eyes continually see suffering and cruelty."** [*The cleansing will take part and affect most, if not all of Western Europe, and even the Church will suffer much during this purification.*]

"**Take warning, Jerusalem, lest I turn away from you and make you a desolation, a land without people. Yahweh said to me, "You shall glean thoroughly as a vine, what is left of Israel. You shall do what the gatherer of grapes does when his hand goes over the branches again."** [*Jerusalem then, and Jerusalem within the Second-Covenant context (the Vatican) will be cleansed and renewed as a result of this thorough gleaning. The hand of God will go over the branches once and again, until only the remnant remains.*]

"**To whom shall I speak? Who will listen, that they may understand? Their ears are closed and they pay no attention. They have only contempt for what Yahweh says and do not want to hear it."** [*Brothers and sisters, this was the question Jeremiah posed to all many years ago, and is posed to us today. 'To whom shall I speak? Who will listen? Who will understand?? I'm sure that even within some of you all, much less others out there that do not understand nor care to understand God's Word, this message is falling on deaf ears and blind eyes. For it is few that will understand and obey God's message to us, but many more that have contempt and apathy for what God says to us, and turn away from his message. Some will become believers when events begin to unfold in the coming years.*]

"**I am full of the anger of Yahweh and I can bear it no longer! Then pour it out on the children in the street and on the circle of young men, for the disaster will befall both husband and wife, both the elderly and those weighed down by years. Their houses will be passed to others, together with their fields and their wives, when I stretch out my hand over the people of the land-it is Yahweh who speaks. All of them-the least to the greatest-are greedy for gain; prophet and priest alike are deceitful. They treat lightly the disaster of my people saying, 'Peace, peace,' but there is no peace."** [*So too today in our modern so called civilized world are there many so called prophets, priests and ministers that are only concerned for their selfish gains and interests. So too today, are there leaders of both politics and religion that proclaim peace, and prosperity for*

their mindless flocks, and lead millions astray with these false notions, even as the
sword, famine and pestilence lie on the fringes of modern societies.]

"They should be ashamed of their abominable deeds. But they have no
shame and do not know how to blush. And so they will stumble and fall with
the others when I come to visit them-it is Yahweh who speaks. *[Many will
stumble and fall when he comes. He that is, will contradict with his mighty hand, all
those that are false leaders of nations and of the faith as well.]* This is what Yahweh
says to you, stand in the roads and look. Question the paths of former times.
Ask where the good way is and take it and find peace for you soul. But you
said, 'We will not take it.' Then Yahweh set sentinels over you: 'Pay attention to the sound of the horn! But you said, 'We will not listen.' *[Few today
ask and question, 'Where have the good ways gone to?' Where have all forms of moral-
ity, faith and decency disappeared to? Where has the family structure disappeared to?
Just as Jeremiah knew, so too do I know that many today will reject these former
times, ideals and beliefs. Most will not listen to these messages, because it will cause
them great discomfort and inconvenience to live or believe in these antiquated precepts
and notions. The sword is at our throats, yet so many still stubbornly refuse to listen
and much less repent and change their ways.]* Hear nations; know what will happen to them! Listen earth! I am bringing disaster on this people! It is the
fruit of their rebellion, because they paid no attention to what I said and
despised my law. *[To all nations, the message is clear. We shall, and have already
started to some extent, to bear and taste the fruit of our rebelliousness of God and his
Word. We all reap what we sow, and we are in for a major harvest from a land that
has sown nothing but sinful seed. What is to come will be the harvest of very bitter
fruit in the coming years.]* I have no use for incense from Sheba or for fragrant
cane from a distant land. Your burnt offerings are not acceptable to me nor
do I find your sacrifices pleasing. This is what Yahweh says, 'I will place
obstacles before this people to make them stumble, fathers and sons, neighbors and friends together. *[The obstacles will be in many forms. Whether financial, climactic, illnesses, famines, and/or wars, we will all be affected in some way or
another by the obstacles that will be placed. Burnt offerings here refer to the external
aspects and forms of worship in attempting to please God. God is pleased with internal
forms of praise and worship, not external ones that attempt to cover up all that is
dead/abominable inside.]*

It is Yahweh who speaks, 'See a people comes from the north, a powerful
nation from the ends of the earth. Armed with bow and spear, they are cruel
and pitiless. Their voice roars like the sea. Mounted on horses, in battle for-
mation they come like one man against you, daughter of Zion.' *[Here again*

we are shown a glimpse of these foreign powers that will be well armed, cruel and merciless. They will come, 'Like one man against you,' meaning they we be united and will attack as one against the daughter of Zion, or the Christian nations. Already we are seeing this occur. Russia, Iran and China have all brokered recent arms and energy deals that enable them to be dependent on one another and therefore need nothing from the West to advance their cause. They are becoming like one, all three, non Judeo-Christian countries are becoming like one man; united. In the next few months, we shall see this alliance become more and more visible. This will be key to the coming alliances of countries in the coming world war.]

When we heard this our hands went limp, anguish seized us like the pain of a woman in labor. Do not go to the fields or onto the roads, for the enemy's sword brings terror on every side. Daughter of my people! Wrap yourself in sackcloth and roll in ashes; prepare to mourn with bitter lament as for an only son, for the destroyer is coming against us. I have placed you as an inspector among my people, that you may examine them and know their ways.

They are all rebels and slanderers. They are like bronze and iron and all corrupt. The bellows blow to burn away the lead with fire, but the smelter works in vain for the evil elements remain. They are called 'refuse silver' for Yahweh has rejected them. *[The message here is crystal clear, with really no need for interpretation. The sword of the enemy will be almost impossible to escape. He is warning us of the bitter mourning and lament we will each endure at some level. We must prepare to humble ourselves as well as do acts of penance for our sins and seek mercy from God. God will reject this refuse silver, or fool's gold, because it is of no value. Intrinsically it has no worth, no matter how hard He seeks to find good/value in it, it has none. This refuse silver symbolizes so many today. They glitter and shine, but in the end will be thrown out as refuse, regardless of what so many today preach, that basically all will be saved (message of Universalism). This would be true, but only if true repentance occurs on a worldwide scale and in true genuine form.]*

Ch7 "These are the words spoken to Jeremiah by Yahweh, 'Take your stand at the gate of Yahweh's house and proclaim this in a loud voice: Listen to what Yahweh says, all you people of Judah who enter these gates to worship before Yahweh. Yahweh, the God of Israel says this; Amend your ways and your deeds and I will stay with you in this place. Do not count on empty words such as; 'Look, the temple of Yahweh! The temple of Yahweh! This is the temple of Yahweh!' *[To all of you my brothers and sisters in Christ, and to all that are currently not in Christ. The message then, now and tomorrow is to repent! Amend our ways! Let us change our thoughts, our words and our deeds! Let us not simply count on the running to the physical buildings that are the churches, or temples of God for safety and security, but instead let us be the temple that houses God and his Spirit for assurance and strength, and not merely on the physical buildings that can be destroyed.*] **Far better for you to amend your ways and act justly with all. Do not abuse the stranger, orphan or widow or shed innocent blood in this place or follow false gods to your own ruin. Then I will stay with you in this place, in the land I gave to your fathers in times past and forever.**

But you trust in deceptive and useless words. You steal, kill, take the wife of your neighbor, swear falsely, worship Baal and follow foreign gods who are not yours. And then after doing all these horrible things, you come and stand before me in this temple which houses my name and say, 'Now we are saved.' *[How many today do all that is offensive to God during the week, or months, or years, and then come to church and say to themselves, 'Ah, now I am saved.' Sound familiar in today's world?]* **Is this house on which rests my Name a cave of thieves?? I have seen this myself-it is Yahweh who speaks. Go to the sanctuary at Shiloh in Israel, where I first let my Name rest, and see what I did to it because of the wickedness of my people Israel.**

You have done all this and not listened when I repeatedly warned you. What I did in Shiloh, I will do to this temple which houses my Name, this holy place in which you trust and I gave to you and your ancestors. *[The punishments God has allowed/caused throughout history are quickly forgotten by people, and therefore reminders are in order to keep them in line. What he has done previously in other times, to other people, will be done once again. He will once again remind us who truly is in charge].* **As for you, I will drive you out of my sight, just as I cast out all your kinsmen of the north, the entire race of Ephraim.**

This is what Yahweh, the God of hosts says to you, 'Add your burnt offerings to your sacrifices and eat the flesh. When I brought your ancestors out of Egypt I did not command them concerning sacrifices and burnt offerings. One thing I did command them; Listen to my voice and I will be your God and you will be my people. Walk in the way I command you and all will be well with you. But they did not listen and paid no attention; they preferred to follow the inclination of their stubborn heart, and they turned away. *[The only thing God really wants of and from us, is simply that we listen to his voice, and walk in his precepts. This is all. It is so simple, yet so many of us choose not to do this most simple commandment. Why is it that we, his people, are always so stubborn, proud and rebellious?]*

Ch8:4 "This is what Yahweh told me, 'You will say to them: Doesn't the one who falls get up? And the one who goes away, doesn't he come back?

Why then do these people turn away in perpetual rebellion? They make a habit of deceit and refuse to repent. I listened attentively; they did not speak truthfully nor did they repent of their wickedness. No one says: 'What have I done!' They all follow their own course like horses plunging into battle. Even the stork in the sky knows her times; the dove, the swallow and the crane know the time to come back, but my people do not know Yahweh's ruling." *[Everything else in this world seems to know when to return, even the seasons of time always return at their appropriate time, but his people, his children, and the nations they make up, they do not. Not only do they not know when to return, but they constantly keep pushing the limits and boundaries and keep going further and further away from Him.]*

"How can you say: 'We are wise and the Law of Yahweh is with us' when the false pen of the scribe has turned it into a lie? [*Today, many so called leaders of the faith practice exactly this. They self-proclaim themselves wise teachers and leaders in the Laws of God, and continuously remind their flocks how God is always pleased with everything they do, but so many do not realize the false pens these scribes are using and misleading many with.*] The wise will be put to shame; they shall be dismayed and caught in a trap. Since they have despised the word of Yahweh, in what then lies their wisdom??

That is why I will give their wives to other men, their fields to conquerors, for all of them, the smallest to the greatest, are greedy for gain. All, from the prophet to the priest, practice deceit. They treat lightly the wound of my people saying 'Peace, Peace!' when there is no peace. *[It is interesting to note here, how in the Virgin Mary's apparitions throughout the past two centuries, she too predicted and correctly foretold that the day would come when priest would oppose priest and bishop would oppose bishop. (The following is from the Virgin Mary's message from Akita (1968, Japan), "The work of the devil will infiltrate even into the Church in such a way that one will see cardinals opposing cardinals, bishops against bishops. The priests who venerate me will be scorned and opposed by their confreres … churches and altars sacked; the Church will be full of those who accept compromises and the demon will press many priests and consecrated souls to leave the service of the Lord."*][1].

Not all men that wear long robes are men of God. The enemy has been very successful in infiltrating the church over the past centuries and is currently very active even as we speak within it. Hence the reason priest would oppose priest and bishop would oppose bishop. One is with the truth, the other with lies and falsehoods. One is with

---

1.   http://www.ewtn.com/library/MARY/AKITA.HTM

humility and the spirit of servitude, the other with pride and arrogance. We are currently seeing this today.] **Are they ashamed of their detestable conduct? They have no shame and do not know how to blush. That is why they will stumble and fall along with the others, when I punish them. I will finish them-it is Yahweh who speaks-for the vine has no grapes, the fig tree no figs, even the leaves are withered. I will hand them over to the passerby. Why do we sit still? Get up! We shall go to the fortified cities to die there. See, Yahweh our God wants us to die and gives us poisoned water, because we have sinned against him.** *[Let us recall that the three main sources for the cleansing will stem from the sword, or wars, pestilence, or diseases, and famine, or the lack of clean potable water. Throughout most of the earth, even here within our country, pure/clean drinking water is quickly becoming a scarce resource, and will be more so in the near future. Contamination of our water supply is also at the root of this current problem and will continue to be. In Chapter9:14, the following regarding our food and water supply is also written,* **"That is why Yahweh, the God of hosts and the God of Israel says, 'I will make this people eat bitter food and I will give them poisoned water. I will scatter them among nations that neither they nor their fathers knew and I will send the sword after them until I have finished with them.'**] **We hoped for peace, but he gave us nothing good! For a time of healing, but terror came! From Dan we hear the snorting of his horses; at the sound of the neighing of his steeds the earth quakes.**

They will come and devour the land and all it contains, the city and all who inhabit it. For I am letting loose against you snakes and adders that cannot be charmed, and they will bite you.

Sorrow takes hold of me, my heart fails me. They cry for help from the daughter of my people *(the Christian countries)* **is heard all over the land: Is Yahweh no longer in Zion? Is her king no longer there?** *[People will call out to God in fear and in terror, but they will ask, is God no longer with us? Does he no longer hear our calls for help?? Why has God allowed such things to happen?? We will all reap what has been sown. It is the fruit of our world's iniquity. This is why now is the time to repent! And be well with God!]*

The harvest is over, summer has gone and we have not been saved. I am torn because of the wound of the daughter of my people. I am crushed and dismayed. Is there no balm in Gilead? Is there no healer there? Why is no remedy given to the daughter of my people? I would that my head were a well of water and my eyes a fountain of tears to weep day and night for the slain daughter of my people." *[Jeremiah is torn and heart broken for what will* *become of God's nations and peoples. He attempts to warn, but few listen. He attempts to show, but few see.]*

Brothers and sisters in Christ, awaken from your slumbers and call to your brothers and sisters, and relay the message to them as well. Let us pray and ask for strength and guidance for the coming times. This will not all happen at once, but over the course of the next fifteen to thirty years, will see these and many other events unfold right before our eyes. Have faith in the Lord our God, and pray for mercy and forgiveness of sins on a worldwide scale.

Letter XXXVI-Ezekiel's First Letter

Good evening brothers and sisters in Christ on this second day of the first month of this New Year in two thousand and six. I come to you in peace and great hope to you all this evening my brothers and sisters, and pray that you all have been continuing your path of preparedness for the coming years.

I realize that the past few letters have been wrapped with a very strong message, but it is one I know and feel must be shouted from the rooftops to elicit a spirit of awareness and awakedness of what it is we as a global community are on the fringe of experiencing.

We must continue to pray brothers and sisters for the forgiveness of sins and for the conversion and repentance of sinners throughout. Let us continue to be strengthened by the Holy Spirit and allow him to come and work through us to help aid in the conversion of others.

Tonight I will continue with the message of the prophets with that of the prophet Ezekiel. He too was called by God to warn not only the First Covenant peoples, but the Second Covenant peoples as well. Ezekiel receives his mission from God almighty and begins the process of warning God's stubborn people, including our world today.

Ch2 "He said to me, 'Son of Man, stand up for I am about to speak to you.' A spirit came upon me as he spoke and kept me standing and then I heard him speak, 'Son of man, I am sending you to the Israelites, to a people who have rebelled against me; they and their fathers have sinned against me to this day. Now I am sending you to these defiant and stubborn people to tell them, 'this is the Lord Yahweh's word.' So, whether they listen or not, this set of rebels will know there is a prophet among them. But you, son of man do not fear them or what they say, for they will be as thorns for you and you will be sitting on a nest of scorpions. Don't be afraid of their words when you are facing this set of rebels. Tell them what I say whether they choose to listen or not, for they are rebels. Listen then, son of man, to what I say and don't be a rebel among rebels. Open you mouth and take what I'm

about to say. *[Here God, through the Holy Spirit, delivers to Ezekiel his mission and reassures him. Throughout the Bible we see countless examples of God's messengers being sent to deliver messages and teachings to his people, whether through the First Covenant, or even now, through the Second Covenant, but people have always rejected, renounced, persecuted or killed His messengers. Those that seek the truth and speak the truth are a nuisance to those who prefer to live in darkness and speak lies or live in half-truths. God reassures Ezekiel and lets him know that this will not be an easy task, for they will be as "Thorns for you and you will be sitting on a nest of scorpions." But even so, God will strengthen his messenger, and tells him not to be afraid of their words. For many will be the highly intellectual, full of knowledge types that will attack Ezekiel and will question his authority to speak on God's behalf, but God will give him what to say through the Holy Spirit, just as he did with Jesus and later with the apostles; who were also reassured by Jesus that when the time came, they would be inspired and influenced through the Holy Spirit to know just what to say/do. So too here, do we see the same assurance by God to his prophet. It always seems that throughout history, God has always utilized the humble, modest, meek and poor to speak against those that carry the full weight of knowledge of the law on their heads like a crown of laurels, and sit in the highest places power protected by the walls (both literal and symbolic) that have been erected to distance themselves and the people they took oaths to protect and serve! Whether it was the prophets, the apostles, the Saints and even Jesus, the World's educated and seemingly knowledgeable, but not wise, have always questioned, ridiculed, and persecuted the men and women God has called upon to deliver his message. But even though the world and mankind has always tried to silence them and their message (like that of Fatima today) God always reassures them, and through the Holy Spirit, gives them the wisdom and the strength to persevere among the symbolic thorns and the scorpions. It has always seemed that the more knowledge certain individuals accumulate, the more methods they seem to come up with ways to veer around, deviate from, and circumvent not only God's Laws, but society's as well. Since knowledge is power, they in effect consider themselves the powerful intellectual elites that always seem to find a reason/motive for doing the evil that they do, and attempt to legitimize it not only to themselves and others, but even to God!]*

"I looked and saw a hand stretched out in front of me holding a scroll. He unrolled it before me; on both sides were written lamentations, groanings and woes."

Ch3 "He said to me, 'Son of man, eat what is given to you. Eat this scroll and then go; speak to the people of Israel.' I opened my mouth and he made me eat the scroll and then he said to me, 'Eat and fill yourself with this scroll that I'm giving you.' I ate it and it tasted as sweet as honey. *[The eating of the scroll here symbolizes the total acceptance and devotion with which Ezekiel takes and accepts his mission. 'It tasted as sweet as honey.' Ezekiel will not feel torn between the sufferings of the people on the one hand, and the Will of God on the other. A similar example is found in the Book of Revelation, when St. John receives his mission.]* **He said, 'Son of man, go to the Israelites; speak to them with my words. Indeed it is not a people with a difficult foreign language to whom you are sent; it is to the people of Israel. It's not to the many nations with difficult and obscure languages which you cannot understand. If I sent you to them, they would listen to you.** *[The message of God to Ezekiel here is one similar that which Jesus spoke of as well. That a prophet or any other messenger of God is usually rejected by his own family, peoples and/or nations. Often times, such was the case with St. Paul. It is usually those of different nations and different tongues that accept God's message and messenger far more readily and openly, than their own.]* **But the Israelites will not listen to you because they are not willing to listen to me; all of them are defiant and stubborn of heart. See, I am making your face as unyielding as theirs and your forehead as hard as theirs.** *[Ezekiel will be as unyielding and as thick-skinned as the people he will do battle against, in order to be resilient and persevere with God's message.]* **I am making your forehead as hard as a diamond, harder than flint; so you shall not fear or tremble because of this set of rebels.**

Ch3:16"**After seven days the word of Yahweh came to me, 'Son of man, I have made you a watchman for the House of Israel. With the word you hear from my mouth you will warn them in my name. When I say to the wicked, 'You will surely die,' if you do not speak to warn the wicked man to give up his evil ways and so live, he shall die for his sin, and I will hold you responsible for his death. But if you have warned the wicked man and he has not given up his wickedness and evil ways, he shall die for his sins, but you will save yourself.** *[The message then, as it is tonight is the same my brothers and sisters. Repent and become converted in Jesus Christ our Lord and savior. The prophet spoke to warn out of fear for his own salvation. For God warns him, just like he does us, 'If you do not help those that are lost, when it is within your power to do so, not only will the lost be judged harshly, but so shall you.']* **When the righteous man turns from what is good to do evil, I shall put an obstacle in his path: he shall die. Since you did not warn him, he will die for his sin. His good deeds will not be remembered and I shall hold you responsible for his death. But when you have warned the righteous man to keep him from sinning and he has not sinned, he will live for sure for he was warned and you will save your life.**

[Here God once again reminds us that we in effect and in truth, are our brothers keeper. How often do we attempt to steer those headed in the wrong direction back onto the right path? Whether young or old, male or female, we should help lead them by example and through prayer, not through force or coercion, like so many fundamental groups try so often to do. Also, God reminds us, that even a righteous person can be lost to sin and die both physically and spiritually, and vice-versa, a repentant sinner can in the end find true and everlasting life. Just as Jesus said, "The first shall be last, and the last shall be first."]

Ch5 **"Son of man, take a sharp sword and use it as a barber's razor on your head and beard. Then take scales and divide the hair you have cut off. Burn a third of it in the middle of the city at the end of the siege, then take a third that you will strike with the sword all around the city; finally scatter a third in the wind and unsheathe a sword and pursue them. Take a few strands of hair and tuck them away in the folds of your clothes; then throw some of them to burn in the fire. Then speak against all Israel: This is what the Lord Yahweh said: That is Jerusalem! I placed her in the midst of the nations surrounded by other countries; she rebelled against my laws and my precepts more than neighboring nations. In fact, she rejected my laws and did not keep my decrees.**

That is why the Lord Yahweh speaks thus: Your rebellion is greater than that of the nations around you-you have not kept my laws, respected my decrees or observed my ordinances but instead have conformed to the laws of neighboring nations—because of that the Lord Yahweh speaks thus: I too have set myself against you. I will pass judgment on you in the sight of the nations, and because of your abominations, I will punish you in a way I have never before done and never will do in the future. That is why fathers among you will eat their children and children their fathers. I will pass judgment on you and scatter your remnant to every wind. *[Here, just like in the previous two prophets, God almighty is once again charging his people with not obeying his laws and decrees, and the punishment for this will be as follows.]*

Therefore, as surely as I live, declares the Lord Yahweh, because you have defiled my sanctuary with all your horrors and abominations, I will strike you without pity! I too will show no mercy!

A third of your people will die of the plague or starve within your walls, a third will fall by the sword outside the city, a third I will scatter to the winds and pursue them with sword unsheathed. *[This part of the text is vital for the following reasons. First of all, this is the symbolic meaning of the hair which Yahweh made Ezekiel cut. One-third will die of famine or pestilence, One-third will die by the* sword or warfare, and one-third will be scattered and living in exile, but even there, they will be followed by an unsheathed sword. Let us also recall what is written in the Book of Revelation. In chapters 8-9, we see basically the same message. In Revelation8:7, **"When the first angel blew his trumpet, there came hail and fire, mixed with blood, which fell on the earth, and a third of the earth was burned up, with a third of the trees and green grass. When the second angel blew his trumpet, something like a great mountain was thrown into the sea, and a third of the sea was turned into blood. At once, a third of the living creatures in the sea died and a third of the ships perished. When the third angel sounded his trumpet, a great star fell from heaven, like a ball of fire, on a third of the rivers and springs. The star is called Wormwood, and a third of the waters were turned into wormwood and many people died because of the water which had turned bitter."** *The messages of Fatima, as well as other apparitions, (through Mary for our Protestant/Evangelical brothers and sisters), also resemble and confirm this dark message. She too talks about massive punishment for the sins of a rebellious world; but also affirms that a small remnant, just as Jesus affirms in the Gospel, will be saved to promote God's message and complete loyalty and love to him, just as the few strands of hair that were tucked away by Ezekiel, which symbolize the chosen few that will be left as a remnant.]* **My anger will spend itself, my fury against them be satisfied. I will have my revenge and they will know that I, Yahweh, have spoken in my jealousy when I have exhausted my fury against them. I will make you a heap of ruins, a reproach among the neighboring nations in the eyes of all who pass by. You will be a reproach, a taunt, a lesson, a warning and an object of horror for the nations near you when, with anger, wrath and stinging reproach, I punish you. I, Yahweh, have spoken. When I send you the deadly arrows of starvation to do away with you and blot you out, I will make you lack all food. Hunger and wild beasts will destroy your children, while the sword and plague will visit you. It is Yahweh, who has spoken.**

Letter XXXVII-Ezekiel's Second Letter

Good evening brothers and sisters in Christ, on this evening of third day of the first month of this year two thousand and six. May the peace and love of the Lord be with you and all your family and friends. Tonight, I continue with this second letter of the prophet Ezekiel and his message to us.

Ch6 **"The Word of Yahweh came to me as follows, 'Son of man, look towards the mountains of Israel and prophesy against them; say to them: Mountains of Israel, listen to the word of Yahweh! To the mountains and hills, to the rivers and valleys the Lord Yahweh has spoken: I am going to bring the sword against you and destroy your high places. Your alters will be become desolate, your incense burners smashed; I will lay your corpses in front of your idols and scatter your bones around your altars.** *[Brothers and sisters, as hard as they may sound to some of you, these messages are directed at the Israel of the New or Second Covenant. This of course being the nations of the Christian Church and its' hierarchical power structures, and all the proud, boastful, shepherds that are no longer concerned for the welfare of their flock, but are only taken up by what benefits them and their motives and/or intentions.]*

Wherever you live, the towns will be in ruins and the high places desolate, your altars demolished and defiled, your filthy idols smashed and ruined, your incense burners knocked all around you and you will know that I am Yahweh. But I shall spare some of you. They will escape the sword and be scattered among the nations. Your survivors then will remember me among the people where they are exiled, for I shall break the adulterous hearts of those whose eyes lusted after their idols *[all that we desire and seek after in the deepest recesses of our hearts. Whether it is material, flesh, or spiritual]*. **They will loathe themselves for the evil they committed, for all their abominations. And they will know that I, Yahweh, have not spoken in vain in saying I would inflict disaster upon them.**

"This is what the Lord Yahweh said, 'Clap your hands, stamp your feet and say and say: Well done! When the people of Israel are falling by the

sword, famine and plague because of their abominations. He who is far away will die of the plague, he who is near will fall by the sword, whoever survives and is spared will die of starvation. Against them I will exhaust my fury! And you will know that I am Yahweh when their people lie slain in the midst of their idols, around their altars, on every high hill, on the mountain tops, under every green tree and spreading oak and whenever they offered fragrant incense to all their idols. I will make their country a desolate wasteland from the desert to Riblah, wherever they live; and they will know that I am Yahweh.'

Ch7 "This Word of Yahweh came to me, 'And you, son of man, listen to what the Lord says to Israel: Finished! The end is coming for the four corners of the land. It is all over for you. I am unleashing my anger against you. I will judge you according to your ways and repay you for all your filthy practices. I will not look on you with pity; I will be merciless. I will bring against you what is fitting for your conduct and your detestable practices and you will know it is Yahweh striking you.

Thus says the Lord Yahweh: Disaster! Disaster is coming! The end is near! It is your turn, you who live in the country. The time has come, the day is near! No joy, only panic on the mountains! Now I am unleashing my fury against you; my anger will exhaust itself on you. I will judge you according to your conduct and call you o account for your detestable practices. I will not look on you with pity and I will show you no mercy. I will give you what your conduct deserves. And you will know that I am Yahweh when I strike you for your abominable practices. *[Again, here we see and read the message the Lord is relaying to us through his prophet Ezekiel. It is the same message that Isaiah and Jeremiah as we have already read, bring to us as well. To all of us, not just some.]* This is the day, the end is coming, the die is cast. For insolence has blossomed, pride bears its fruits and violence reigns. No one will escape. *[Let us be prepared my brothers and sisters with all our hearts and all our souls.]*

The time has come, the day is here! Let not the buyer rejoice or the seller regret, for the punishment will fall upon all. The seller will not get back what he has sold, even though he survives, for the sentence regarding the multitude will not be reversed. They may sound the trumpet, make preparations, but no one will go to battle, for I am indignant with all. Outside in the open is the sword; plague and starvation in the houses. Those in the country will die by the sword, those in the city will be victims of famine and plague. *[This particular point is also made in Native American[1] Prophecy; in reference to the vision that great stone villages (cities) will be left desolate due to great famine and plagues.*] **Those who escape will go to the mountains; they will be like doves, each one moaning because of his sin.**

Every hand will be limp, every knee as weak as water; they will put on sackcloth and shudder. All will be covered with shame and every head bald. They will throw their silver in the streets and their gold will be dropped like filth. Silver or gold will not save them on the day of Yahweh's anger. It will be useless to satisfy their hunger and to fill their stomachs, for it was their stumbling block, the cause of their sin. They became proud of their splendid jewel, but they put into it their loathsome images and idols; that is why I will make foreigners and as booty to the most wicked of the land, and they will defile it. I will take away my protection from them and people will profane my treasure. *[God himself is acknowledging that He will allow the profaning of his treasure, the Church and its people; Christians! Not only this, but He is constantly letting us know exactly why He will do this, so that there will be no question as to why?]* **Robbers will enter and desecrate it and within it there will be massacres, for the land is full of violence.**

I will bring the most cruel of the nations to take possession of their houses. I will break the pride of the violent and their sanctuaries will be profaned.

Anguish is coming; they will seek peace but there will be none. Disaster will follow disaster, rumor will follow rumor. In vain will they demand a vision from the prophet. The PRIEST will have no answer; the elders will be unable to advise. The king will mourn; the princes will be overcome with grief, and the hands of the citizens will tremble. *[Neither the clergy, nor the politicians throughout the land will have the answers, because the majority are blind and deaf to the truth and only pursue that in which they can indulge in; power, money, fame, etc. Citizens throughout will tremble when they see what approaches.]* **I will treat them as their conduct deserves and judge them according to their deeds, and they will know that I am Yahweh.**

Ch9 Then he shouted loudly in my ears saying, 'The punishment of the city is near; see each one of these has in his hand his instrument of destruction.' And six men came from the direction of the upper gate which faces north, each one with his instrument of destruction. With them was a man clothed in linen with writing material at his side. They came and stopped near the altar of bronze. *[Here we clearly see the image of Christ accompanied by these other men, or perhaps helpers or angles, similar to the vision in Revelation chap-*

---

1.   Waters, Frank. <u>Book of the Hopi</u> New York: Penguin Books Publishing, 1963.

ters 6-10. The man clothed in white linen is none other than Jesus himself and he is described as having writing material by his side, or in other words, the Book of Life, just as it is described by St. John in the Book of Revelation. Yet Ezekiel wrote this circa 599-590 b.c., almost six hundred years before Christ. In Rev10:6, the following confirms that the full message of the prophets will be fulfilled during this coming period. The message of these Old Testament prophets has not been completed, but will in the coming times. "He said, 'There is no more delay; as soon as the trumpet call of the seventh angel is heard, the mysterious plan of God will be fulfilled according to the good news he proclaimed through his servants the prophets."

Then the Glory of the God of Israel rose from the cherubim where it rested and went to the threshold of the house. Yahweh called to the man clothed in linen who had the material for writing at his side, and he said to him, "Pass through the center of the city, through Jerusalem *[both in literal sense and symbolic sense in relation to the Second Covenant Jerusalem]*, and trace a cross on the forehead of the men who sigh and groan because of all the abominations committed in it. *[God the Father here gives authority to the Son to go through and mark the foreheads of all who fear, know and do the Will of God. Let us also see this reference in Rev7:3,* "Do not harm the earth or the sea or the trees until we have sealed the servants of our God upon their foreheads. *Here again, we see that the prophet's message coincides with the end of times book of Revelation. If we read a little further in Rev7:9, we read the following,* "After this, I saw a great crowd, impossible to count, from every nation, race, people and tongue, standing before the throne of the Lamb, clothed in white, with palm branches in their hands." *Jesus, throughout Revelation is always described as wearing white linen, and carries with him the Book of Life, in which he writes all the names that will be saved.]*

I heard him say to the others, 'Now you may pass through the city after him and strike. Your eyes shall not look with pity; show no mercy! Do away with them all—old men, young men, virgins, children and women—but do not touch anyone marked with a cross.' *[God the Father relays the message to those accompanying God the Son, to go through and destroy men, women and children of all ages, BUT to NOT harm those with the seal/mark on the forehead. It is interesting to note here, how we as Catholics are also marked with this cross on the forehead at Baptism, and there after during the start of Lent, on Ash Wednesday every year.]* And as they were told to begin with the sanctuary, they struck the elders who were in front of the Temple. *[God the Father here actually tells the men accompanying Jesus, or the man dressed in white linen, to begin the cleansing, with the elders in the Temple or sanctuary. This message does not bode well for those in the upper hierarchy of the church today, in the modern day temple, of the modern day Second Covenant Jerusalem.*] **Yahweh said to them, 'Let the courts be filled with the slain and the Temple be defiled with their blood; go out!' They went and slew the people in the city. It happened that while they were slaying the people, I was alone (referring to Ezekiel). I fell on my face and cried out saying, 'Ah, Lord Yahweh! Are you going to destroy all that is left of Israel, and unleash your fury against Jerusalem?' He said to me, 'The sin of Israel and Judah** *(both the Catholic and Protestant nations)* **is very great; the land is filled with blood and the city full of perversion. For they say, 'Yahweh has forsaken the land; Yahweh does not see. I too will be without pity; I will show no mercy and I will bring their deeds upon their heads.' Then the man clothed in linen who brought the writing kit reported, 'I have done what you ordered."**

[*Here Jesus, or the man dressed in white linen, reports back to God the Father, and relays to him that he has done what has been ordered of him.*]

Letter XXXVIII-Ezekiel's Third Letter

Good evening once again brothers and sisters in our Lord Christ. I come to you this evening of the ninth day of this first month, on this two thousand and sixth year. May God's blessings descend upon you and your families today, tomorrow, and always.

I truly hope that your preparation has been going well, and pray that this may be the case. I too ask for your prayers and ask that you keep me always in your thoughts and prayers, as I too do the same for you all.

Tonight's message is a continuation of the book of Ezekiel and will start off in chapter 12.

Ch.12 **"This word of Yahweh came to me, "Son of man, you live in the midst of a house of rebels: they have eyes for seeing but do not see; they have ears for hearing but do not hear, for they are a house of rebels. Because of this son of man, prepare for yourself and exile's baggage and leave by day in their sight as an exile does; and go as an exile to another place in their sight. Would that they may understand, because they are a house of rebels. You will gather your things, an exile's baggage, by day to be seen by them, and you will leave in the evening in their sight as for a departure of deportees. While they look on, dig a hole in the wall and leave from there. As they look on, shoulder your baggage and leave in the dark. Veil your face and do not look at the land for I have made you a sign for Israel.** *[The message of God to Ezekiel is that he should he should demonstrate to them, by portraying himself as an exile, the future that each and every citizen in that city faces; that of they themselves becoming an exile. Where they too will have to leave their homes and security, for that of the unknown and foreign due to the invading forces that will cause many to flee.]*

I did as I was ordered, gathering my things by day, an exile's baggage, and in the evening I made a hole in the wall with my hand. I left in the dark, in their presence, shouldering my baggage. In the morning the word of Yahweh came to me: 'Son of man, did not the Israelites, these rebels, ask you, 'What are you doing there?' Answer them on behalf of the Lord Yahweh: This ora-

cle concerns the prince in Jerusalem and all the Israelites remaining in the city. Say, 'I am a sign for you,' for what I have done will happen to them: They will be deported, exiled. The prince among them shall shoulder his baggage in the dark and depart. They will dig a hole in the wall to let him leave by it. He will cover his face because he must not see the land with his eyes. I will spread my net over him and he will bee caught in its mesh. I will bring him to Babylon in the country of the Chaldeans, but he will not see it and it is there that he will die. *[Let all those who have eyes see what this means, and all those who have ears, hear what the message here is. This passage refers to the prince of Jerusalem. Both in literal sense and symbolic as well. For them and for us today. Look also in what St. Malachi[1] wrote about the last pope on a list of 112 popes, written by him, in 1139 a.d.]* As for all those who form his court, his guard, his troops, I will scatter them to the winds and pursue them with the sword. They will know I am Yahweh when I scatter them among the nations and disperse them in other countries. I will however allow a small number of them to escape the sword, famine and pestilence so they may confess their abominations among the nations where they will go and they will know I am Yahweh.

Is it not a false vision you have seen? Have you not uttered lying divinations? You say; Oracle of Yahweh when I have not spoken. But this is what Yahweh says: Because of your false and lying revelations I will oppose you, word of Lord Yahweh. My hand will strike the prophets whose revelations are delusions, whose predictions are lies. They will not be accepted among my people's assembly nor will they be inscribed in the register of the nation of Israel. They will not re-enter the land of Israel-and you will know that I am the Lord Yahweh. These prophets have misled my people saying 'Peace!' where there is no peace. The people build a wall and these prophets daub it with whitewash; but say to those who daub it with whitewash: The wall will fall. I will send torrential rain, huge hailstones and stormy winds and see: the wall will fall! Will they not say to you: Where is the whitewash with which you daubed it? *[Similar today, where thousands of Christian ministers, preachers, and other leaders of the faith are preaching a message of 'Universalism,' or basically a message where all are saved. Everyone is perfect, and everyone is good, and everyone is going to receive a reward in the end, without ever having worked for it. If all are saved, then what's the point in even trying to do the will and work of God?? Because after all, all are saved and all are good, so in that case, I suppose no one is*

---

1.   http://www.catholicplanet.com/future/future-popes.htm.

going to receive any punishment. This is the dangerous message that is currently being floated out there my brothers and sisters, and it is one that that basically says, 'As long as you believe in God, then you are saved.' I'm sorry to disappoint, but just believing in He that is, will not get you into paradise. For even the devil believes in God, but that doesn't mean he does the will of the Father, nor does it mean he will ever be saved. Jesus himself said that most would take the wide and easy road/path, but very few would take the narrow and difficult path, but you would never hear that being preached today, because it might offend someone. Just as it is written in Ezekiel13:10, "The people are building a wall and these prophets daub it with whitewash." This is exactly what is happening today in so many congregations, both Catholic and Protestant.]

That is why the Lord Yahweh speaks thus: In my fury I will make a violent wind break out and in my anger I will send a torrential down pour, and my wrath will hurl destructive hailstones. I will destroy the wall you daubed with whitewash; I will level it to the ground and its foundation will be laid bare. It will fall and beneath it you will be utterly destroyed and you will know that I am Yahweh. I will exhaust my anger against the wall and against those who daubed it with whitewash. Then they will say to you: Where is the wall and where are those that whitewashed it, the prophets of Israel who prophesied to Jerusalem and who had visions of peace when there was no peace? *[This is directed exactly to all those that help build that wall of confusion, and was whitewashed/painted with false preaching's, teachings and messages from these religious leaders.]*

Ch15. The word of Yahweh came to me, 'Son of man, in what way is the wood of the vine superior to that of any other tree in the forest? Do they take its wood to make anything? Do they use it to make a peg for hanging a tool? But now they have used it as fuel and the fire has burned it at both ends leaving the middle charred. Is it then of any use? If it was of no use when it was whole, of even less use will it be when burnt in the fire. That is why Lord Yahweh speaks thus, 'I took the vine from among all the trees of the forest, and I gave it to the fire to be burned. This is how I have just dealt with those living in Jerusalem. I will turn my face against them. Though they escaped from the fire, the fire will burn them and you will know that I am Yahweh when I turn against them. I will make the land a desolation because they have unfaithful'-word of Yahweh. *[Here Ezekiel, just like Isaiah, compares God's church and the world as a vine that has become useless and therefore must be burned. It is also interesting to note how St. Peter, in 2nd Peter3:6, also concludes the same outcome of what is to be,* **'by the same word of God, this world perished in the** *flood. Likewise, the Word of God maintains the present heavens and earth (God's Vine/Vineyard) until their destruction by fire; they are kept for the Day of Judgment when the godless will be destroyed. Do not forget, brothers, that with the Lord, one day is like a thousand years, and a thousand years is like one day. The Lord does not delay in fulfilling his promise, though some speak of delay; rather he gives you time because he does not want anyone to perish, but that all may come to conversion. The day of the Lord is to come like a thief. Then the heavens will dissolve with a great noise; the elements will melt away by fire, and the earth with all that is on it will be burned up."* St. Peter's message is the same as that of Ezekiel, Isaiah, and Jeremiah. Water brought about the first cleansing, and **fire will be bring about the second great cleansing.**]

Ch19. As for you, son of man, intone a lamentation for the princes of Israel *(all the princes of the Church today)*. Say: A lioness among lions was your mother! Crouching among the cubs she nursed her whelps. One of these she pushed forward and he grew to be a young lion, able to tear his prey and became a man-eater. But the nations heard about him and he was trapped in their pit; and they brought him with hooks to the land of Egypt. *[Symbolic of the First Covenant]*.

When she saw that her hope had come to nothing, she took another of her cubs and made him a young lion. He strutted among the others for he had become a strong lion, able to tear his prey and be a man-eater. *[Symbolic of the Second Covenant, the Christian Church]*.

He destroyed their strongholds and ravaged their towns. The country and its inhabitants were alarmed at the sound of his roar. But the nations came against him from the regions round about. They spread their net over him and caught him in their pit. They put him in a cage with hooks and brought him to the king of Babylon. There he was put in custody so that his roar was no longer heard in the mountains of Israel. *[This refers to all the countries that are allying themselves against the U.S., and her allies, even as we speak. The Judeo/ Christian Lion will be trapped in Babylon. Modern day Iraq/Iran, and the rest of the Middle East region.]*

Your mother was like the vine of a vineyard planted near water. It became fruitful and leafy from being so well watered. It produced a vigorous branch that became a royal scepter towering above the foliage. It was outstanding for its height and its numerous branches.

But the vine was uprooted in fury and cast down to the ground. The east wind dried it up and stripped it of fruit. *Its vigorous branch withered and was burned by fire.* It is now planted in the desert, in an arid land of

drought. Fire from its stem has destroyed its branches and fruit. No vigorous branch or royal scepter has been left. This is the lament that people will sing." *[Symbolic of God's chosen, both Jews and Christians (First and Second Covenants), and how both will be uprooted in fury and cast down to the ground]*.

Brothers and sisters in Christ, this concludes this series of evening letters that have been brought back, by the prophets, to warn us today, the people of the Second Covenant. This has all been written in hopes of eliciting a spirit of awareness, as well as for further preparation for the coming dark years. Through prayer, penance and meditation, we can perhaps stave off this period for an undeterminable period of time, but we cannot completely stop the Will of God.

As always, these messages have been brought and presented for your discernment. Do not take my word for it, but instead research for yourself if what I have said is truth or fiction, and allow the Holy Spirit to guide you in your journey.

Continue to pray my beloved brethren, and continue to act as Christian role models so that all may know that you are true followers of Christ by what you do, and not just by what you say.

The following was said by the apostle James2:16, "You have faith and I have good deeds; show me your faith apart from actions, and I, for my part, will show you my faith in the way I act. Do you believe there is one God (he applies this question to all those that believe faith as being the sole method of salvation and believe that just believing in God is enough)? Well enough; but do not forget that the demons also believe and tremble with fear!" For it is through our faith, that leads us to doing good deeds. Otherwise, faith without deeds is dead.

Your brother in Christ,
Horacio.

Letter XXXIX-Remain Vigilant

Good afternoon brothers and sisters in Christ, on this cold and cloudy nineteenth day of this second month, I come to you all once more with a message of hope and faith for the coming times.

This is the thirty-ninth letter in a series of forty and I am nearing the end. It has been a while since my last letter, but I hope that since then, you and your family and other loved ones have been doing well. I pray for you all my brothers and sisters, and ask that you all pray for me too. The last few weeks have been especially trying for me, and foresee the coming months as trying as well. So I pray that you all please pray for me, and I will pray for you too.

Brothers and sisters, in the previous letters, I have laid out for you to see and discern the reasons for internal preparations and why it is of the utmost importance now and for the coming years. I see a sea of faces that are on the wrong path, and only a small stream that are on the right one.

I see all the things that have been written about in Scripture, Native American prophecy, Nostradamian prophecy, the Koran, and the Marian apparition messages all happening now, yet very few others realize this is happening right now.

I have mainly focused on and written about the message as written in Scripture, but I also highly suggest looking into these other sources to see how they too coincide with what has been written in Scripture.

What are happening now are only the birth pangs of what is to come. We must not allow our financial security and other materialistic sources of wealth to be our only sources of security. Instead, let us be rich and have an overflowing abundance of wealth as God disperses.

Let us be filled with faith and love for He that is, and He will protect us as he sees fit. Let us not be filled with arrogance, pride, anger, jealousy, and contempt, but instead be filled with the gifts as God sees fit to deliver to us through the Holy Spirit.

Let us be filled with a meek and humble spirit that is willing to serve others, and not be concerned about being served ourselves. After all let us keep in mind that Christ came to serve and not be served. He came show us what the true meaning of sacrifice is, and not that of selfish self-motivated interest.

Yet today, sacrifice has become an antiquated notion and selfishness as the accepted norm. How can children ever learn the meaning of sacrifice, when the parents only practice selfish acts? How can they ever learn what it is to be giving of oneself, when culturally, through television, radio, etc, they are constantly bombarded with messages of self-pleasing and self-indulgence? They enemy has been hard at work in our world, and continues to take many with him.

This is why my brothers and sisters in Christ, it is up to us to lead others in these battles that we face on a daily basis, and will continue to face in the future. Let us comfort, nurture, support and reassure those that are on the fringes of being swayed by the more popular or prevalent notions. It is so easy to destroy something or someone, yet so challenging to build and create. It is so easy to flow with the contemporary current, yet so hard to flow against the current.

But we must, as faithful followers of our master Jesus Christ, continue to abide by and follow God's will. Let him be our guide, our strength, and our wisdom. After all, with God on our side, who or what can stop us? But, we must not arrogantly assume that He is on our side, but rather know He is by acknowledging that we are on his side first.

Know brothers and sisters that the time for repentance on a personal, national, and global basis is here. We must repent of our sins, by acknowledging them before God, and then humbly asking for forgiveness. Yet even as these things that are to happen, many will refuse to repent.

In Mthw24:1-14, the following is written, *"Jesus left the Temple and as he was walking away, his disciples came to him and pointed out the imposing Temple buildings. But he said, 'you see all this? Truly I say to you: not one stone will be left upon another here. All will be thrown down.' Later, when Jesus was sitting on the Mount of Olives, the disciples approached him privately and asked, 'Tell us when this will take place. What sign will be given us before your coming and the end of history?' Jesus answered, 'be on your guard and let no one mislead you. Many will come, claiming my title and saying: 'I am the Messiah,' and they will mislead many people. You will hear about war and threats of war, but do not be troubled, for these things must happen, but it is not yet the end. Nations will fight one another and kingdom will oppose kingdom. There will be famines and earthquakes in several places, but all these are only the beginning: the first pains of childbirth. Then they will arrest you, and they will torture and kill you. All nations will hate you for you bear my name. In those days, many will stumble and fall; they will betray one another and become enemies. False prophets will appear and mislead many people, and because of such great wickedness, love will grow cold in many people. But the one who holds out till the end will be saved. The Good News of the Kingdom will be proclaimed throughout the world for all the nations to know; then the end will come."*

Brothers and sisters, no one knows the time, day, or year, but Jesus warned us to Mthw24:42, *"Stay awake, then, for you do not know on what day your Lord will come. Just think about this: if the owner of the house knew that the thief would come by night around a certain hour, he would stay awake to prevent him from breaking into his house. So be alert, for the Son of Man will come at the hour you least expect."*

So let us continue to prepare and remain vigilant. Let us continue to pray for all those that are on the wrong path, that they may be influenced by the Holy Spirit and see the error of their ways and repent of their sinful ways. Let us continue to be hopeful and remain strong in Christ, and he will remain strong in us. Let us also pray for the intercession of saints and the blessed Virgin (through the Rosary for all good Catholics), that they too may help us in interceding on our behalf.

I too pray for you all my brothers and sisters in Christ, and ask for your prayers as well. That God continue to enlighten your paths and strengthen your preparation, amen. Your brother,

Horacio.

Letter XL-Love and Sacrifice

Good morning brothers and sisters in Christ, on this beautiful morning of this twenty-fourth day on this third month of this 2006 year. I come to you my beloved brothers and sisters to relay and give from my heart, this final letter of preparation.

It has almost been to the day, a year since I began these series of letters, and it has been a work of love and sacrifice that I hope have benefited most of you all.

Throughout the process, I would often wonder and question what it was I was supposed to write and bring to you all. But every time, my questions were always answered by He that is the All mighty. He guided, strengthened and enlightened me throughout, even when the message I was delivering was somewhat of a harsh and frightening one.

I would often times find myself being intimidated by the message myself and asked him, "Are you certain this is what I am suppose to deliver?" And every time the answer would be yes.

Letters one through thirty were all letters of preparation, and letters thirty-one through thirty-eight, were letters of why the preparation is necessary. These were all letters that were written in the evening hours, seeing how these letters were written in reference to the dark years ahead.

It is with deep love and concern that I wrote these forty letters, so that you all and many others, could perhaps be exposed to and influenced by, this message of preparation. While the world sleeps, God calls us. While the world is blinded with messages of power, fame, sex and money, He gently taps us. While the world indulges itself in what is pleasing to the physical, He reminds us that we are spiritual souls on a journey through this limited, physical, temporal plane.

But why is that so many of us do not, or cannot hear when God is calling? This is a question on so many people's minds today. Why can't I hear a response to my prayer? Why doesn't God answer me? Why?

Most of us have forgotten of how exactly it is that God communicates with us. He does not come with trumpets and horns like so many expect him to come, but rather he comes to us as a whisper. He comes to us as a gentle breeze that blows by and around us. His answers come to us in stillness and in emptiness.

We cannot hear or capture his message to us, if our lives are full of distractions and other worldly attachments. We have to empty ourselves brothers and sisters and be still. Hence the reason why so many of us never hear Him calling us, or responding to our prayers.

In 1st Samuel3:2, we see how God called Samuel, *"One night Eli was lying down in his room, half blind as he was. The lamp of God was still lighted and Samuel also lay in the house of Yahweh near the ark of God. Then Yahweh called, 'Samuel! Samuel!' Samuel answered, 'I am here!' And ran to Eli saying, 'I am hear, did you not call me?' But Eli said, 'I did not call, go back to sleep. So he went and lay down. Then Yahweh called again, 'Samuel!' and Samuel stood up and went to Eli saying, 'You called me, I am here.' But Eli answered, 'I did not call you, my son, Go back to sleep.' Samuel did not yet know Yahweh and the Word of Yahweh had not been revealed to him. But Yahweh called Samuel for the third time and, as he went again to Eli saying, 'I am here for you have called me,' Eli realized that it was Yahweh calling the boy. So he said to Samuel, 'Go, lie down, and if he calls you again, answer: 'Speak, Yahweh, your servant listens."*

How many times has God called us, and we have not heard him. Or perhaps we heard, but could not understand. Or it may even have been that we heard, understood, but did not obey.

God called Samuel three times and each time Samuel hear the voice of God, but believed it had been Eli that had called him. After Eli advised Samuel how he should answer, then Samuel was able to finally comprehend and retain God's message with humility as God's servant.

Mother Teresa also said the following, "It is in the silence of the heart, that God speaks to us. If you seek God in prayer and in silence, God will speak to you. Then you will know that you are nothing. Only when you are aware that you are empty, can God begin to fill you with his love and glory. The souls of prayer are souls of great silence."

It is in this emptiness and silence that we can begin to know God and be filled by him. It is only then that we can begin to hear him call us, or perhaps respond to the many prayers and questions that we have asked of or to him. It is here where fasting also plays a vital role in the emptying of ourselves.

During this Lenten time of year, many of our non Catholic brothers and sisters, throughout my life have always asked me what the importance or significance of fasting is? For even Jesus fasted for forty days, and hence the reason we celebrate Lent with fasting and sacrifice, so as to become spiritually strong.

Fasting is somewhat like the following example; let us imagine that we have a full glass of water or perhaps clay jar that is full of water, all the way to the top.

This vessel not only is full of water, but remains constantly full, and when ever more water, or any other liquid or substance is added, there is no more room for it, so it begins to spill over the brim.

Our lives and many of ourselves are similar to this vessel that is constantly full of water. We are constantly full of distractions, and other concerns that keep us constantly full and there fore with no room or space for anything that can be added that will benefit us. But let us say that we temporarily shut the source that is constantly filling this glass, and we leave that glass out on the table for several days. As each day progresses, the glass begins to have more space, due to the evaporation of the water. IN STILLNESS, IT BEGINS TO EMPTY ITSELF. After several days, the glass finally has enough space for anything additional that may be added, without spilling over.

Likewise is the case with ourselves. If we choose to seek Him, we must shut the valve that is constantly keeping us filled with physical sustenance, but no spiritual sustenance. After doing so, we begin by denying the body physical needs and wants, and begin to control it, instead always being controlled by it. This is where great will power, through prayer, begins to strengthen our spiritual selves. Just as the glass became empty after several days, so too do we begin to empty ourselves and therefore begin to create space for God and his messages to us. Because otherwise, whenever he tries to give or add something to us, it will just continue to spill over and out.

Over the last century, great importance has been given to our physical sustenance needs and wants, but little or not importance has been given to our spiritual ones. How can God communicate with us, if we are constantly full and overflowing with this world's problems and distractions?

Yet so many today keep searching for this elusive answer and cannot figure out why they are so depressed, angry, or just out of balance, when there is no longer a balance between the spiritual and the physical (there is a unity, but no harmony between the two). All of the attention has been focused on the physical. We were all made in His image, to love and be loved.

In Scripture, Jesus demonstrates and conveys to us the importance of penance through fasting. In Matthew 17:14-21, it describes how Jesus healed an epileptic boy. Even though his disciples had attempted to free the boy of this evil spirit, they couldn't. Jesus finally commands the evil spirit to leave the boy, and afterwards addresses his disciple's questions as to why they had not been able to, and Jesus says to them, "Only prayer and fasting can drive out this kind of demon." In other words, penance coupled with prayer, brings about great blessings and grace. (Also read Mttw6:16, 4:1, for further validation of the power and reasons for doing penance through fasting.)

Native Americas too would fast for three-four days before journeying on their vision quests, where they would receive messages to their prayers from the all mighty creator.

This is why brothers and sisters in the Lord, it is necessary for us to always pray in silence and pray so that we may be filled by his grace and love. But, the key here is that before we can accept these gifts and answers from him, we must empty ourselves and become vessels that can hold and retain these gifts, and not have them overflow due to the fullness of our selves by the valve that stems from the world and its problems. The emptier we become, the more we can take away from His bountiful goodness.

Today's world of modernity has, especially in industrialized countries such as the one we live in, left many marginalized homeless and hungry on the street. But even they are outnumbered by those are dying of starvation for love, caring and acceptance of the spiritual kind. It is they that in most cases need the most prayers and love.

In Matthew6:43 Jesus says the following, *"You have heard that it was said, 'Love your neighbor and hate your enemy.' But I tell you: Love your enemies, and pray for those who persecute you, so that you may be children of your Father in Heaven. For he makes his sunrise on both the wicked and the good, and he gives rain to both the just and the unjust. If you love those who love you, what is special about that? Do not even the tax collectors do as much? And if you are friendly only to your friends, what is so exceptional about that? Do not even the pagans do as much?"*

It is this type of love and example, we should try to promote and set as our own personal standards. Especially in today's world of selfishness, greed, violence, perversion, and so on.

Brothers and sisters, I will leave you all with a brief caption from my **first letter**,

"The reason I am writing to you all this morning is to prepare you for what has been written in Scripture, and to allow you all my brothers and sisters in Christ to continue more than ever to live a Christian lifestyle, in the face of modern materialism and self indulgence. If your relationship with the Almighty is well and healthy, then help spread the wealth that you have amassed through him. Talk to friends, family and neighbors that perhaps may not be as wealthy as you in Christ's teachings and love, so that they too can be prepared. If on the other hand, your relationship with God is not as healthy, then begin to build it now, before the flood comes, and then it will be too late. Read the Word of God as written in the Bible (but always through the lens of sacred tradition and the teaching of the church), and let it's words and teachings grow within your hearts. Love your neighbors and pray for your enemies, for they need prayers more than anyone else.

My dear friends, the time for preparation is now. The storm clouds are hanging low, the lightening is getting closer and louder, and the time to repent and be well with God through Christ is Now! Don't leave it for tomorrow. Pray to God, and ask that the Holy Spirit guide and enlighten you. Do not continue being a Christian of Mouth, but be one of Heart."

Finally, *"Be strong in the Lord with his energy and strength. Put on the whole armor of God to be able to resist the cunning of the devil. Our battle is not against human forces but against the rulers and authorities and their dark powers that govern this world. We are struggling against the spirits and supernatural forces of evil. Therefore, put on the whole armor of God, that on the evil day, you may resist and stand your ground, making use of all your weapons. Take truth as your belt, justice as your breastplate, and zeal as your shoes to propagate the Gospel of peace. Always hold in your hands the shield of faith to repel the flaming arrows of the devil. Finally, use the helmet of salvation and sword of the spirit, that is, the Word of God. Pray at all times as the Spirit inspires you. Keep watch, together with sustained prayer and supplication for all the brothers and sisters."* (Ephesians 6:10)

Brothers and sisters, I pray that God continue to guide, enlighten and strengthen you and your loved ones. Be strong and vigilant that you may stand in defiance of this world and its ruler.

All forty are complete and the message of preparation has been given to you all. Pray brothers and sisters, pray for me, for the Will of God to be fulfilled as he wills it.

Your brother in Christ,
Horacio.

978-0-595-48542-0
0-595-48542-1